GIUSEPPE - - only in America

by

Joseph Francesco Levanto

Printed by

FRANKLIN IMPRESSIONS INC.   NORWICH, CONNECTICUT

First Edition

J. Levanto Publishers, LLC. 18 Wayne St. Norwich, CT 06360

Library of Congress Control Number: 2002095747

Levanto, Joseph.
Giuseppe -- only in America / by Joseph Francesco Levanto.

ISBN 0-9725529-0-1

Cover: Giuseppe - age 3

Photography by Cody McKeon

Cover design by
Merrill Keeley and Debra Sminkey

Printed in the United States of America
by
Franklin Impressions, Inc., Norwich, Connecticut

To Very Special People in My Life

*My devoted and lovely wife, Dorothy, mother of
our children,
who, for over fifty-years has been my guardian angel
and is my nominee to sainthood.*

*Our daughters, Jacqueline, Jeannette, and June,
and son Joseph,
all of whom make us justly proud.*

*Our grandchildren, Christopher, Cailynn, and Cody
who have blessed our lives with so much joy.*

*Our newest blessings, grandchildren Sierra and Mia,
who we hope the good Lord will allow us time
to see them grow.*

*I thank them all
for making me the "richest man" in the world.*

Contents

Prologue *1*

I   From 1929 to 1938

A Humble Beginning *3*
A Wartime Citizen *5*
A Marriage Arranged *5*
Ellis Island -- 1926 *6*
Home and Family *7*
Homemade Medicine *9*
A New Neighborhood *12*
Giuseppe Goes to School *16*
Joseph Moves Again *19*
Broad Street School *21*
The Big Storm *24*

II   From 1938 to 1943

A Very Sad Day *26*
Fun Times *27*
Hitching Free Rides *32*
Hunting at a Young Age *34*
The Home Entertainment Center *36*
From Joseph to Joey *36*
Stashu's Market *37*
Neighborhood Gangs *41*
Raiding Parties *43*
Second Time Around *45*
A Lesson in Responsibility *47*
Broadway School and Work *49*
Boat Building *50*
Joey's First Kiss *54*
War Is Declared *55*
Working the City Streets *57*
The Bowling Alleys *60*
Cow Flop Stadium *62*
Good-bye Broadway School *64*
A New Kid in the Neighborhood *66*

III   *From 1943 to 1952*

A High School Freshman   *68*
No More Street Fights   *74*
Someone Cared   *76*
An Army Experience   *82*
The Academy Senior Year   *84*
The College Experience   *91*
The Dating Game   *97*
Joe Buys His First Car   *99*
The College Senior Year   *100*
A Wedding Day Disaster   *103*
Back to Work   *106*
An Important Lesson Learned   *108*
Don't Put Off 'til Tomorrow What You Can Do Today   *111*

IV   *From1952 to 1960*

The First Born   *114*
The Beginning Teacher   *117*
Joe Returns to His Alma Mater   *127*
A Shocking Situation   *129*
Get Even Time   *130*
Freshman Football Begins   *131*
Oh My! Not Again   *132*
New Recruits   *134*
A True Fish Story   *136*
Trouble in Football   *139*
Number Four Arrives   *140*
Time for a Change   *141*
Lost at Sea   *143*

V   *From 1960 to 1975*

A Computer Guru   *146*
A Fabulous Job Offer   *150*
A New Beginning   *152*
Time to Start Graduate Studies   *153*
Halloween Night Security   *155*
Elmer's Folly   *158*
Being an Administrator Has Its Ups and Downs   *161*

Students Are Not Always the Problem   *164*
A Shooting in the Cafeteria   *167*
Attendance Records Are Important   *168*
A Riot in the Lunch Room   *170*
Earned Student Respect   *173*
A Dual Life and More   *176*
Real Estate Business Was Good   *180*
On the Way to a Doctorate   *182*
Launching a Ph.D.   *189*

VI   *From 1975 to 1988*

A Change in Command   *192*
The Mansion   *197*
The Honeymoon Is Over   *200*
Principal and Builder   *201*
A Year's Salary Earned in One Day   *205*
A Trick for a Track   *210*
The Big Fire   *214*
Snowballs Snowballing   *217*
A Picnic on the Green -- Eating Crow   *219*
Bees but No Birds   *220*
A Nightmarish Day   *223*
Police Are Always at Your Door   *225*
I Got a Disease   *228*
The 'Godfather' Image   *230*
A Rewarding Profession   *232*
Five Years In and Out of Court   *235*
The End of a Thirty-five Year Career   *250*

VII   *From 1988 to 2002*

The Retirement Years   *258*
A Hole-In-One -- Not One but Two *261*
Gregor Turns a Big Seven-O   *264*
Gregor and the Turkey   *269*
The 50th Celebration   *271*

Epilogue *277*

Acknowledgments

I would like to thank Eleanor Buehrig, a talented and gracious lady. She gave generously her time, and encouragement. Her teachings were invaluable lessons in learning the mechanics of writing this book.

Eleanor made this book eminently more readable than it otherwise might have been. She was incredibly helpful, spending many hours, checking and rechecking the manuscript. Never tiring and always with a pleasant attitude. Her sense of humor and her smile made a mammoth task bearable. To her, I am deeply indebted ... to my new friend.

A thank you to Ed Dunn, a highly respected editorial manager for the local newspaper, who was the first to volunteer to read my original manuscript. His early reaction and positive comments served as an incentive to keep me moving ahead with this project.

I also want to thank Dorothy Richards, school librarian, who early on in the project, was able to give me some sincere, enthusiastic feedback that kindled the fire to keep on writing.

To my respected colleagues, Dr. Larry Fenn and Bill Stevens, a thank you for taking the time to review my manuscript and providing me with much appreciated testimonials.

GIUSEPPE - - only in America

by

Joseph Francesco Levanto

PROLOGUE

Life has been good to me and fond memories give me satisfaction beyond description. To share, particularly some of them with my children and grandchildren and those to come, hopefully, will be a legacy to be appreciated and enjoyed. Not everyone will agree that the way I was brought up as a child was best, but as I look back upon my upbringing it was rich in love. I am eternally grateful for all the guiding hands that influenced my life and brought me into adulthood.

It's snowing outside as I sit in my overstuffed chair, looking out the window high on a hilltop, overlooking the snow covered fields and treetops. I think of what a lucky man am I. The beautiful scenic picture triggers both a sense of wonderment of what may come next in my life and a realization that my seventy-three years on this earth have passed too quickly. Having lived a good life blessed with a loving family who, without any doubt, radiates a sense of pride in having me as their father. This is a gift I would wish for every father.

My family members are three lovely, talented daughters, a son said often to be just like me, a loving spouse of more than fifty years who is also my best friend, always at my side, and the best mother our children could ever hope for. My adorable grandchildren are always with me whenever "Gregor" has occasion for celebration. ("Gregor" is the name my oldest grandson labeled me when he first learned to talk; he just could not say Grandpa, it kept coming out as "Gregor").

I am still in a state of awe from a recent dedication ceremony naming a building in my honor at my Alma Mater. For me this was the crowning experience of a lifetime. My entire family and many friends shared in the honor as they have many times before at similar occasions . My grandchildren were especially impressed. A few days after the dedication, my ten-year old grandson really touched my soul when he told his mother he wanted to change his name to be the same as mine and to include the Ph.D. after his name ... she laughed and said to him the name change was a possibility; but, the Ph.D. he would need to earn for himself. Several days later, he went so far as to telephone a lawyer friend of the family to ask if changing his name might be an expensive process. I am certain he was never aware of what a wonderful message he was sending to me.

Now, I feel it is time, before it passes me by and my memory may begin to fail, that I should commit to writing some of my life's experiences because, as fate would have it, the story of Giuseppe's life could have evolved only in America.

I

From 1929 to 1938

~ A HUMBLE BEGINNING ~

The year is 1929, the year Giuseppe was born to immigrant Italian parents. It was a cold day in January and Giuseppe's parents were unable to afford a hospital stay nor a physician. He drew his first breath in a cold water flat in an old apartment house, next to a commercial laundry on Franklin Street. It was not an uncommon event to give birth at home in those days, so Giuseppe came into this world into the arms of a neighborhood midwife . Two Italian families resided in this Franklin Street house, one on each level. No one would have dreamed that from such humble beginnings two prominent and highly respected individuals would emerge from these families -- one, an honorable and popular Judge; and Giuseppe, who became a prominent educator. This section of the city housed mostly Italians who emigrated to this country in search of new beginnings and opportunities. There were no single family residences in the neighborhood, only multi-family dwellings. No one could afford to own a house without some means of generating additional income to meet the mortgage payments. The Italians, like many other ethnic groups, clustered together in neighborhoods that served as support and a connection to the old world they left behind. In Giuseppe's neighborhood, families living in a block of houses within a stone's throw of each other, ultimately produced respectable and outstanding professionals: lawyers, surgeons, musicians, educators, and business people.

Today, many of the remaining houses stand in disrepair. No longer is there a vibrant community of Italian immigrants bustling about. There is no music, nor the aroma of Italian cooking, heavily seasoned with garlic and onions, flowing from the open windows. Along the street the open storefronts are gone and with them the aromatic odors of provolone cheeses hanging from the ceilings. People don't gather on the sidewalks nor sit on doorsteps and porches during the early evening hours anymore. The gatherings of old men smoking their stogies and arguing about the woes of the world have disappeared. The sounds of mothers calling out to their children or talking to their neighbors through an open window have long been silenced.

The old immigrant generation has passed on and so have many of their children. The others have moved away from their early neighborhoods; all that remains are old memories and possibly a few haunting ghosts who walk the streets.

~ A WARTIME CITIZEN ~

Giuseppe's father, Francesco, first ventured to America, penniless, just prior to the United States' entry into World War I. Soon he would be faced with a decision; be drafted into the U.S. Army or return to his native land and be drafted into the Italian Army. Having already served his time in the Italian Army, under a mandatory service requirement for all Italian young men, he chose instead, to serve the United States. He soon found himself in the battlefields of cold and muddy trenches of France fighting as a soldier in a distinguished machine gun battalion. Being an Italian, uneducated and not fluent in the English language, he drew some of the worst and most dangerous battlefield assignments.

Upon his honorable discharge at war's end, he automatically was granted his U.S. citizenship and a driver's license. *He earned them the hard way.* Francesco had no more than six months of schooling in Italy and not one day in America. Workdays left no time for schooling nor was it readily available. Every ounce of energy needed to be saved for the next day's work. Unable to read nor write, his destiny would be a life of hard, physical labor with pick and shovel. However, the railroad, his employer, gave him as it did for many Italians in those years, a financial opportunity to save some money. He sent money to his homeland to help his mother support their impoverished family in Tusa, Sicily.

~ A MARRIAGE ARRANGED ~

After a few years of labor he returned to Sicily to visit his mother. Before leaving Sicily again, his mother insisted that he should not return to America without a wife. Within a few weeks a bride-to-be, twenty year old Concetta, was found for him. A marriage was hastily arranged between these two strangers and within a few days they boarded ship in Naples, Italy, headed for America. *Next stop, Ellis Island ....* The sea journey was a frightening experience for Concetta. The story of the many tears she shed during the crossing, the first experience of sea travel, the confinement to the lowest travel class on ship with a man she hardly knew who was fifteen years her senior, had to be torment beyond comprehension. Further compounding this anguish was that she left behind her entire family to travel to a strange land with a stranger for a husband and with absolutely no knowledge of the language and customs of her new world. The crossing across rough seas was truly a sickening experience. She blamed her many days of sea sickness on the food served aboard ship.

Only a woman with a strong constitution and deep religious conviction could have survived the torment of the times. There was no one to turn to for help or consolation. It was a solitary confinement on a turbulent sea.

~ ELLIS ISLAND - - 1926 ~

Sighting the Statue of Liberty had to be like seeing the pearly gates of heaven. This euphoria was to be short-lived because of what awaited Concetta on Ellis Island. Here, she was separated from her husband and herded like an animal with hundreds of other immigrant women to be examined for contagious diseases and other medical conditions. The processing of immigrants was crude and rude and

6

FRANCESCO and CONCETTA
Wedding picture - 1926.

subject to the personal whims of inspectors. Those suspected to have conditions undesirable for entry into the country would be labeled with a chalk mark on their backs. She quickly learned a chalk mark made on an immigrant's clothing meant serious trouble and it could result in a rejection of entry into the United States. She watched in fear as many before her were "chalked" and pushed aside bewildered and with teary eyes.

Concetta did not know nor understand one word of the English language. She, like her husband, had very limited schooling in Italy -- approximately a total of one school year. Between the two of them they could amass a total of a year and a half of formal education -- that is all the formal education they would ever have in their entire lifetime. It is a wonder this frightening circumstance did not lead to complete mental breakdowns.

Imagine being lost in a sea of strangers, in a strange country, looking for the only one familiar face you know, who is nowhere in sight, and not being able to communicate your plight.

~ HOME and FAMILY ~

Francesco and Concetta settled in Norwich, Connecticut, in 1926 and within a few months their first child was conceived. The birth of this child was a traumatic experience. Francesco left for work in the early morning hours of that eventful day, as he did every working day, to return home late in the evening. He could not afford to take time out from work for fear of losing his job or losing an hourly wage. He left his wife in the care of a midwife during those expectant hours. During the birthing process the midwife was unable to induce the birth. In desperation she called in a physician who used metal forceps in delivering the baby. In doing so, severe brain injury resulted and the family was left with a son who was bedridden for nine years requiring constant care until his death.

To hear Concetta recall this horrible event, one can only wonder whether the physician really did his best or just didn't care because she was an Italian; discrimination and disrespect for Italian immigrants were rampant in those days.

• • •

The next born was Giuseppe followed by two sisters, the first of whom died suddenly at the age of eighteen months. The death certificate stated cause of death, " inflammation of the intestinal tract". *Most likely this was a viral infection for which there were no wonder drugs in those days.* Giuseppe's last vivid memory of her was watching her run along the sidewalk holding an ice cream cone in her hand on the night before she died.

Curly-headed Giuseppe quickly became the shining light in the family. He was quick to learn to speak Italian, full of energy, and amusing to the older Italians who marveled at his command of the Italian language and particularly of expressions that flowed effortlessly from his lips. His hand and body gestures were perfect imitations of those displayed by old-world Italians. Older neighborhood girls always welcomed the opportunity to take him for a walk and watch over him because he amused them.

Growing up on Franklin Street was truly an old-world experience. Primitive ways and customs made a lasting impression on Giuseppe. To hear him tell of some of his childhood experiences may seem far fetched at times but they are, none-the-less, true and many older Italians readily relate to them.

Medical attention was mostly a do-it-yourself affair.   Not many immigrants could afford to call in a physician. There was an old-world remedy to take care of most anything. Giuseppe will tell you that his mother invented the band-aid. Whenever he got cut, Mama would go to the basement, gather a handful of cobwebs off the ceiling beams, rip strips of cloth from an old, clean bed sheet, put the cobwebs on the open wound and wrap it with the cloth strips. The bleeding quickly stopped and amazingly no infection ever set in.

Whenever Giuseppe came down with a cold it was time for Papa to bring out his own homemade penicillin, a half cup of hot coffee with a hefty shot of anisette made from one hundred proof vodka and anise flavoring. Immediately he would be tucked into his cold bed -- there was no heat in the bedroom, only that which came through an open doorway. Mama would cover him with piles of blankets and heavy woolen army coats. *No child could roll over under this weight.* Giuseppe would awaken in the morning in the same spot and position he took when he entered the bed.

Most likely, he would awaken the next morning soaking wet from all the germs sweated out during the night ... so he was told by Mama.

• • •

One time Giuseppe fell off a wall injuring his leg and nose. He was carried across the street to the home of an old woman who always dressed in black and was known to have a cure for most any serious injury. She prepared a fried egg. *It had to be a special fried egg because during the cooking process there was a lot of low voice mumbling over the frying pan.* She was actually praying. Then, the fried egg was placed directly on a thin white cloth that covered the injured area -- *now, that gave another pain that made one forget the original and soon the injured was up and jumping or running away* -- Giuseppe's nose never did get fixed. Not incidentally, this old woman happened to be a grandmother to two Italian boys who later in life distinguished themselves as prominent and highly respected general surgeons in their community, one of whom served as Chief of Surgery at the local hospital.

There must have been something good in the old woman's genes that got passed along.

• • •

Of all the "treatments" Giuseppe was exposed to, the *mal occhio* (translation: bad or evil eye) was his favorite. Whenever he was sick with a fever, the old woman in black would be summoned to the house and perform a ritual that was supposed to rid the body of any evil spirits that may have entered his body and caused him to become sick. A large cupped dish was partially filled with cold water and a small dish of olive oil placed nearby. The dish of cold water was held in place on his head while a few drops of the olive oil were sprinkled onto the water. The formation or shape formed by the oil on the water determined what prayers were recited while the dish, now held with two hands, was rotated on his head. Giuseppe can recall the soothing feeling of a cool dish moving about on a feverish head and always looked forward to this comforting treatment.

As with Giuseppe, the children of many Italian immigrants were taught how to combat the *mal occhio* by simply carrying a bit of salt sewed into a tiny bag, the size of a quarter, and keeping it in a pocket. Another cure was to hang a sprig of garlic around ones neck.

10

According to Giuseppe, as you grew older not only would this practice ward off the evil spirits but it could discourage an encounter with the opposite sex.

• • •

The most common and easiest method of fighting off the *mal occhio* was to form a set of horns with one hand by extending your index finger with your little finger. You could be discreet about this by keeping your horned-shaped hand in your pocket whenever the need arose. If you have ever seen a Texas University Longhorn football game you most likely saw forty thousand fans with their hands held high giving the *mal occhio* sign. Concetta, in her later years, seeing the Longhorns on national television for the first time, did not understand the significance of this massive show of horned-shaped hands and was totally shocked.

She would say <u>Gesu Cristo</u> and bless herself by making the sign of the cross.

• • •

One time, when Giuseppe was visiting cousins in Massachusetts, he wanted to go outdoors to play and it so happened the family dog was by the door waiting to go out also. When the door was opened he inadvertently jammed the dog's tail under the door. The dog turned on him and took a bite out of his arm. During the commotion that followed the dog ran out the door. Immediately, the family's oldest son was sent outside to fetch the dog and bring it back into the house. As soon as it was brought into the house, the old woman of the house grabbed a pair of long blade scissors, collared the dog between her knees, and with one hand grabbed its snout raising its head high exposing the underside of its neck. At this point,

Giuseppe expected the worst -- *a bloody end for this nasty animal?* Instead, the old woman cut a chunk of clean fluffy hair from the underside of the dog's neck, then let go of the dog and proceeded to place that batch of fluffy hair directly on the open wound. The arm was wrapped with a strip of white cloth and soon everything was back to normal. When Giuseppe tells this story, people often ask if any infection or other ill effects followed. *His reply is always, "no, but for the longest time after, I had this strange urge to stop and raise a leg every time I walked by a water hydrant."*

~ A NEW NEIGHBORHOOD ~

With three young children the time was right for a move to a larger home. Soon, Giuseppe would be ready to attend school so a rental was chosen closer to school and on the outer edge of the Franklin Street neighborhood; up the hill to lower Boswell Avenue, next to a small Italian grocery store. The store occupied the front half of a house with the grocer and his family living in the remaining rooms. The grocer was robust in stature and always dressed with a full white apron, white shirt and black bow tie, and wearing a flat-top straw hat. In good weather the door was always open allowing the aroma of the hanging cheeses to spill out onto the street. He stood outside by the front door until a customer came in.

One of the grocer's adult sons, Naady, was severely handicapped. He too suffered from apparent brain damage from a forceps delivery during birth that left one side of his body paralyzed from head to toe. His mother and Concetta would often talk and lament the burden of hardship they both had to bear. Unlike

Giuseppe's brother who was bedridden, Naady had limited ambulatory control of his legs, dragging one foot as he moved forward rapidly, holding his withered arm, and looking as if he were stumbling and about to fall. This motion would only allow him to move a distance of ten to twenty feet before he would need to grab onto something so he would not fall. He always held a handkerchief in his good hand because he drooled profusely when he tried to utter a few words. His days were spent on the sidewalk near the store leaning against a fence while holding his withered arm. He was kept away from the store entrance so as not to discourage or bother potential customers. Because he was unable to groom himself, his unruly hair and twisted face made his appearance frightening to the youngsters in the neighborhood and a pitiful sight to older people. Giuseppe and his friends would run and hide whenever one of them would yell, "lookout, Naady is coming to get us." The older kids often taunted him.

This was a form of cruelty that greatly saddened Giuseppe.

• • •

Giuseppe's "new" house was a four tenement home with two families on each floor. Two Italian families and two Negro families (in those days the term Black was seldom used). Giuseppe's family occupied the second floor and across the hall lived one of the Negro families. The four families lived in harmony, each keeping to themselves.   Race nor skin color never was an issue. The landlord was a Polish undertaker who had his undertaking parlor as part of his home a few houses away. The basement level of the house where Giuseppe lived was used by the undertaker to store his inventory of coffins. The basement level opened under the front porch which spanned the entire length of the house, a long, windowless area open at one end only. It was always dark and spooky. The lower quality coffins, with some empty crates, were stored here under the porch outside the locked basement room. This area was easily accessible and declared off limits for play. However, Giuseppe and his friends often found the inside of the coffin crates a great place to hide during a game of hide-and-seek. Only a few brave players had the courage to venture into this dark area. When they did and thought they heard low tone moans coming from inside a coffin crate and saw the movement of a lid that was about to open, the excitement of the chills and screams that ensued would be a thrill long remembered.

Although the boys received several scoldings from their parents for playing there, the practice would then be suspended for awhile only to be revived when things got boring. There was a day when Giuseppe's redheaded friend, Dennis, hid in one of the coffin crates not knowing that the undertaker had arrived, unannounced, to check his inventory only to have the living daylight scared out of him when he saw and heard the unexpected. Needless to say the undertaker, recovering from his heart stopping fright was furious, grabbed Dennis by the collar, dragged him up the stairs to the street level and with the inside of his shoe literally kicked his butt all the way home -- three houses away.

Can you imagine doing that to a kid today? One could get jail time for child abuse, but not in those days.

• • •

Behind Giuseppe's house was a city playground bordered on the opposite side by Lake Street where some of the toughest Italian kids lived. At one end of the playground, the Broad Street end, the Italian neighborhood lines became blurred and a more diverse population resided at that end. The playground was Giuseppe's first experience with non-Italian speaking kids. It was here he was to encounter his first taste of discrimination against Italians. He was called "dumb wop," "dago," "stupid guinea," whenever he attempted to venture beyond the play area occupied by his Italian friends. It wasn't long before he was taught by the older, tougher kids to defend himself against those derogatory remarks. He became a formidable opponent and blackened a few eyes and bloodied several noses at the Lake Street playground. Giuseppe was not a violent kid. His father taught him to avoid starting an altercation, but when push came to shove, he was encouraged to follow through and finish the job. This he did. It was not long before he was to earn the admiration of the older Italian boys who delighted in watching him fight. He swung like a windmill in action, swarming nonstop all over his opponent until blood was drawn or his opponent fell. In those days fights were supposed to be "fair." You never hit anyone who wore glasses or who may have fallen to the ground.

There was a time when one of these encounters got out of hand. Giuseppe, while getting the best of the other kid, was soon confronted with his foe's older friends who joined in to help their pal. Soon the Lake Street gang came to Giuseppe's aid. The free-for-all was witnessed by Giuseppe's father who jumped over the backyard fence, ran over and became involved in the fracas with some of the older combatants. It was not long before the police arrived with their green paddy wagon, arrested Giuseppe's father, Francesco, and carted him off to the police station.

Giuseppe was left behind being restrained by the older kids as he cried.

~ *GIUSEPPE GOES to SCHOOL* ~

Boswell Avenue School was a small red brick building with four rooms housing four grade levels, kindergarten through grade three. Neighborhood schools in those days were within walking distance of home. There were no cafeterias nor gymnasiums. Everyone had an hour to go home for lunch. This time in Giuseppe's life was a most difficult one. Knowing and understanding but few words of the English language caused his early school years to be difficult.

Giuseppe started school at the age four. Two years in kindergarten were spent to ready him for the first grade. His only recollections of kindergarten were the many hours he spent playing in its sand box and that his name somehow became Joseph. First grade left lasting impressions that would stay with him throughout his life. Some memories would be forever etched in his mind. In first grade he would try to learn basic reading and writing.

Whenever Joseph was called upon to read aloud it became a most dreaded moment. The snickering and laughing by his classmates at his mispronunciation of simple words was a form of cruelty that on many days would send him running home, after school, with tears in his eyes. At times the teacher would also laugh along with the class. This would really hurt even though she would be quick to apologize and try to comfort him with a hug.

One day in memory, while marching out the back door for recess time in the school yard, Joseph spotted a dime on the floor. He quickly picked up the coin and pocketed it. Upon returning from recess, one of the girls in the class told the teacher that someone had *stolen* her dime. It was common practice in those days to encourage thrift by having a banking day when those who could afford it would bring a dime to school to be added to their own bank account maintained at the school. What apparently happened was the dime was placed on the corner of her desk and got knocked off onto the floor as the class passed along the aisle to go outside. The teacher questioned the class as to who took her dime. After lecturing the class about taking something that doesn't belong to you, Joseph sheepishly raised his hand and said he had found a dime at some distance from her desk.

The teacher's reaction was one that fostered a sense of guilt in Joseph's mind. He felt his classmates were now looking upon him as a crook. This incident was not the only one that would leave him guilt ridden.

• • •

One day while with his mother, shopping in a Five and Dime store, Joseph wandered over to a display of eyeglasses. His childish fascination with eyeglasses led him to try on several pair. He found one that met his fancy, and unbeknown to his mother, he slipped it into his pocket. They left the store. As they walked along the sidewalk, Joseph who lingered behind her decided to put on the new glasses. When she turned to see where he was she was surprised to see him wearing a pair of glasses, disoriented and weaving from side to side. Quickly, she grabbed him and demanded to know where he got the glasses. Apparently, whatever the explanation, it infuriated her and she grabbed him by the ear. With a painful twist she led him back to the store by his ear as he held onto her arm with both hands trying desperately to alleviate the stinging pain. She made him return the glasses to the store clerk with an apology.

Telling the truth can, sometimes, be a painful experience ...especially when there is a lesson to be learned.

Later in the spring of that year, a new Italian immigrant family arrived in Norwich. The family's oldest boy, who was about eleven years old at the time, was placed in the first grade and Joseph, who spoke Italian , was assigned to serve as an interpreter for him. This arrangement delighted Joseph as it made him feel important and helped, not only the newcomer and the teacher, but Joseph himself. After several weeks in this arrangement, the eleven year old was promoted to the fifth grade in another school. Joseph had difficulty understanding why he could not join his new friend at the fifth grade level. This became somewhat of an argument with the teacher because Joseph thought it was his own efforts that made the "promotion" possible and he was deserving of the same treatment.

The schoolyard at Boswell Avenue School was mostly cinders and gravel and enclosed with a chain link fence. Girls played on one side and boys on the other. Baseball was strictly a boy's game; the only game played by them in the schoolyard. If you did not play you watched as you stood along the fence. Joseph came to school one day sporting a new baseball cap. On the front was imprinted a picture of a uniformed baseball player swinging a bat and the caption under it read *Home Run*. The first time at bat Joseph was subjected to some verbal abuse and ridicule about his hat, but, that would soon change. He hit a home run over the fence. From that point on the hat became a *must wear* for every player at bat. A home run over the fence in this schoolyard was a rare event and was remembered and talked about for several years. Twenty years later Joseph returned to the school yard to savor the feat he had recalled so many times before. He was not only dismayed but disappointed when he found the distance between home plate and the fence could not have been more than sixty feet. Notwithstanding, his home run had to be a great hit considering that baseballs of the day were called "nickel brickers." They were cheaply made baseballs with covering that easily became unstitched and then held together with several layers of heavy cloth-like electrical tape. Often, a ball would be water-soaked and heavy from being left in the rain. Hitting it with a bat was like hitting a brick; thus, "nickel bricker."

~ JOSEPH MOVES AGAIN ~

Little else is remembered about the Boswell Avenue School years except that at the end of the third grade the family moved again to upper Boswell Avenue into a predominantly Irish neighborhood. This time it would be a new home built during the depression under the watchful eye and apparent envy of Irish neighbors. His father, Francesco, purchased a piece of land, better described as a piece of rock, considered by many as not suitable as a home building site.

By this time Francesco had worked himself up the construction trade ladder to where he could obtain a blasting license. His on the job training and experience qualified him for a license even though he could neither read nor write. Home building began with drilling of blasting holes in the rock ledge. After school and weekends saw Joseph developing early stages of a strong work ethic, helping his father while other boys his age were playing ball in the nearby fields. Many times he was carefully lectured about the dangers of some of the construction practices and the horrible consequences of carelessness.

Most work assignments became interesting and fascinating for Joseph. He learned to respect and handle sticks of dynamite. His job was to slit an opening in the side of a dynamite stick with a jackknife, hand the stick over to his father and watch while he inserted a red metallic colored blasting cap into the slit; then wrapping and tying the two wires from the blasting cap around the stick of dynamite, then stuffing the loaded stick into the blasting hole with a long wooden pole. The thrill and reward for a job well-done was to allow Joseph to actually set off the charge. The detonator would be placed at a safe distance behind a protective shield; the wires would be connected to the detonator and the detonator handle raised. Joseph would be allowed to give three long warning blasts on an air horn and then, with help of his father's hand, would push down hard on the detonator handle and watch the resulting blast as it raised into the air a heavy protective wire mesh with the blasted rock beneath it

What a thrill it was to hear the boom and see the rising cloud of smoke and dust.

• • •

The new home slowly began to take shape. Francesco built the foundation with the blasted pieces of stone. Carpentry work would be contracted out. The contract for labor was written on one sheet of paper in the simplest terms: $160 due when the rough framing was complete, $160 due when roofing and window installation were complete, the final $160 due when the inside was finished. Total labor cost $480. This contract covered all carpentry work for a two story, four bedroom house with two bathrooms. All materials were to be provided by the owner. Total cost for labor and materials came to a little under $5,000. These are late depression era prices. This home sold fifty-five years later for $89,000. The actual building of the house went smoothly; however, relations with the Irish neighbors on both sides became quickly strained.

On one side lived a big Irish cop who would delight in harassing Francesco particularly after popping a few drinks. There was a time Francesco found him roaming, uninvited, in the upstairs bedrooms. An argument ensued while the big Irish cop kept a threatening hand on his holstered revolver. They did not speak to each other for many years thereafter. On the other side lived an elderly Irish couple. Joseph loved to talk with the old man and seemed to get along fine with him, but didn't care much for his wife who would always complain about Joseph's dog, especially when the small beagle mongrel was turned loose to play with Joseph's friends. When not playing with the kids, the dog was always chained to his dog house and never allowed to roam. There would come a time, because of a complaint filed by his elderly neighbors, most likely the wife, the dog would be taken away from him by the dog warden because it was not licensed. The loss of his favorite pet proved to be a very traumatic event in Joseph's early years.

It would be the first time, ever, Joseph could recall a sense of deep anger and long-lasting hatred for another person, particularly an old woman.

~ BROAD STREET SCHOOL ~

Joseph remembers his fourth grade teacher, Miss Shields, at Broad Street School as the first teacher who conveyed a caring attitude toward him and one that he recalls fondly. She was a kind person who gave him the personal attention he needed. He began to

BROAD STREET SCHOOL
Top - front view. *Bottom* - rear view; with fifth-grade classroom
on lower level and sixth-grade classroom above.
(Building now condominiums)

enjoy and excel in school. This would end with his passing to the fifth grade. Here, many difficulties began to develop. Joseph sensed a dislike for him by his teacher and soon would find himself acting out and spending many afternoons staying after school -- *detention was an unfamiliar word in those years.*

The perceived dislike for him seemed to begin early in the fifth grade during a history lesson. The topic was a picture of George Washington standing at the bow of a boat being rowed across a river. The class was asked to identify the river by name. The teacher's question was easily answered with a show of several hands. However, when all the hands went down, there was Joseph frantically waving his hand. The teacher called on him and he blurted out, "He crossed the Shetucket River in Greeneville too!" The class enjoyed a hearty laugh. The Shetucket was a dirty local river that flowed through a section of the city called Greeneville. This did not set well with the teacher who took Joseph's comment as a disruptive joke. She harshly reprimanded him and told him his comment was not appreciated and he should keep his "stupid remarks" to himself. *Little did she know, as with most likely 99+% of the local residents,* George Washington *did* cross the river. Joseph knew this because he frequently passed a small stone monument on his way to play in the river. It had an inscribed bronze plaque attached that gave credence to the crossing.

Today, the monument is still there obscured by tall grass in a spot where hardly anyone can notice -- a piece of history that has managed to escape the great majority of local residents.

• • •

"The straw that broke the camel's back," or should be said, the teacher's back, came one day during fifth grade music time, when the class was singing along with the teacher who was seated at the piano

22

GEORGE WASHINGTON MARKER
George *did* cross the Shetucket.
Top - marker obscured by weeds.

in the front corner of the room. She was seated on a piano stool, the swivel type, with her back to the class. Joseph was seated in the outside row nearest her in the second seat from the far end of the row. He thought he would be funny and whenever she struck a high note he would sing low and whenever she struck a low note he would sing high not realizing that she could hear him. This action delighted his friends seated nearby. Suddenly, in the middle of a song the teacher grabbed the thin gray colored music book she was reading from, whirled around on her stool, and hurled it through the air, along the entire length of the row, hitting the top of Joseph's desk where it bounced into his chest. This action brought about some snickering laughter from his friends. Joseph, somewhat embarrassed, without missing a beat, back-handed, scaled the book back in her direction. Obviously, this unexpected reaction did not make her a happy camper. That day was one of those stay-after ones, only this time she kept him very late until about 5 p.m.

Joseph became concerned because it was getting dark outside and having no phone at home there was no way to call to let his parents know he was still in school. Furthermore, the rule in his house was that he always had to be home before the street lights came on or the punishment could be severe. The teacher decided to drive Joseph home. He thought this was great. After all, it was not very often he got to ride in a car, and this was also an opportunity to offer his parents a valid excuse for his lateness. Once there, however, she wasn't about to say goodbye. To Joseph's surprise, she turned off the engine, got out and walked him to the door. *A dreaded moment for him -- she wanted to meet and talk with his parents.*

She introduced herself and was cordially greeted by his parents, invited in, and offered a glass of wine which she readily accepted and drank. She proceeded to explain her disappointment in

Joseph's school work and behavior. Joseph could see the fire developing in his father's eyes. He knew this meant big trouble was about to arrive. Immediately after she departed there were no questions nor discussion only a very short enraged comment by his father, who quickly pulled a large leather belt from his work pants and administered a tanning to Joseph's butt, sending him off to bed without any supper.

~ THE BIG STORM ~

The 1938 school year was the year of the big storm known as the great "38 hurricane." There was no warning whatsoever. It turned out to be the worst storm in history to hit New England with winds of 120mph to over 180mph. Nearly six hundred people died in New England shoreline communities. All teaching and learning quickly halted when the fury of the storm howled by outside in the schoolyard. Huge trees began falling over in the school yard as if some monster were pulling them out of the ground. All the students quietly sat in class and watched, mesmerized with fear. It seemed as though everything was flying by the windows -- garbage cans bounced along and empty cardboard boxes looked like they had wings. The teachers did not know what was happening nor the severity of this storm. They kept school in session until about two o'clock and then dismissed everyone. As it happened dismissal time came near the end of a normal school day and at the height of the storm. Joseph, with several of his classmates, began to walk the usual route home only to be stopped a block from the school by National Guardsmen because fallen, live power lines were sparking on the street. Huge fallen trees blocked the streets and everyone had to find an alternate way home. Students turned and walked in opposite directions looking for side streets that were passable. Eventually the trek took them far out of their way through the downtown area where flood waters were rising rapidly, store windows were broken, window display items were strewn on sidewalks and streets. Boxes of store goods began to float by with the rising flood waters. Huge river rats, some the size of rabbits, displaced by the rising waters, were scurrying about. For Joseph it was more an exciting time than a fearful one. He had not seen anything like this before. To his young mind it was more like an adventure. Nearing home Joseph stopped and watched as a huge tree hit the side of an auto and sent it rolling over several times, like a toy tumbling down a hill. It was a struggle to walk, going from pole to pole and fence post to fence rail, holding on tightly to keep from blowing away. The usual fifteen minute walk home took nearer to three hours.

For several days after the storm, schools were closed while streets were cleared of fallen trees and downed power lines were repaired. These no school days certainly were not a vacation for anyone. Every able bodied person, young and old, was expected to pitch in and do a part in the cleanup. It was hard physical labor from sunup to sundown. There were no chain saws in 1938 and everyone helped in the clean up with axes and hand saws. Joseph's father had a two-man saw and he and his father began a task that seemed to have no end. Joseph was required to help by guiding one end of the saw, keeping it straight so it wouldn't bind in the cut, while his father did the heavy work of both pushing and pulling. Many times during the process Joseph would tire causing the saw to bind. This made his father very angry. *Today, that saw hangs on a wall as a decorative memento of his father and the great '38 hurricane.*

25

II

From 1938 to 1943

~ A VERY SAD DAY ~

Promotion day for the fifth grade at Broad Street School was a sad experience for Joseph. The practice was, on the last day of school that students in a class would rise together and march into the next grade level room as those from the lower grade level marched in to occupy the seats that had just been vacated. Joseph had to stay in his seat as his classmates moved on, upstairs, to their new sixth grade room. He remained seated, it seemed like forever, sitting quietly waiting for the students who had just been promoted to enter his room. *There he was for all to see, the dummy who stayed back, seated alone in an empty classroom.* Retention was not a word used then -- if you were not promoted it was said you "stayed back." To this day, Joseph can recall the awful, sickening feeling he had seeing his classmates slowly filing out of his room, waving good-bye to him and he sheepishly waving back, as they left him behind. He sat quietly waiting, ashamed to meet the incoming class. His eyes filled with tears. He quickly wiped away the tears that trickled down his cheek and his thoughts turned to summer vacation that would begin with the next day.

The cruelty of that day would never be forgotten. It would serve Joseph well in the years to come. He developed a keen sensitivity and a respect for young minds.

~ FUN TIMES ~

Summers were great fun even though Joseph's family never went on any trips nor vacations. As with many, they had no car nor money to spend on such foolishness. There were plenty of chores to be done before any playtime was granted. Behind Joseph's house were acres of woods called the *Company Woods* (*Comps* for short) which provided all the entertainment needed by kids neighboring this wooded oasis. It was bordered mostly on the far side by Polish families and a few Greeks. Joseph gravitated to them because he was not accepted by the Irish kids and further he thought of them as a bunch of sissies. Games were plentiful and never boring.

Baseball: they played in an open area with so many rocks protruding from the ground that sometimes the ball hit one of them and it would come directly back to the hitter or glance off in a direction making fielding the ball almost impossible. A hit would require the batter to run uphill to first base, then uphill to second base, downhill to third, and almost a level plane to home plate. Everybody played, good players along with the bad players, no matter if there were four or fourteen on a team.

Boxing: when the kids had their fill of baseball, a boxing ring would be staked out with freshly cut tree limbs fashioned into poles. Four holes would be dug, the poles placed in them to form the ring and then laced together with pieces of twine for the ropes. The kids would strip off their shirts. Matches would be arranged by the older boys who delighted in watching the younger kids beat each other until one bloodied the other's nose -- *that would end that match.*

Peggy Stick: was another game fashioned from an old broom handle. Two pieces were cut, one about six inches long and whittled to a point at both ends, this was called the "peggy;" and the other a piece about eighteen inches long called the stick. A circle was drawn using the stick as a measure of the diameter. The stick was then held upright in the center of the circle while from a line drawn ten paces away the "peggy" would be thrown at the stick. Using the length of the stick, end over end, the number of lengths to the "peggy" would determine the number of swings allowed to hit the "peggy". Should the stick be hit while being held upright in the circle, the one holding the stick would lose his turn to hit. The "peggy" would be hit, from where it landed, by striking the tapered end of the "peggy" with the stick making it rise, in a forward or backward direction, and while spinning in the air it would be swung at and hit, *hopefully.* At the end of the number of swings allowed, the "peggy" would be thrown back toward the circle and from where it landed, using the stick end over end as a measure, the number of sticks to the center of the circle determined the points earned -- lowest score wins.

Johnny Blueballs: was another game that proved very exciting. In this game a long switch was cut from a small tree and marked by stripping pieces of its bark to give it an easy recognizable appearance. A large circle was drawn which was to serve as a safe harbor. Everyone stayed in the circle while one person hid the long switch. He would then return to the circle to stay while the others went out to search for the switch. Whoever found it would yell "Johnny Blueballs," pick up the switch and race after anyone not in the circle, whipping them only below the waistline, until they reached safety within the circle.

Joseph quickly learned if he spotted the switch, it was not wise to reveal his find until the very last moment when he was certain someone was near enough to enable him to get some good licks in before his victim raced into the safety of the circle. To yell "Johnny Blueballs" and not being able to raise some good welts on someone's calves made one the laughing stock of the day.

What a hilarious sight it was to see the unlucky one jump and yell as the switch made stinging contact with its mark.

• • •

Buck-buck How Many Fingers Up: another game played when at least eight players were available. Teams were chosen the heaviest and biggest kids always picked first. A sturdy tree was found just big enough to enable one's arms to be completely encircle it and comfortably support a shoulder to lean against it. The first kid would bend over with his back parallel to the ground and wrap his arms around the tree. The rest of the team would assume the same parallel position, locking onto each other with their heads in tight against the hips of the kid in front and with their arms tightly wrapped around his thighs. This made for a long straight line of human bodies locked onto the tree. The other team would line up directly behind, but far enough away to get a good running start. The best jumper would be the first yell out "buck-buck" and run as fast as he could and as he approached the end of the treed line, he would put both hands on the last person's back side, who was in a parallel position with the ground, and propel himself, leap frog style, as far as he could onto the back of someone further along the line. You had to stay on where you landed and wait for the next teammate to do the same until everyone had his turn. *Sometimes, a kid would purposely let out some gas and the ensuing laughter would cause the line to collapse.* Should someone fall off, or if everyone did not make it onto the line, the other team would assume the treed position and the game would continue. If a team was able to get all its members up on the backs of the other team, then, the first man on would yell "buck-buck, how many fingers up," holding up fingers on one hand. The person holding onto the tree would have one guess If he guessed correctly, his team would get bonus points and their turn to jump. The real hero of this game always turned out to be the fat kid who could also jump. Many a line would collapse under his weight. Everyone had a good time and, surprisingly, injuries were rare.

Grinder Sandwich Tree: these were only a few of the games that occupied idle times. Imaginative minds were always at work and they needed no one to organize or supervise them. Many games were invented whenever the need arose. The "grinder sandwich tree" game was one where a tall, young sapling was climbed to the point where it would bend over and allow the climber to hang from it by one arm. The climber, while holding on with one hand, would use the other hand to simulate each step in the making of a grinder (also called a sub sandwich) from cutting the bread length wise, adding all the ingredients one at a time, to finally wrapping and bagging it. Many times the participant would tire before he could finish, and not being able to hold on any longer, would fall to the ground. He lost the game.

Swimming: on hot summer days, sometimes the gang would venture down to the river for a quick swim. This was forbidden territory for most kids including Joseph. The river was not only filthy with raw sewage but also dangerous. Not one parent would ever approve of their kids using the river. Anyway, it was an adventure to

30

sneak down to a swimming area, where a Tarzan rope swung high over the river, and go skinny dipping. Not many kids had access to their bathing suits because the parents kept close watch over them thinking this would keep them away from the river. All the kids knew the Australian Crawl style of swimming, but swimming in this river one developed what became known as the Shetucket River Crawl -- the same as the Australian except for the hesitation at the beginning of the overhand stroke when a quick flip of the wrist pushed aside the nasty stuff that often came floating by.

When the river became too dirty, the kids would move upstream to a set of canals feeding into one of the riverside mills. Here, the water was screened as it entered the canal and appeared somewhat cleaner. This was another dangerous place to swim and the kids were often chased away by police and observant mill workers. Often, when no one was watching, one of the older and stronger boys would crank open one of the flood gates, opening into the river below, and the water would come rushing out with such force it would nearly wash away the brave ones who thought this was a great way to take a shower. Joseph and his smaller friends knew enough, or were scared enough, not to try this stunt.

On one hot summer day, an older boy swam too close to the turbulent waters exiting the end of the mill. He was trying to retrieve a piece of wood floating in a small circular pattern. It was to be used in building a raft. Everyone there that day watched as he was dragged under, and after much searching by the local fire department, he eventually surfaced as a lifeless body. The dangers of the river were vividly etched forever in the minds of everyone watching that day. That ended Joseph's swimming in the river. A new swimming hole would be found in a small, snake infested pond located closer to home. The abundance of water snakes, although harmless but scary,

THE CANAL
Top - A dangerous swimming place.
Bottom - Flood gates opening to river below.

soon discouraged the thoughts of swimming there.

    <u>The Comps:</u>   the woods were a source of enjoyment for kids from the poorer families. The more affluent families, of which there were none in Joseph's neighborhood, could afford memberships in the YMCA, Boy Scouts, Girl Scouts, Sea Scouts and summer camps. It seemed as though the rich were the lucky kids who got everything. There were no Little Leagues or any other organized play programs with the exception of a few city sponsored playgrounds located in the more densely populated neighborhoods. Playgrounds were too far away and most of Joseph's friends were required to stay close to home and within calling range. Police-like whistles and bell ringing were some of the methods used to summon kids home. When playing after supper, Joseph was programmed to head for home when the street lights came on. Joseph and his friends were able to organize their own games and have fun without parental interference and the squabbling between parents often encountered in this day and age in organized activities.

It would be years later that Joseph and his friends would come to realize their own lives were greatly enhanced by a freedom in childhood that molded them into strong-minded individuals who were able to handle most challenges that life would bring their way.

~ *HITCHING FREE RIDES* ~

In the 1930's, a trolley line ran by Joseph's house and terminated its run at the next intersecting side street. It was here, at the end of the line, where the trolley would stop and the conductor would prepare the trolley car for the trip back. Because the trolley car could not be turned in the opposite direction, the conductor would remove the fare box and carry it to the other end of the car and fix it to a stand mounted next to the controls at that end of the car. He would then proceed to walk along the aisle and move the seat backs from the previous position to one where a passenger would be allowed to be seated facing the new direction of the car. This was a relatively easy task as the backs were hinged in such a manner as to enable them to move from the back of the bench seat to the front and vice versa. The final preparation required the conductor to exit the car and pull down a long arm with a wheel on the end of it. This wheel made contact with the overhead electrical wires, providing power to the trolley motor. The attached rope pulled the arm down and anchored it. Then, at the other end of the car, another connecting arm with a wheel on its end, was released to make contact with overhead wires which would allow the car to move in the opposite direction. Many times Joseph would wait at the end of the line and help the conductor change the position of the seat backs. He was happily rewarded with a free ride to the next corner.

Another opportunity to hitch free rides came during the summer months when horse drawn ice wagons came by, carrying blocks of ice covered with canvas. The heavy canvas served to protect the ice from the sun. The kids would hide and wait until the wagon passed. Trying to avoid being seen by the driver, they would carefully rush out and hitch a ride by hanging on the back end of the wagon as it moved along. With their feet placed on the back axle and holding on with one hand, they would quietly lift the canvas cover and search for small chunks of ice; ice that may have splintered off from an ice pick cutting a block to size for a home ice box. *Few people owned, or could afford, a refrigerator.* Many times the driver would snap his horse whip over their heads and yell at the kids to get off. *Sometimes the crack of the whip came so close it would set an ear ringing.*

The rag man also came by in a horse drawn wagon. As he moved slowly along the street he would ring a bell and yell out,

"Rags ... rags ... any rags?"

He would buy old rags and stuff them into huge burlap bags heaped on the back of his wagon. He provided another opportunity for a chance at a free ride. With him, it was a challenge as to who could ride the farthest without being detected. Again, a masterful snap of the horse whip was used to discourage the unwelcomed rider.

~ HUNTING at a YOUNG AGE ~

Kids learned from each other, usually the older ones teaching the younger. Joseph learned to hunt with homemade bows and arrows and spears fashioned from young saplings. A long finish nail was inserted into the end of an arrow and held in place with a wrapping of fine wire. He would make slingshots cut from a small tree branch shaped like a Y with strips of old rubber tire inner tube carefully tied to the top ends of the wooden Y and the other end to a square leather patch, to hold a stone missile, cut from the tongue of an old leather shoe. Using these crude weapons, sometimes, Joseph proudly brought home squirrels and frogs. Joseph's mother would cook squirrel and add it into the spaghetti sauce but she refused to cook frog legs. *She would say they were food for the Frenchmen and they really knew how to properly cook this delicacy.*

These crude weapons, although dangerous, were never used on each other and never used to damage anyone's property. It was like an unwritten law that no one would ever aim at anyone even in jest. Slingshots were commonly carried in a back pants' pocket. Broken windows were indeed a rare event and should anyone have the misfortune of accidentally breaking a window, there would be hell to pay even after the window was repaired and paid for.

Along with hunting, fishing was always an adventure. It provided a form of relaxation and enjoyable quiet time. It was also an opportunity to bring some fresh fish to the table. Fancy fishing rigs were not affordable and like most kids in the neighborhood, Joseph would make his own rig. A pole would be cut out of a young maple sapling and fitted with a winding of store string connected to a fish hook. Eventually, Joseph found a discarded, bent fishing reel that he was able to fix and fastened it to a crude pole. Using screw eyes as guides for his fishing line, he had a fishing pole that lasted for many years and now stands in the corner of his den as a lasting memento of many happy days.

War games were a common pastime. Weapons used in this activity were also homemade and harmless. Guns that fired rubber bands cut from rubber inner tubes were made from a rectangular piece of wood. A nail was hammered into the bottom edge and used for the trigger finger. Half of a clothes pin was used for the hammer and was tightly banded with several rubber bands to the end of the gun. Squeezing the trigger nail together with the clothes pin would release a rubber band "bullet" that was stretched along the top length of the barrel held in place by the clothes pin pressing against it. *The rubber inner tubes of old were made of real rubber and easily stretched making for good travel distance and accuracy.*

~ THE HOME ENTERTAINMENT CENTER ~

There was no television to occupy idle time. Many households, as with Joseph's, had neither telephone nor car nor subscription to the local newspaper. Contact with the outside world was the radio. It was usually a big hunk of furniture, about three feet high, that sat in a corner of the living room where the kids would gather on the floor to listen to favorite programs. Programs like The Shadow, Jack Armstrong - the All American Boy, and The Green Hornet were some favorites. Kids would lie on the floor in front of the radio listening and allowing themselves, through their imagination, to be transported into the adventures and descriptive scenes of the program. They appeared so real in their minds they transfixed the listeners directly into another world. On Sunday evenings, families would sit together in front of the radio and listen to popular weekly programs like The Jack Benny Show, Edgar Bergen with Charlie McCarthy and Mortimer Snerd, and The Fred Allen Show.

The radio programs had to be one of the greatest learning tools for developing an imagination in the minds of that generation. Unlike today where the graphic details of television leave little or nothing to one's imagination.

~ FROM JOSEPH to JOEY ~

By now, most of Joseph's friends called him Joey. The name, Joseph, was used mainly in school by his teachers. Some of the older kids nicknamed him "Shindy" a name he disliked and couldn't do

much about because they were bigger and stronger than he.   The
name came about one day when one of the older kids asked Joey
where he lived. He pointed to his father's shed in the distance and
said, "over there by the ... (a Sicilian slang word for shed that sounded
like shindy)."   Everyone laughed. The name stuck and was used
many times by the older boys to agitate Joey. It seems all names of
that era used two syllables: Eddy, Frankie, Charlie, Benny, Stevey,
Mikey. Even Joey's dog, who was named Hooks was called Hooksy,
name earned by always stealing the ball during a game. Another word
for steal was "hook." If one said you "hooked" something it meant
you stole it. Hooksy was seen one day eating his own excrement and
from then on the older kids called him Shithooks, a name that
offended Joey and made him very angry.

~ STASHU'S MARKET ~

Joey lived three houses away from the neighborhood grocery
store. The store was a typical Mom and Pop operation that was very
common in that generation. It occupied the front part of their house
and sold all the essentials needed in most homes. Everything from
floor mops to all cuts of meats, canned foods, and ice cream cones.
The entire family worked in the store. Stashu was the oldest son and
at sixteen he had quit school to work full time in the store. He had a
driver's license and on designated days of the week he would fill
orders for home delivery. Many times he would ask Joey if he wanted
to take a ride and help with the deliveries. Joey would jump at the
opportunity to ride with him. Not having a car in the family, a ride in
a motor vehicle was a special treat. Besides, Stashu always had

interesting stories to tell. The delivery truck was a small panel type truck with only one seat -- the driver's. A passenger sat on the floor or on a box usually filled with bottles or groceries.

Saturday was the busiest day in the store and Joey, sometimes, got a chance to help out. The store experience would turn out to be his first introduction to sex education. One day, Joey was behind the counter when a customer came in with her order. As she read from her shopping list he would get the item off the shelf and take it to the counter for bagging. One of the items she asked for was a box of table napkins. All napkins and light weight items were stored on the higher shelves. This was an opportunity for Joey to make use of one of the long sticks with spring-loaded jaws that could be opened to grab onto out-of-reach items. He had seen them used before to remove items from the high shelves and then skillfully caught as they dropped. It looked like fun. Along the top shelf he spotted a display of blue boxes with the words "sanitary napkins" printed below the company logo. Down it came and the catch was perfect. As he turned and placed the box on the counter the customer said, "no, no, I don't want those, I want table napkins." Joey, trying to be a good sales clerk, pointed to the box and replied, "but, Ma'am, these are good ones, see, it says they're sanitary ones right here." The lady held her hand over her mouth. She was speechless. By this time Stashu's father came to the rescue. He apologized to the lady and they both enjoyed a good laugh. Joey, somewhat confused by the whole affair was sent outside to help with loading the truck. The next trip with Stashu was when he learned all about Kotex, the sanitary napkin. *Of course, the explanation was expanded and interesting.*

Thursday afternoons was chicken day at the store. On this day chickens were readied for processing on Friday. Little or no meat was consumed on Friday since it was an eat fish day for most Catholics and some Protestants too. *With no refrigeration, fishing smacks came in on Fridays to serve the towns. Fish was fresh off boats. Residents of coastal towns could buy from wells on boats -- fish gutted, wrapped in newspaper and taken home.* On Saturday the chickens were ready to be sold. The store had their live chickens in a large chicken coop in the rear yard. Joey and Stashu's younger brother, Henny, would chase all the chickens into the coop and close the door. Stashu would wait outside, with a short length of steel pipe in his hand. Henny would go inside and close the door behind him. He then would open a small door near the floor, normally used by the chickens to enter and exit the coop. One by one, he would coax them outside where Stashu waited with a hunk of pipe in hand. As the chickens exited the coop, he would clobber them unconscious and then bleed them by slitting their throats. The feathers were plucked while their bodies were still warm making for easy removal without the use of hot water.

When darkness set in Joey and Henny would often climb onto the roof of the chicken coop and lay there quietly, hanging over the edge with a forked spade dangling from their hands. They waited patiently for rats to emerge from under the coop searching for bits of chicken left on the ground. It was a contest as to who could spear the most rats.

Henny's ready access to the store provided cigarettes and other goodies unbeknown to his parents. He would open a new pack of Lucky Strike cigarettes and he and Joey would have a smoke behind the garage. The remainder of the pack would be hidden in an outside wood pile stacked along the side wall. After a rainstorm the wet, yellow-stained cigarettes were removed from the pack and laid out to dry to be smoked another day. It was Stashu who caught them smoking one day and told them if they continued to smoke that stuff it would dry up their blood and they would die. That was enough to scare them and it put an end to their smoking. Henny decided to try chewing tobacco instead. A rectangular plug of golden colored tobacco, wrapped in a clear cellophane package with a big red apple printed on it, labeled Apple Honey, looked like it would be a sweet treat. The plug was split in half, Joey and Henny, each taking a half. Not knowing only a very small piece was used by chewers, they put the entire half plug into their mouths and started chewing. It didn't take very long before they swallowed enough tobacco juice to make them both very sick. Henny quickly ran into his house and Joey, dizzy headed and holding his stomach, in a whispering voice was quietly calling for his mother's help as he struggled to walk home. *It seemed that he would never make it home as he held onto a wall, inching along.*

Stashu's parents were very religious and regularly attended the local Polish Catholic church. Often they would ask Joey if he went to church especially on religious holidays. Most of the time he would answer, " no," only to be chided and lectured to. Joey's parents were not church goers because his mother was constantly caring for his bedridden brother and his father's only day off from work was Sunday and he needed that entire day to attend to the needs of his small farm. However, Joey was encouraged to attend church by himself. His mother would give him a nickel and send him off to Sunday mass. After mass he was to attend catechism classes in preparation for his First Communion. This arrangement was short-lived. During attendance in his second class, the teacher, a young girl, asked him to leave because of his fooling around with some other boys and not paying attention to what was being taught. Joey never did return to class. That time would be spent in the nearby woods watching a crap game which was a regular fair weather event, for several young adults, after a Sunday mass. They would gather in a secluded area using the younger kids as lookouts and fetchers of discarded cardboard boxes which would be flattened and used as a surface to roll the dice on. Sunday crap games would periodically be moved to a different locale in the woods to avoid police detection.

After watching what appeared to be huge amounts of money changing hands (impressive hunks of folding money, not change), Joey decided he would skip Sunday mass and save his nickels so one day he could play the game. He never did accumulate enough money to get into the big game, but he did learn the basics of shooting craps. When he attended church services, he observed that the priest, who was noted for his fire and brimstone sermons, was a frightening figure. It seemed his sermons captivated the entire congregation's attention to a point where one might hear a pin drop or the breathing of the person seated next to you.. This terror ended Joey's church going for a long time.

Joey never did get to make his First Communion or his Confirmation until much later in life -- after graduating from college.

~ NEIGHBORHOOD GANGS ~

Gangs were not formal organizations but rather a group of kids from the same neighborhood, mostly from the same ethnic group. There was no rivalry among many gangs, no secret meetings nor initiations, nor any of the ill conceived practices we hear about in this day and age.   It was a rare occasion when one gang would visit another to play a game of baseball or tackle football. All encounters were friendly and seldom were there fights. If there were a fight it would be between two individuals but never a gang fight.

There was one gang, however, that everyone stayed away from. It was the River Street Gang. One of its members, a kid named Rollie, was well-known for shooting at others with a 22 caliber rifle. He had to be a terrific shot because he never hit anyone. He always seemed to manage a near miss that would kick up the dirt and pebbles around his target sending everyone nearby scurrying for cover as he enjoyed a good laugh. Joey had a school friend named Eddy who lived within a few houses of Rollie. One day on his way to visit Eddy he took a shortcut dangerously near Rollie's hangout and subjected himself to some of Rollie's fancy shooting. *Needless to say, all track records were broken that day and Joey's feet hardly touched the ground as he raced for the shelter of Eddy's house.*

Rollie had many encounters with the law and served several terms in, what was then called, Reform School. On one of his many escapes from Reform School, he was caught at home and convinced his captors to wait while he went to his bedroom to get some personal items to take back with him. He then climbed out the back window of his bedroom and hid inside an empty garbage can. The resulting momentary search for Rollie proved futile. However, this deceptive move gave Rollie a few more days of freedom.

On another of his escapes he led the local police on a chase that was to see him attempt a swim across the local harbor in an effort to elude capture. This was to be the last time police would be bothered with his antics. He was captured and returned to the State Reform School. A few weeks later, he was found dead in his room hanging by the neck -- *an apparent suicide at a very early age.*

~ RAIDING PARTIES ~

No matter what season of the year, kids would find something to do. Family vegetable gardens were plentiful and provided an attractive lure for raiding parties. At the edge of the *Comps* an old man, called Bubbles by the kids, had a small apple orchard in the midst of a large garden. Bubbles was stone deaf and because of his old age he could not move very fast. Sometimes the desire to get some of his delicious apples was too great to ignore so Joey and a few of his friends would lie in wait in the high grass area outside a six foot high wire fence. When Bubbles was far enough away and had his back turned, the fence was climbed and the low branches of the trees were carefully relieved of their fruit. The old knickers style trousers came in very handy. Everyone checked for holes in pockets and the one with the biggest hole would be designated as the carrier of extra apples. If the hole weren't big enough, it quickly became bigger with a little help. The baggy legs had plenty of room to store many apples. Overloading was always a concern because it could hinder running and getting back over the fence.

A lookout was always left behind to keep an eye on the old man. Should he turn and spot what was going on, the lookout would yell "Bubbles" and the race for the fence started. An escape plan was always in place prior to the raid. Everyone had a place along the fence, distanced from each other, so as to confuse Bubbles and make it difficult for him to catch anyone.

Gardens bordering the *Comps* also provided potatoes and corn silk. Potatoes were dug out with bare hands, washed in a nearby brook, and cooked in an open fire a safe distance from their point of origin. They were cooked until the skin became black and crusty thick. Most of the blackness was then wiped off or knocked off with a stick.

Cornfields provided corn silk, the dry dark-colored kind was removed from the ear and rolled into the shape of a cigar using strips of brown paper from a discarded grocery bag. Sometimes these cigars would burn so hot it was almost impossible to take a drag without creating a burning sensation in the throat. For some unexplained reason the ear of corn was never stolen, perhaps because the kids didn't know it could be cooked on an open fire *There's nothing like a burnt, tasty potato meal followed with a good cigar.*

Sometimes the older boys would come by and throw a handful of live 22 caliber bullets into the fire just to watch everyone scatter and hit the ground for cover as the shells exploded. No one ever got hurt because the fire was always set in a dish shaped cavity in a rock ledge and when the shells exploded the fragments were directed up and out.

There was a time when one of these raiding parties did not go as planned. This time the owner, an old man, not as old as Bubbles, came out his back door just as the raiders were climbing back over the fence. The old man was quick to catch Frankie, with his knickers loaded with apples, just as he was about to make it over the fence, grabbing him by his trousers while Frankie held onto the fence for dear life. His trousers came apart along the seams down to the knees. Another good yank and they were completely down spilling the apples all over the ground. There was one embarrassed kid with one irate, old man who made him pick up every apple while his pants were down around his knees. He had to carry the apples to the back door and hand them over to the man's wife who stood there laughing. When he finished, he got a swift kick in the butt and told never to come back.

The last laugh of this escapade would come on Halloween night. It was *get even time.* An old Campbell Soup cardboard box was obtained from the corner grocer, then, half-filled with the dirtiest and most foul smelling garbage that could be found topped with a few shovelfuls of chicken manure.

Joseph can remember the careful and detailed planning for "operation get even." Several heavy garbage cans were quietly placed on the old man's bulkhead door leading to the basement. A length of clothesline was tied to the back doorknob with the other end tightly secured to a porch post. Now, anyone attempting to get out the back of the house would have a difficult time. The Campbell Soup carton with the foul smelling slimy garbage, its covering flaps folded closed as if it were a new carton, was carried to the front porch and quietly and carefully turned bottom side up and placed directly in line with the front door in the center of the porch floor.

Everyone went across the street and found a place to hide behind a tall hedge and observe what was about to happen. Frankie rang the front door bell and, to be sure he would be heard, gave a few extra loud bangs on the door. He jumped off the porch and ran to a hiding place across the street and watched. As planned, the front door opened and the old man, seeing the upside down carton, gave it a terrific boot sending it flying across the porch floor and down the front steps, spilling its foul smelling contents all over the place. . To everyone's delight it was a mess to behold. *None of he kids would go near this house again for months thereafter.*

~ SECOND TIME AROUND ~

Repeating the fifth grade was probably one of the easiest grade levels in Joey's early education. He and another boy, Orrin, became the teacher's favorites. Orrin was really smart and Joey obviously knew the teacher's routines from the year before. The lessons were old stuff. Joey captured several awards that year. Perfect attendance, never late, best wild flower collection, and best penmanship were some of the awards remembered. The teacher awarded him with a new Boy Scout knife for his wild flower collection. *Can you imagine a teacher giving a student a knife these days?* The knife would be treasured for life and to this day the knife is still in his possession. Joey soon convinced his mother to buy him a new pair of hi-cut boots that came with a sewed on side pocket to hold his new knife. Hi-cuts were high-laced shoes, almost reaching the knees. Further, it was the style of the day for boys to wear hi-cuts with knicker style pants. Very few boys in the early grades had long pants. Long pants were a luxury that eluded Joey until he entered the seventh grade at Broadway School.

The schoolyard became a very competitive area of play. Many arguments would be settled by a fist fight after school on the way home, out of sight of the school grounds. The event would be anticipated by many classmates who heard earlier that day of the impending fight. One such day would involve Orrin. During a rough-housing session in the schoolyard Orrin had the misfortune to hook onto Joey's hi-cut shoe tearing the closing snap off the pocket holding Joey's knife. Fighting words developed and the big event was immediately scheduled for after school hours. A couple a blocks away, Orrin removed his glasses and handed them to a friend -- *that meant he was ready.* Joey wasted no time in starting his, now famous, windmill action in motion, Orrin, back stepping as fast as he could, quickly went down to the ground and refused to get up -- *it was over and settled and they became friends, never to fight each other again.*

The next day, the teacher heard about the fight. She was told that Joey beat up Orrin badly -- *a greatly exaggerated story*. To make matters worse, Orrin was not in school that day and Joey was subjected to an old time grilling by his teacher and the sixth grade teacher who also served as the school principal. This was not a good situation for Joey because she was to be his next grade level teacher and already he was in trouble with her. It turned out Orrin was out because he was sick and not because of any injury -- *the only injury he could have suffered was to his pride or a good case of wind burn from the whirling windmill attack -- the great majority of swings having missed their mark.*

~ A LESSON in RESPONSIBILITY ~

On the walk to school one snowy winter day, Joey and some of his friends decided to throw snowballs at the girls walking in front of them. The snow was wet and it packed nicely to form icy snowballs. During a bombardment of snowballs, Joey threw an icy ball that found its mark near the hemline, in the center of the back, of a transparent plastic-like raincoat. It penetrated the coat leaving a gaping hole in the plastic-like fabric. When the girls arrived at school they reported the incident to the principal. All the boys involved were called to her room and the interrogation began. No one would admit to throwing the snowball that did the damage. When it became apparent they would all be punished, Joey raised his hand and said,

"I'm sorry ... me did."

With an infuriated tone in her voice she replied,

"Poor English, Joseph, it's I, I, I, not me."

She paused awhile staring him straight in the eye and then said,

"You need to pay Winnie for a new coat *and* apologize to her."

The replacement cost was determined to be approximately two dollars. Joey went home that afternoon dreading the thought of telling his father what he had done, and especially needing to ask him for two dollars. That evening at the dinner table, and after the radio news broadcast, (Joey's father always demanded everyone be quiet during the radio news broadcast -- no one was allowed to talk), it was time to tell him what happened on the way to school that day. Joey told his father he needed two dollars to pay for some damage he had accidentally done. As expected, this was not well-received. After a very short discussion, Joey's father said to him,

"You broke da coat ... you pay ... no me."

His "no" always meant "no" and that was the end of the conversation. *An appeal process was never allowed and Joey knew too well it was not a wise move to challenge his decision.* Upon return to school the next day, Joey reported to the principal that he was unable to get any money from his parents; however, he would be willing to pay for it himself from money to be earned shoveling snow. This turned out to be an acceptable arrangement and Joey was to make a payment to the principal after each snow storm. Shoveling snow from neighborhood sidewalks in those days earned him anywhere from twenty five cents to fifty cents for each job. The higher amount usually included shoveling a long driveway. It took several snow storms and many early morning risings, before leaving for school, to earn enough money to pay for the coat.

This escapade served as a great lesson for Joey. Not only did it earn him the respect of his teacher / principal for his determination to live up to his promise to pay, but it also clung with him throughout life as a constant reminder that he, alone, had to take responsibility for his own actions.

Years later, he tried to instill this in his own children, during their formative years.

~ BROADWAY SCHOOL and WORK ~

Broad Street school housed only six grade levels so eventually Joey was off to Broadway School for the seventh and eighth grades. This was a very large school, located downtown, housing students ranging from kindergarten through the eighth grade.   It had classrooms on each of its four floors.   The top floor had been renovated because of the damage caused by the '38 hurricane.   A good portion of its roof, shingles, including roof boards and framing, had been blown off by the hurricane winds.

The seventh grade year was a good school year for Joey. Here he encountered, for the second time, his former fourth grade teacher, Miss Shields, who now was one of his seventh grade teachers. She was his favorite and the most helpful teacher of his entire elementary school experience. Her interest in him motivated him to seek new heights in all his subject areas with all four of his seventh grade subject teachers. Miss Shields was to inspire in him a special interest in geography and social studies.   Joey, with her guidance, became deeply involved in a class project building a model of the Panama Canal that spread across the entire raised teaching platform in front of the room . He would spend many after school hours in the local public library researching the canal and its design.   Sets of working locks were built including a huge lake with its surrounding landscape.

49

Paper mache' was used extensively and painted by the class. This massive undertaking was on display for the entire school year and Joey was hailed as one of its great engineers -- *what a tremendous boost to his ego and sense of self worth. Miss Shields seemed to have magical powers over Joey.*

Broadway School also provided Joey with another positive experience. It would be his first exposure to basic carpentry. It was called manual training. Because of his good work ethic and interest he was chosen to help in building world globes to be used in many of the classrooms. These globes were huge, about three feet in diameter. It would be his first introduction to a geometric problem. Joey would experiment at home by slicing the skin on an orange in such a way as to simulate the pieces needed to be cut to form a spherical world globe.

Another project, this one was for himself, was to build a bookcase. It turned out to be bigger than he could carry and the biggest individual project made in school that year. It was finished at year end and now he was faced with getting it home. He borrowed a wagon and rigged it to carry the bookcase in such a way as not to damage the hand rubbed finish. Then he struggled pulling it home -- *it was a long, up hill pull all the way.*

~ *BOAT BUILDING* ~

Whenever Francesco, his father, was working on a construction job where used lumber was headed for the dump, he would arrange for a truckload of the reusable lumber to be delivered to his home. It was Joey's job to pull out the nails, straighten and save them, and sort and stack the reusable lumber by size. Hours and days were devoted to this chore; however, there was a bright side to this monotony. It allowed Joey an opportunity to experiment in building a few projects. He started with bird houses and lawn chairs and soon moved on to bigger projects. One such project was a boat. Had he known, Francesco never would have approved of such a project, so Joey was careful not to divulge his plans and proceeded to find an obscure place, behind an old barn, where his building activity would not be easily detected.

Tongue and groove boards were selected and hand cut to size. There were no screws available; used nails had to suffice. The construction went smoothly until it was time to form the bow. Not knowing how to bend lumber and wanting his boat to have a pointed bow, he built an angled bow separately and nailed it to the open side of what was, at that stage, a three-sided box. A nearby roofing company provided the tar used to seal the joints. Two kinds of tar were always available; the soft, pliable kind used to seal small voids and the brick-hard kind that was melted and applied to flat roofs. Chunks of the brick-hard tar were often smashed into little pieces by the kids and chewed like candy chewing gum. *It's a wonder no one became ill or died. It didn't taste that good, but it certainly gave your jaw muscles a workout.* Oars were fashioned out of old, discarded auto license plates nailed to long sticks. The finished boat turned out to be monstrous in size and much too heavy to be lifted or carried. No problem. Old carriage wheels were fastened to the ends of two 2X4's and they were tacked to the bottom of the boat, now it could be pulled and pushed to the river for launching.

Joey and his friend, Eddy, picked a launching site near the Gas House at the river's edge. Here the river was closest to the roadway and the boat could be wheeled in easily, they thought. However, after crossing the railroad tracks, they encountered a retaining wall with a six foot drop to the shore level below. There was no way that Joey and Eddy could slide this monstrous boat down to the shore level by themselves. It was just too big and too heavy. Just then, an older big kid came along, he had to be about fifteen years old, and they asked him to help.

"Sure," he said, "I'll get down there and you guys push the boat over the side."

The big kid waited below, the wheels were hammered off the bottom, and the boat was nudged over onto the pair of waiting hands outstretched over his head. The boat was too heavy and could not be controlled by the brave helper. Down he went, with the bow of the boat leading the way, crashing onto a rock, splintering several floor boards in the bow section. Joey was prepared for emergencies with hammer, nails, bailing can, and a can of soft tar. The tar was carefully spread over the splintered areas, loose boards were hammered tight and the boat was then shoved into the water. *What a joyful feeling. It floated.*

Joey and Eddy climbed in and began to row the boat across the river. About in the middle of the river, the bailing can was put to use to clear some of the water that had seeped in. As they were bailing they noticed the soft tar covering the splintered boards was beginning to form big bubbles. The bubbles got bigger and bigger and more of them start forming. Soon, they burst and the water came in faster than they could bail it out. Sitting in waste deep water, they decided they had better abandon ship. Luckily for them the river at this point was not very deep. They waded to shore as they watched the partially submerged boat float down river, never to be recovered.

The following summer, Joey went to the local public library and researched kayak building. Painstakingly, he built a frame, got some old canvas to cover it, and sealed it with a water proofing dope that resembled tar. Again, license plates on a long stick would serve as paddles. The small pond at Mohegan Park was chosen as the place for its maiden voyage. The kayak, being much lighter than the previous wooden monster, did not require special wheels for transport. A regular wagon would do the job. On the way to the pond, Joey stopped at his friend's house and convinced Buddy to come along. They both pulled the kayak to the pond. When they got to the pond they both lifted the kayak into the water and checked it out for any leaks. Joey was a bit leery of his new vessel, never having been in a kayak, he said to Buddy,

"Do you wanna go first?"

Buddy replied, "Yeah, I'm not chicken."

Joey steadied the kayak while Buddy climbed in. Off he went, gliding smoothly. Not even twenty feet from shore, the kayak turned over on its side and Buddy struggled to free himself. As he was thrashing in the water and turning over and over, Joey couldn't help but laugh. He laughed so hard he was holding his side in pain. Buddy was getting madder by the second, cursing the kayak until he was able to finally free himself. He dragged the kayak ashore, and being a hot tempered kid, he cursed at it again and kicked a major hole in its side. Then, together they both kicked it apart and tossed the remains into the nearby woods. *Joey went home with an empty wagon.*

Joey, not to be discouraged by these adventures, decided, the next time, he would build a butter box style boat. A simple, rectangular structure with a square, sloping bow. Construction was not hurried on this project because summer's end was approaching and there would be ample time to do an especially good job and be ready for next summer. This boat never made it to the river because the secret shipyard was discovered by his father and the boat, nearly completed, was quickly turned into firewood. *Thus ended Joey's boat building career.*

~ JOEY'S FIRST KISS ~

The schoolyard at Broadway was very small, always crowded, and limited to playing games requiring little space. Playing baseball and football were prohibited. Girls played on one half of the area and boys on the other. One day, during a girl's dodge ball game, the ball rolled onto the boys' side and directly toward where Joey was standing. He picked up the ball and was about to hand it to, Carmela, the girl who chased after it. Before he knew what was happening, she grabbed him with both arms and planted a big kiss right on his lips. She then took the ball and ran back to her game. Joey stood there in a state of shock and embarrassment while his friends laughed, hooted, and hollered. *He could not get to the boys' room fast enough to wash off the remains of what was a very wet kiss.*

It would be days before he could live this one down. From then on he would avoid Carmela as if she had the plague. He would avoid making eye contact with her. In fact, he got in trouble one day because he refused to dance with her. As part of the physical education program in those days, the visiting physical education teacher would teach dancing by forming two lines side by side around the perimeter of the room. Boys and girls were paired together with boys on the left and girls on the right. The room was very large, it contained four classes totaling close to a hundred twenty-five or more students. Joey would always spot where Carmela would be standing and try to position himself, far enough away in line, so he would not wind up with her as a partner. Dancing started and when the music stopped the boy moved ahead to the next girl in line and so it went. Well, as luck would have it one day, when the music stopped, Carmela, somehow, got to be next in line for Joey. He refused to dance with her and tried to skip over her to the next girl but the boy who just moved ahead from her would not relinquish his spot. The teacher was quick to notice the commotion and Joey was in hot water again. *A few years later he realized, that maybe, he had made a mistake. Carmela turned out to be a really good looker. However, she got herself into trouble in high school and quit school.*

~ WAR IS DECLARED ~

War with Japan was declared while Joey was enrolled in seventh grade at Broadway School. He was to learn of that infamous Pearl Harbor Sunday when he was sent to the neighborhood grocery store to buy a yeastcake for his mother. The Polish grocer, in his accented voice, said to him,

"Joey, I think you go in da army pretty soon."

Joey was confused by his comment and would not know its full meaning until the next day in school. The teachers made the surprise bombing of Pearl Harbor the subject of the day. *These were scary and exciting times.*

Joey learned several weeks later that his former next door neighbor, Mikey, was trapped on a battleship, the Arizona, when it was bombed and sunk. Mikey was killed in the attack and would be forever entombed on the Arizona. In the years prior to joining the armed services, Mikey and his brother, Jimmy, would sometimes entertain Joey, as he peered over the backyard wooden fence. He enjoyed watching them kneading bread dough for their mother in a large galvanized tub which was placed on two rickety wooden saw horses. They took great delight in punching what was imagined to be a giant's big belly in the tub.

Mikey's mother, to her dying day, refused to believe her son was dead. She could be seen, for hours on end, standing on the sidewalk in front of her house waiting for him to come home. When Joey's mother would stop to talk with her, Joey would listen in amazement as she would sobbingly express her sincere belief that Mikey was alive and well. In her mind she believed he was living in the ocean with a mermaid. For years she stood in front of her house, waiting for Mikey to come home. Eventually, she was committed to the State Hospital where she died, still waiting. Mikey's father also was never the same after the loss of his oldest son and he also would carry this sorrowful belief to his grave.

Thirty six years after Pearl Harbor, Joey visited the Arizona Memorial. He stood over the sunken battleship, looked down through the water at one of the ship's smoke stacks and experienced an undescribable, eerie feeling. This was Mikey's tomb and he could envision Mikey dancing around the big tub and laughing while punching the giant's belly.

• • •

Young men were drafted and went off to war. Women went into defense work programs. Scrap iron was collected for war use. All kinds of activity kept the city bustling. The entire country was quickly mobilized for war. Air raid drills were practiced in all schools.; blackout drills at home at night. Cars and trucks were required to have their headlights painted black with only a small opening for light to shine downward limiting the amount of light that could possibly be spotted by enemy aircraft flying above.

Joey attended airplane spotters' classes held at Broadway School at night. Here, he learned to spot and recognize silhouettes of enemy aircraft and be able to report them quickly to air raid wardens. On the way to school in the morning he would walk by the State Armory Building and watch the buses loaded with young men, who had been drafted, leaving for service in the armed forces. After tearful good-byes with their families they would be handed packs of cigarettes and loaded onto their bus. Joey thought this was great, all those cigarettes for free. Silently, he wished he could be one of them. As the buses left the curbside, many inductees would be hanging out both sides of the bus windows frantically waving to their loved ones until out of sight. Left behind were mothers and fathers, wives and children, friends and girlfriends, many standing and sobbing trying to comfort each other. Slowly, the crowds seemed to vanish and Joey would run to school because, now, he was late. *No one was ever punished for being late for watching the boys go off to war.*

~ WORKING the CITY STREETS ~

The war years provided many opportunities for youngsters to earn a few pennies.   Joey tried to earn some money.   The local newspaper had an afternoon edition of the news which was quite popular in those days. Not many kids could afford to buy a route so it was either work for someone who owned a route or "hack" newspapers on the city street corners.   Joey tried both and soon found he could make more money "hacking" newspapers on street corners yelling,

"Paper, paper, get your paper here."

At four in the afternoon a crowd of ambitious youngsters would gather in a distribution room at the rear of the newspaper building waiting, with heavy white canvas carrying bags, for a huge roll-up window to open. The big push was on to be one of the first to buy newspapers to be resold on the streets. The bigger kids would always beat on the smaller ones with their heavy bags for a more advantageous position. After suffering a few stinging defeats at the hands of some of the bigger kids, Joey while on his way to buy his papers one day passed by a driveway paved with small pea-sized stones. He grabbed a handful of stones and put them in the bottom of his bag. When the bag swinging started he was ready. It didn't take much effort to make his way up front.

Newspapers were purchased at the counter with cash only, three for a nickel. They would be sold on the street for the same price as the news stands, two cents each, a penny profit when three were sold. However, many customers would pay with a nickel and not require any change so a handsome profit was made. Joey made it a practice to sell to people getting off buses at transfer points because they would be in a hurry to get a seat on an awaiting bus and did not want to wait for change. Unsold newspapers would not be discarded but taken home where a good use for them could always be found. *Many homemade kites were to be made from old newsprint.*

• • •

Shining shoes on a busy downtown streets was another money maker, especially on a Saturday. The competition for a good spot was fierce and required one to get to it early. Joey made his first shoe shine box from remnants of wooden boxes used to ship grapes to his father for wine making. A carrying shoulder strap was fashioned out of a discarded belt from his father's trousers. Brown and black shoe polish came from a Five and Dime Store where they were purchased for a nickel per can. A shoe brush and an polish applicator brush were unaffordable and therefore considered a luxury. Instead, bare fingers dipped into an open can of polish were used to rub the polish directly to the shoe and a strip of old, soft cloth would be used to apply the finishing shining touches. Joey could always tell who the experienced shoe shiners were by the loud snap of the polishing cloth as it crossed the shoe. The real pro would spray a little bit of spit on the face of the shoe to give the shine more luster.

A good spot was directly related to how much money was earned. Joey was quick to learn how to discourage newcomers; therefore competition, from moving in on his territory. He learned from his friends to put numbers on his box. Metal numbers used to number houses were obtained from the Five and Dime Store and nailed to the end of the shoe shine box. When newcomers came along without a number displayed on their new box they would be quickly spotted and stopped by the veteran shoeshine boys and told they needed to get a license and a number before they could shine shoes in the city. They would be told to go to the Court House and for a one dollar fee a license and number would be issued. This was enough to discourage new competition. *After all, who could afford a buck for a license?*

Many Saturdays, in winter and summer, Joey would spend hustling shoe shines for a nickel a shine. A two dollar Saturday was considered a fantastic day. Many Saturdays he would go home with cuts on his fingers from the sharp edges on the cans of polish, cold and disappointed with less than that magic number of a two dollar day.

~ THE BOWLING ALLEYS ~

Joey and his friend, Dicky, found jobs as bowling pinsetters in what was known then as The Alleys -- *no automatic pinsetters in those days.* Their starting pay was three cents a string and soon they would become two of the best pinsetters in The Alleys and their pay was raised to five cents a string. It was illegal to work in The Alleys if you were under sixteen years of age. The owner would carefully drill all the underage employees as to what to do should a state inspector decide to check his establishment. The owner rigged a buzzer system that would ring in the pits warning the underage pin-setters that they were to stop immediately and leave through an opening in back of the pits and go out the back door and directly home. The system worked well because the underage pinsetters work on the second floor and before the inspectors reached the second floor the warning buzzer sounded and everyone vanished to return another day. Big Tony, the owner, took good care of Joey and Dicky, gave them sodas and snacks, drove them home on late nights and physically threw out anyone who could have injured them, as would sometimes happen, when a drunken bowler decided to throw an extra ball down the alley while they were still picking up pins in the pits.

Ladies bowling leagues were fun nights at the alleys. Certain nights of the week were reserved as ladies nights and Dicky and Joey looked forward to being the regular pinsetters for the ladies league. It didn't take them long to recognize the good bowlers and the not-so-good. It seemed that every time a not-so-good bowler scored well, there would be much hoopla and hollering expressed as a form of encouragement for the bowler. Whenever a match seemed to be in a lull, it was time for the pinsetters to inject some excitement. They would wait for a not-so-good bowler's turn and set the pins in such a manner as to give her an advantage over her teammates. Unbeknown to the bowlers, the pins would be set in what was called a "combination setup." The two middle pins in the back row were moved closer to the third row of pins, along each side of the center pin. This arrangement made for a clustering of pins near the center of the formation that would be almost impossible to detect from the bowler's position at the other end of the alley. Now, a hit anywhere on either side of the formation would result in many more pins falling -- *and lots of hoopla and hollering.* The more fun the girls had was directly proportionate to the size of the tipping.

Dicky and Joey were masterful "combination" pinsetters and they often would give this advantage, unbeknown, to bowlers they thought needed some help, especially, the female gender of a couple who had an apparent show-off partner. *The tips in these cases were not so good -- and most often non-existent.*

Joey, to this day, has what is called pinsetters fingers. The index fingers on both hands curve inward. Setting duck pins day after day, picking up two in each hand, at such an early age affected the bone growth of his fingers. His earnings were saved by his mother and when he accumulated his first one hundred dollars, he bought his own, new bedroom set that is still in the family sixty-five years later.

Earning three to five dollars for six nights of work was not too shabby in those days.

~ *COW FLOP STADIUM* ~

Joey's good friend, Dicky, lived nearby on a small farm. The farm had a few cows and pigs, chickens and ducks, rabbits, a very large vegetable garden and a small fruit orchard. Dicky's mother, who emigrated from Poland, struggled to raise her thirteen children on this farm after her husband died at an early age. As with many immigrant families, they often purchased a home with land that could be farmed to supplement their family needs. Vegetable gardens provided food for canning and many families never had a need to purchase canned foods from a store.

Their farm had several pasture fields and often one became a play field when the cows were grazing in another. The play field was often called Dicky's field and many of the neighboring kids delighted in playing there because the fields were relatively flat and covered with a lush carpet of green grass. The field also provided a special challenge with its deposits of cow manure that the kids called cow flops. Years later, Dicky's field was referred to as Cow Flop Stadium. A game of touch football often turned into a rough tackle football game as the ball carrier tried to dodge stepping in a cow flop while the pursuing tacklers tried to knock him down into one of those land mines. There were a lot of near misses and sometimes a few unfortunates got messed up and had to use a nearby brook to clean up before heading home. *It didn't take much practice on this field to learn the art of fancy footwork.*

A cool, crisp fall day will always be remembered. During a game of football, Dicky was hit, slipped on a crusted land mine and fell. The laughter quickly ended when it became apparent something was very wrong. He lay on the ground with a leg under him that was in a sickening, grotesque position. His leg was broken. One of the boys spotted an old wooden platform wheelbarrow near the barn, ran over to it, removed its sides and ran back with it to where Dicky was laying. Carefully, the kids lifted him onto it and then wheeled him back to his house which was a considerable distance away. Dicky was carried onto the front porch and laid on an old mattress which happened to be on the porch floor. All the kids stood by on the front lawn and waited for the only Polish doctor in town to arrive.

The broken leg was set by the doctor there on the porch floor while Dicky, held down by family members, screamed in pain. The screams raised goose bumps on everyone's neck.

• • •

Another unforgettable day would see Jimmy, one of the tough kids in the neighborhood, making tackle after tackle. He always seemed to enjoy being rough and tough. This day he had the misfortune of being in the wrong place at the wrong time. He was attempting a tackle on a ball carrier from behind. The ball carrier was faster than he and in desperation Jimmy took a leap at the fleeing ankles only to catch the heel of a shoe under his front teeth. It was an ugly sight. Several of his upper front teeth were pulled straight out and still remained attached to his gums. A nearby lady came to help. She ran to her house, came back with a towel and Jimmy, bleeding profusely with the towel held over his mouth, ran home. He was immediately taken to a dentist who, somehow, was able to save every tooth. It was a long healing process with a mushy diet. He always joked about the mushy food whenever the kids would ask about the condition of his teeth. When Jimmy turned sixteen he left school and went to work to help his parents with their large family. He later joined the Army, worked his way up to the rank of an infantry Captain and, as fate would have it, lost his life in the jungles of Viet Nam.

63

Jimmy and his family were very poor and their life was truly a struggle, but, he was never without a smile.

Dicky and Joey remained close friends until many years later when as a young adult, during a labor strike, Dicky got himself into serious trouble with his employer. He was arrested and fined and could never obtain work again as a newspaper pressman. He became despondent and spent the rest of his life on his farm as a recluse. He did maintain a constant interest in following Joey's career path by often checking with Joey's mother until the day he died.

~ GOOD-BYE BROADWAY SCHOOL ~

The eighth grade was to see Joey get started on the wrong foot again. On the first day, one of his four teachers at that level who also served as Principal, called out his named and asked in a rather nasty manner if he was related to Cosmo. Cosmo was Joey's cousin who apparently had given her some grief a few years before. She lectured Joey in front of the entire class about how she would not tolerate anything from him that would resemble Cosmo's behavior. It seemed that from that day on, Joey could not do anything right for her. He dreaded attending her class and thought of her as a nasty old lady. Two of the other three teachers were a joy in his eyes and they were able to motivate him to perform well in their subject area. The third teacher was a bore.

Students were grouped by ability into four levels, A, B, C, and D. It didn't take long for the students to figure out the brightest students were placed in the D-group and the dumbest in the A-group. *A clever mind must have developed this system.* Before the year ended Joey had been placed in each of the four groups; totally confused as to whether he was dumb or smart or in between. *By today's standards he most likely would have been labeled as a special needs student.* At year's end it was time to choose a course of study for the first year of high school. Joey had no one at home to advise him as to what he should choose so he decided the nasty Principal had all the answers and he would ask her. The answer she gave him will follow him to his grave. She said, with a mean look in her eyes,

"Joseph, you know what I think? I think your wasting your time going to high school."

She hastily turned away from him to help another student. *What she probably meant, but didn't say, was he should go to trade school and learn a building trade. He was destined to prove her wrong.*

Joey decided the best path for him was to choose the commercial studies program. He was thinking this would prepare him for a respectable office job and he would not need to work hard the rest of his life like his father.

Graduation day from elementary school was a major event. For some, those who were sixteen years of age and there were a few, this was to be the end of their formal education. An elaborate graduation program was planned to be held in a church directly across the street from the school. Everyone was required to dress in Sunday best for this very special occasion. Joey's mother took him shopping and bought him a new white shirt, white trousers, and white shoes. As always she would insist on buying clothes he could never outgrow -- *about three sizes too large.* Joey will always remember the disappointment of that day because his father could not take time off from work to attend the afternoon exercises. It seemed that all the other kids' fathers were there.

~ A NEW KID in the NEIGHBORHOOD ~

As a reward for having graduated from grammar school, Joey talked his mother into buying him a set of eight-ounce boxing gloves. This was a big event because it was to be the most expensive gift he had ever received. Not even at Christmas time would he receive a gift of comparable value. The purchase of playthings, in his household, was considered to be a waste of money. Besides, Joey always seemed to manage the acquisition of used gifts through his friends or by making his own toys which he sometimes would use to work a trade with others. Joey was a master at making sling shots, bow and arrow sets, and guns that shot heavy rubber bands cut from discarded rubber tire tubes.

Allie moved in across the street. He was a pudgy, blond haired kid who had a brother in the Marine Corps, who when on leave, was like a neighborhood hero, always dressed in his colorful uniform decorated with impressive ribbons. Allie apparently had been drilled by his brother on some self-defense moves used by the Marines. He tried a few of these moves on Joey and managed to hurt him a few times. Having had enough one day, Joey talked Allie into putting on the boxing gloves. Allie, a bit younger in age, obliged. It didn't take long for Joey to enjoy sweet revenge. After taking a couple of clean shots to the head,   Allie had enough and would lie down. Joey would talk him into getting up. As soon as Joey started swinging again and before any punches could land, down he would go again. Up again , down again, Allie behaved like a yo-yo.

Allie never did learn how to box, but he did become an accomplished pianist and a talented artist later in life.

• • •

Allie was a good natured kid and frequently they would play together. Joey's father had several goats and whenever he had to work late, it was Joey's job to milk them before dark. He told Allie he would show him how to milk goats and they both went to the goat shed. Allie was reluctant to enter the shed with all those goats and decided to watch from the doorway. Joey proceeded to show him how. As Joey sat on the milking stool, he turned the goat's teat in Allie's direction and with a quick squeeze he fired a long stream of milk that hit Allie square in the face. The warm milk dripped off his chin and onto his shirt. *That would be Allie's first and last visit to the goat shed.*

III

From 1943 to 1952

~ A HIGH SCHOOL FRESHMAN ~

It's 1943, during the middle of Word War II.   Joseph enters
the ninth grade at the academy. Most teachers and friends call him
Joe now. Some of his older friends still call him Joey. He's starting
to sprout some facial hairs but not enough to use a razor.   The
freshman class reports to school a day before the rest of the school.
Excitement is everywhere. The academy is one huge four-year high
school, one of the largest in the state, drawing students from ten
different towns. Never before did Joe see so many new faces. The
freshmen class, alone, numbers between four hundred and five
hundred students. Everyone is dressed in new clothes and walking
about the campus bewildered by the awesome sprawl of buildings that
seem to be everywhere. Classes are scheduled in many different
buildings and most kids were forewarned not to ask directions of just
anyone if they become disoriented or lost.   Instead, they are told to

refer to the campus map posted in each building. The campus is teeming with upperclassmen who are waiting to have some fun with any unsuspecting freshmen who become lost in this maze of buildings and people. Some unsuspecting freshmen are asked to buy elevator passes so they can get to their new class on time, only to soon find none of the buildings have elevators and they have been duped. Others are sent to the far ends of the campus when the room they seek may only be a few feet away. Still others are told to go onto the athletic field and look for the scrimmage line. The building they are looking for is at the end of that line. *Many laughs and many tears will forever mark this day.*

Joe was a savvy kid and well-prepared for his first day. He knew, from others, what to expect on the first day. For him it was an uneventful one until a note was received by one of his classroom teachers requesting he be sent to the principal's office immediately. *What could that be all about ? He had done nothing wrong on this first day.* As he made his way to the principal's office located on the second floor in another building he suddenly became worried because he had heard that the principal, known as Bulldog George, was one tough hombre. He arrived in the outer office and politely informed one of the student office workers that he was told to report to the principal. She asked him to have a seat and wait because he should be arriving shortly. The office was a busy place and Joe sat there watching the activity. He also noticed how pretty the girl was who asked him to have a seat. As a matter of fact, there were several student office workers there who were good lookers. Soon, a big man came in, gave a glancing look at Joe, and went behind the counter to a side office. Joe knew this had to be Bulldog George. His face had jowls just like a bulldog and he was mean looking. A short while later the pretty girl summoned Joe to come in. He entered a small office and was greeted with a scowling look staring over a set of half glasses,

"So, your Joe the trouble maker," he said.

Joe replied, "I'm sorry sir, I don't understand, what did I do? It soon became apparent that on the way to school that morning, Joe and some of his friends took a shortcut through the Broad Street School yard. His former fifth grade teacher, *you know the one who held him back a year*, -- still had her ground level classroom and observed what she thought were uncomplimentary gestures coming from a group of boys as they passed by her window. Recognizing Joe as part of the group she called and reported his name to Bulldog George. Joe had said nothing and done nothing other than enjoy a few laughs as he passed by. However, he was guilty by association and sentenced to spend a few hours on the bench in the office. *What a way to start off your high school career.*

Joe never before had a male classroom teacher. *There was no such thing as a male elementary school teacher. They were all unmarried females. In high school, married females were allowed to teach. However, should they become pregnant they would be required to leave before any physical showing became apparent.* The first year at the academy would provide him with four male teachers out of the six he was assigned. All but one were interesting and well-liked by him, as well as his classmates. Half way through the school year, one of his best liked teachers, Mr. Kells, was drafted into the army. He was an excellent role model, very personable, and a former athlete. After the war ended, he would be the one to introduce a new course into the curriculum, it was called Personal Hygiene. His course required signed parental permission and was open only to boys. Today, fifty five years later, this course would come under the guise of sex education. Joe never did take the permission form home to be signed. It would be too difficult to explain to his parents and if he could they probably wouldn't sign it anyway, so he forged the signature line as did many of his friends. This bird and the bees course emphasized the perils of venereal disease and gave everyone something to think about.

The pictures were so gruesome it would most likely slow down a young boy's sex drive.

• • •

Joe thought of himself as a fairly good athlete and looked forward to the tryouts for the frosh football team. The first day of tryouts would long be remembered. He was asked what position he wanted to play and the reply was the backfield. So he lined up with all the other hopefuls trying out for backfield positions. The coach and his new student manager, Orrin, (*remember him from the fifth grade? ... the kid Joe "beat up"...*) would make note of their observations ultimately to be used to determine the selection to the team. Each day the roster would be posted on the gym bulletin board and if a line were drawn through your name, it meant you were not selected for the team and not to bother reporting for the next day of tryouts. On the second day, the posted list had Joe's name lined out. How could that be? He proved himself as the fastest sprinter the day before; however, he was unable to catch the only pass that was thrown to him which was thrown so far behind him it was impossible for any human to catch. That S.O.B., Orrin, finally got even was his first thought.   After stewing about it for a few days he was encouraged by some of his friends, who did make the team, to go and talk to the coach. He did, but, it was too late. According to the coach, all the available uniforms had been assigned. Eventually, the head varsity, Coach Wills, heard about what happened to Joe from other players and his display of respectable speed during tryouts. The coach sent for him and invited him to come out for spring football training with the varsity team.

Talk about being high on cloud nine, Joe's cloud had to be much higher.

Spring football turned out to be a quick growing up experience. Joe, a one hundred twenty pound (soaking wet) freshman banging heads with upper classmen twice his size turned out to be a painful experience. The varsity coaches were impressed and delighted with his speed and footwork when he carried the ball.

Little did they know it was not his talent for running that made him look good, it was his fear of being hit by those huge upper classmen who delighted in catching a freshman and piling all over him.

• • •

The locker room was a dreaded place for a freshman. Sometimes, particularly when Joe had a good running day, he would be picked up by the big boys and stuffed into a locker and left there until most everyone went home; then someone would be kind enough to set him free. Exiting the gang showers often was a torture in itself as the snap of a stinging towel hit its mark. Joe's father did not understand the game of football and thought of it as a barbaric and dangerous sport. He was not pleased to learn his son was a participant and warned him several times he'd better not come home hurt. One day, as part of a practice session, a head-on tackling drill was the order. Ball carriers were allowed only to run full speed, straight on, at a linebacker who was ready and waiting to make the tackle. As luck would have, bad luck that is, the meanest and toughest linebacker, who never before could catch Joe in the open field, was ready and waiting for an easy kill and the opportunity to avenge a prior embarrassing time when Joe was able to get by him with some fancy foot work. As Joe tells it, this was like feeding raw hamburg to a starving lion. He was hit so hard his entire body went numb and he didn't even know if he still had possession of the ball or if it was fumbled. *When the birds in his head stopped chirping, he knew he still had control of the ball.* On the way home that day, Joe was hurting badly and limping. When he came within sight of his home he attempted to make his approach by hiding any trace of a limp because he feared what the reaction by his father might be. Luckily, for now, he made it home before his father arrived from work. After supper, it was homework time and then off to bed. The next morning, Joe had difficulty getting out of bed and told his mother he wasn't feeling good and wanted to stay home for the day. His father came into his bedroom to ask why he was not going to school. Soon he would learn Joe was badly bruised and football was to blame. This very angry father gave him a fiery tongue lashing, got him out of bed and sent him off to school, limping worse than ever, and with strict orders he was to give up football immediately, or else.

The or else, was something that had to be reckoned with. This ended what might have been a promising high school football career. However, the relationship he had established with Coach Wills during this short time would last for many years and play a major role in Joe's future.

• • •

Joe's academic performance in his first year was marginal. He did just enough work to get by and struggled through his business elective course. The subject was a complete bore to him and any

73

concentration on its subject matter was nearly impossible. Time was spent day dreaming of being a football hero. This was to put him into his first and only conflict with an academy teacher. Not paying attention in class one day, during the spring football season, resulted in the teacher, Mr. Cassid, telling Joe he had to make up the wasted time after school. That did not set well with Joe because he knew if he reported late for football practice the punishment would be many running laps around the field, so he blurted out,

"I'm not staying after."

Mr. Cassid, paused briefly, staring at Joe, then pointed to the door and said in a soft but firm voice,

"Out. Get out, I'll see you in the office."

He followed Joe to the office and the two of them stood in front of the Bulldog's assistant administrator, Mr. Gray, to explain the nature of their visit. Joe's explanation must have been impressive, his apology to Mr. Cassid was reluctantly accepted, and the stay after school assignment was canceled. It was sometime latter he would learn this teacher was married to a distant relative and this fact most likely earned him a passing grade. A passing grade in those days was a numeric grade of 70 in order to receive credit for the course. Joe had just barely made a 70 in each of his subject classes.

~ NO MORE STREET FIGHTS ~

Joe's high school years would see the end of his fist fights. He learned not to be so quick with his hands and that arguments could be better settled by talking than hitting. Up until high school, Joe was able to hold his own with most boys. There were two exceptions when Joe found himself on the receiving end. One was during a sand-lot football game when the game became a little dirty and an argument led to some old fashion fisticuffs. It was a surprise to him when his opponent, who was somewhat smaller than he, got the better of him and ended with Joe nursing a bloodied nose. When both gladiators calmed down, they shook hands and play resumed as if nothing ever happened.

The other encounter, when Joe came out on the short end of things, involved a neighborhood girl who he had a crush on. It became obvious that someone else also had her eye. He was considerably bigger and stronger than Joe and this encounter ended quickly with a bloody nose. A handshake ended the bout and they became good friends. Soon after, they both would learn the confrontation was for naught because neither was in her favor. There was another, much older boy, who had captured her interest.

Joe's last two fights would come during his freshman year on the way home from school. There was a boy called Whitey who was older and bigger who always bullied anyone smaller than he. Whitey kept poking Joe from behind with a long stick and after being told to knock it off several times, he said to Joe,

"Are you gonna make me?"

Joe said nothing and kept walking. On the very next poke, Joe turned quickly, grabbed the stick from his hand and hit Whitey across the side of the head. The element of surprise made it easy for Joe to pummel him until he finally said,

"OK, OK, I give up."

Joe never had to fear him again and the word quickly spread that Joe's temper was to be respected.

• • •

The last fight came one winter day on the way home from school when two boys decided to throw snowballs at Joe from across the street. Snowballs were exchanged and what started as a friendly battle quickly soured when one of the boys got hit square in the face. Joe laughed and they responded by calling Joe a f---'n wop. Joe ran across the street, grabbed one kid and stuffed his head into a snow bank. The other boy jumped on Joe's back and the fight started. The fight did not last long before the two decided they had enough and went their way; one sporting a fat lip and the other, what turned out to be the next day, a beauty of a purple and black shiner (black eye).

This was Joe's first and only time he had fought two boys at the same time and it was to be the last of his street fights.

~ *SOMEONE CARED* ~

The next year the business courses of study were again a bore and any passing grades earned were more a gift of kindness than achievement. Joe didn't know his assets from his liabilities and didn't care. The only interesting class was the one with a cute teacher, Miss Eyena. Joe was enamored of her. She taught bookkeeping (called accounting today). That relationship ended one day when Joe, unable to balance his books because he was one penny off, in frustration took his worksheet to her desk, reached into his pocket and said,

"Here -- here's a penny, now we're balanced."
She didn't think that was funny and became very upset with him. *That ended the fantasy with this teacher.*

Joe looked forward to the end of the school day when he could go to work and earn some money. He had gotten himself an

76

after school job cutting grass and hedges for a lady who lived near the school. Little did he know, this experience was to have a major impact on his future. The lady, Mrs. Geril, took a special interest in him. She had a son also named Joe who happened to be confined to an army hospital in France suffering from wounds received in battle. Joe reminded her so much of her own son when he was his age. Joe had a talent for fixing most anything that required some mechanical ability. She noticed this and one day asked him what he planned to do with his life. When she heard he had chosen to follow a business course of study and was not happy with it, she sat him down and said to him,

"Young man, with your mechanical ability you should be studying and preparing yourself for a career in engineering. You need to change your course of study so you can go to college when you graduate."

Joe replied, "But, I don't think I'm smart enough to do that."

"Young man", she said, "you can do it. Never say you can't. Remember that."

Joe thought about their conversation all the way home and over the weekend. He respected and liked Mrs. Geril and did not want to disappoint her.

Monday morning Joe was in the office to see the only one guidance counselor the school had. He told her he wanted to change over to the scientific program of study so he could go on to college. She immediately pulled Joe's file and it wasn't very long after she opened the folder she looked at him and snickered, then paused and said,

"How do you expected to pass the scientific courses of study when you just barely passed the easy courses your in now ? Furthermore, you cannot earn a Scientific Diploma at this late date because you will not have time to meet the program's four year requirements."

She strongly suggested he forget about changing programs and stay with the courses he had already chosen.

Joe didn't know how he was going to tell Mrs. Geril the bad news. He knew she would be disappointed and he also feared she would think the lesser of him for not being as smart as she may have thought. *He never did tell her he barely earned passing grades.* A few weeks passed and Mrs. Geril noticed that he seemed to be avoiding her, and he was. He was quick to leave when he finished his work and would not stay to have his usual soda drink and sit and chat with her. Soon she would confront him to ask,

"Joe, is there something wrong ? We haven't talked in some time. How are you doing in your new courses?"

He sadly explained to her he had done what she told him to do but they would not allow him to change his courses. She looked him squarely in the eye and asked,

"Who wouldn't make the change?"
Joe told her, and she said to him,

"I want you to go directly to the Principal, Mr. George, I know him well, and be sure to tell him that Mrs. Geril sent you to see him and I said he should change your course of study."

The manner and tone in which she spoke to him, he knew she was somewhat upset and now it was up to him make the next move.

Joe dreaded the thought of facing Bulldog George again. He also dreaded the thought of disappointing Mrs. Geril in not following her instruction. He felt he was trapped. The only way out would be to quit working for her and that he could not do. He thought about it for a few days and finally mustered enough courage to do it. It had to be done before he would see Mrs. Geril again. There was no way to duck her. When nervous Joe walked into the principal's office and faced the Bulldog again, he was greeted with a pair of glaring eyes looking over the same half glasses positioned half way down his nose,

"Haven't I seen you before?" he said.

"Yes Sir" was the reply and in the same breath Joe said, "Mrs. Geril told me to come in and say Hello."

"Oh, how is she? I haven't seen her lately," he said with a smile.

What a relief this was for Joe. The Bulldog could smile. He was human. Joe was asked to sit down in front of his desk and he proceeded to tell the principal exactly what Mrs. Geril told him to say. Mr. George rose from his chair, went over to a file cabinet, pulled out Joe's file, went back to his desk and sat down. As soon as he opened the folder Joe detected a change in the expression on Mr. George's face and heard him grunt a short hmm sound. Joe knew this was not a good sign. He said to Joe,

"You know, what you're asking for is a very difficult course of study and you will need to do much better than the record shows here."

"Yes sir, I know, but I want to be able to go to college."
The Bulldog paused and thought awhile, then said,

"OK, ... I'll change your program so you can get yourself into college. If you do well in your college prep studies you might be accepted at the university."

Then for a short while he stared Joe in the eye and Joe couldn't help but think what must be going through his mind, *I'd rather not face Mrs. Geril. If this dummy wants to fail, so be it.*

Joe left the office much relieved and was anxious to see Mrs. Geril again. The next two years would see a surprising transformation in Joe's study habits. With a loaded schedule of college prep courses crammed into a two year time frame, he was able to graduate with a

90 average in his senior year.

Joe would be forever grateful to Mrs. Geril for her powerful and caring influence that put him on the right road at just the right time in his life.

· · ·

Before Joe turned sixteen years of age he had developed an excellent work ethic. Jobs were plentiful and his reputation as an excellent and reliable worker made it easy for him to get a job. Even though he was legally underage for employment, when asked his age he would always say he was sixteen. Most employers sensed he was lying, but didn't seem to care. The war created a shortage of workers and kids who wanted to work could. Nobody seemed to be checking ages and many underage kids were paid in cash "under the table." It was a win-win situation for the kid and the employer. Joe's pre sixteen years included work as a baker's helper in a large bakery, a grocery store clerk, an usher in a theater, a dishwasher in a restaurant, and at age fifteen a shoe store salesman.

The shoe salesman job was Mrs. Geril's doing. Her husband was the shoe store manager of a large fashionable chain store in the city. The city in those days was the shopping mecca. (Shopping malls had not yet been developed). Mrs. Geril must have convinced her husband Joe would make a good shoe salesman. He asked Joe to come to work for him and this became Joe's part time job throughout his high school days and later his college years. He did turn out to be one of the best salesmen in the store. His playful antics also managed to get him fired several times; but, was always rehired before he could get out the door. Mr. Geril would yell at him, just as he was about to exit the store,

"Joe. Get back in here, we've got customers waiting."

Mr. Geril treated Joe like he was his own son even though Joe got him in trouble with government inspectors a few times. They came in, unannounced, during the war years to check on stores to see if they were complying with government rationing regulations. During the war years, all leather shoes required a ration stamp before they could be sold; similarly, butter, meats, sugar, and gasoline. It was the store operator's responsibility to collect a ration stamp from each customer for every purchase of regulated items. A few times Joe was so busy talking to customers, he would forget to collect the stamps, *especially if they were girls*. Periodically, government inspectors would come in to check by purchasing one or more pair of shoes and it was expected and required that the salesman would collect a stamp for each pair of leather shoes sold. Joe sometimes would sell two pair and collect stamps for only one or none. He got caught twice and Mr. Geril had to answer the warning citation that was issued. Joe quickly learned how to manipulate the system to his advantage. Some of his friends worked in other stores and he would often trade off shoe stamps for some other rationed goods needed at home.

Women's nylon stockings were a hard to find item during the war years and when the store did receive a shipment, usually a small allotment, they were seldom put on display. They were saved, under the counter, for special customers and friends. Joe would also trade some for butter and sugar. *His ready access to girls' sheer nylon stockings made Joe a popular guy with a lot of young girls.* The shoe store was an interesting place to work. It attracted a wide variety of people because it carried the latest fashions in men's and women's shoes. The store was often frequented by stage and film stars who were in town to perform in summer theater productions. Joe often talks about the day movie star Veronica Lake walked in and he sold her a pair of baby doll style shoes. During bragging sessions

81

with his friends, he would let them know he had his hands on Veronica's legs. Actually, it was her ankles when he was trying to fit her for shoes, but legs sounded better. There were other movie stars like Nina Fochs and Mae West, but Veronica was his favorite.

Joe was an excellent part time salesman. Many times he would be the top salesman on Saturdays, the busiest sales day of the week. He would accommodate two and three customers at the same time when it got busy. On some days after school, he would come in to help the company window decorators set the seasonal window displays. He would often stay after the store closed to help with taking inventory. Eventually, his good work ethic reputation reached the central office administrators and upon graduation from high school he was asked by company officials if he would be interested in entering a training program for store managers.

It was tempting, but Joe had his sights on college.

~ AN ARMY EXPERIENCE ~

Toward the end of the war, Joe, still in high school, decided he would like to join the Connecticut State Guard. The regular guard, known as the National Guard, had been mobilized and sent off to war earlier. The State Guard was organized to take its place. Not yet seventeen years old, the age requirement to join, Joe joined Company H at the age of sixteen. Drill nights were held once each week in the local armory. There were also some weekend maneuvers and summer camp requirements. This experience was exciting, patriotic, manly, and an opportunity to show off. Sometimes they were allowed to wear their dress uniforms to school. Joe proved himself to be a good soldier and was soon chosen to become a member of the Guard's firing squad. This special squad was commissioned to participate in local military funerals. It was good duty and payed extra money for each funeral, of which there were several toward the end of the war, when the war dead began arriving home.

During the summer months, a caravan of army trucks would take several company units to camp. Hard work, marching drills, weapons schooling, and training on the firing range left little time for fun. Joe did manage to have some fun. When assigned to the pits on the firing range, he would often take one of the flag assignment while someone else would move the targets up and down. His job was to signal the shooter by waving a colored flag on a long pole that was extended above the pit whenever the target was hit or missed. A missed target flag, white in color, was named Maggie's drawers. Many times when a good shooter on a competing team scored a hit on the target, Joe would signal the opposite and give him the Maggie's drawers flag. A few of these wavings and the shooter would adjust his gun sights causing him to really miss the target resulting in an increased frustration level for the shooter.

There were very few sharp shooter medals awarded when Joe worked the pits.

• • •

Most everyone looked forward to firing sub-machine guns. The Thompson sub-machine guns were a real challenge when it came to target practice. Life-like targets would be placed about thirty yards out. The firing started with single shot firing, then moving on to short burst of rapid fire, and finally a long, continuous burst of fire. The latter was a real challenge because the gun, under rapid fire, tended to pull to the right and up on angle. It was a struggle to keep it on target. Joe did manage to keep the gun from taking an angle upward direction, but wasn't strong enough to control its tendency to move to the right. Thus, many times he would begin firing at his own target and in struggling to keep the muzzle on target he would wind up cutting the adjacent target in half, *only to be yelled at by his superiors.*

~ *THE ACADEMY SENIOR YEAR* ~

World War II was over and the returning service men were being replaced with occupational troops in Europe and in Japan. Joe wanted to quit school and join the armed forces before starting his senior year in high school.   Joe's plan was to spend two years in the service, earn his high school diploma while in the service and then, after discharge, he would use the G.I. Bill benefits as his ticket to a tuition free college education with a monthly living allowance.   In those days, all the returning service men were eligible for educational benefits under the G.I. Bill.   The Bill was extended to cover new recruits for a few years after the war. His plan would be short-lived. When he told his father about the plan, his father reached across the table and grabbed him by the forearm with a hard iron-like grip, and said, (in broken English)

"Ifa you leava school before you finish, you no needa worry 'bout geta kill ova there, because I killa you myself ova here."

A man of few words, the answer was clear.   End of discussion.

. . .

Senior year began with some of the discharged veterans returning to high school classes to finish their high school education. It was an interesting mix of students: the mature young men, and kids still wet behind the ears. The war stories served as a motivation for the younger students emphasizing the importance of furthering one's education. Joe wanted to make the most out of his last year especially in athletics. Being a senior with no previous team experience proved to be a disadvantage to making a team. Most coaches felt one season to learn the basics of the game and their system of play would not suffice. A first time senior was considered excess baggage with little or no value to a team effort. Joe did find himself a place on the track team where he was able to compete. The track experience was bittersweet. It took time away from his part time employment and because of this it did not meet with favor by his parents. Work was always considered most important and sports were of no value in their eyes.

Joe always thought of himself as a good sprinter and wanted to run in the dash events; however, he did not have a pair of spiked track shoes. His running shoes were ordinary sneakers. Spiked shoes were a necessity on a cinder track surface allowing the runner to move quickly out of the starting blocks. Wearing sneakers was a definite disadvantage in a situation where every fraction of a second was crucial. One day his teammate, Mo, brought a pair of his older brother's spikes to school for him to use. In time trials that day, Joe begged his coach to let him try one of the dash events. To everyone's surprise, he was able to place second in the 220 yard dash. Mo wrote to his brother, who was stationed in Germany at the time, telling his brother that his shoes, with Joe's feet in them, took an impressive second place.

Joe learned of this letter some thirty years later when he met

Mo's brother who mentioned receiving that bit of news from home.

What Mo didn't tell his brother was the shoes were too big and not only did they provide Joe with an impressive performance, but impressive blisters on both feet as well.

. . .

Joe's parents would not purchase track shoes for him and he soon found himself running events that did not require starts using starting blocks. Although Joe's performance enabled him to add to his team's point score during a meet, his heart was not in his efforts. He was discouraged and could never bring himself to understand why his parents would not buy him track shoes when in fact they bought a pair for Joe's uncle a few years earlier. His uncle was held in Africa as a prisoner of war by the British. He requested a pair of track shoes from his sister, Joe's mother, so he could participate on a prisoner of war track team. Ironically, it was Joe who went shopping with his mother and advised her as to which shoes to buy. He also helped his mother with their packaging and then walked to the post office to mail them. This experience fueled many arguments with his mother during his time on the track team. Joe was careful not to pursue any argument with his father on this issue because his stand was clearly understood and Joe's only chance appeared to be with his mother.

This chance bore no fruit and this circumstance would be remembered for a lifetime.

The last track meet of the season was the state meet. It was an all day affair held on the university campus with all large high schools in the state competing for honors. Joe knew he was scheduled to run in a medley event, a relay race, some time that day but did not know what part of the medley he was running nor the time of the event. The medley race consisted of two dash events interspersed

86

with a quarter mile and half-mile race. Joe was hoping he would not be assigned the anchorman position. It was a long day and the medley race would come late in the afternoon. During the long wait, Joe and some of his teammates did some things with their idle time that upset their coaches. Instead of resting, they ate peanuts and popcorn and went swimming in the university pool. All the things that should not be done before a race, they did. At race time the positions were announced and Joe, as he surmised, was selected to run the anchorman position ending with a half-mile race.

The race started with a dash event and the baton was passed to the next runner who ran his part of the race and then passed the baton on to the next runner and so on until it finally reached Joe's hand. When Joe grabbed the baton he noticed the closest competing runner in front of him had a thirty yard lead and the runner behind him was about the same distance away. In Joe's mind he wasn't about to try to beat the front runner, nor give any ground to the back runner. He just wanted to finish the race in the same position. At the end of the first lap and into part of the second and final lap, several dogs who were playing on a hillside near the track decided to chase after the runners. Down the hill they came and for some unexplained reason they only chased after Joe while ignoring the other runners in the race. Joe was so preoccupied with the dogs chasing him, swinging his baton at them as they tried to nip at his heels, he didn't realize he had put on an extra burst of speed that sent him past the runner in front of him; the one who was leading him by a good thirty yards. Suddenly, the cheers of his teammates and fans became very loud as Joe approached the finish line. He felt a rush of internal energy never experienced before.

I guess it can be said Joe was indeed a motivated runner on that day.

The senior year, academically, was a success beyond anything Joe could have imagined. Any free time in his class schedule was filled with elective subjects such as mechanical drawing and jewelry. This was far better than sitting the time away in a study hall. He excelled in all his subjects and carrying high grades during the entire year made him eligible to be excused from all his senior year final exams. He earned an overall average of 90 for his last year of high school despite the fact he was carrying a full and demanding college prep load. In jewelry he was awarded the Carnegie Institute Prize for his design and construction of a sterling silver floral display. This woman's lapel pin was displayed in a statewide exhibit and later became a gift to his mother. *She wore it with great pride for many years.*

The senior year was also the first year Joe began dating. He was rather shy when it came to girls and could never seem to find the courage to ask anyone out. Accessing a telephone was not easy. His home was without a phone and there were no pay phones nearby. One day he expressed his desire to date a particular girl in his class to one of his friends. Somehow, the word got back to her and the romance started. No car, no phone, only city buses for wheels, and the local movies as a destination, the relationship was one of mutual admiration. They enjoyed each other's company and neither was madly in love. She did put an end to Joe's shyness and helped him to take a big step toward building his self confidence in the presence of girls. She was a good looking girl and a classy dresser who always turned heads whenever she walked by. When Joe walked her home from the movies it was a difficult maneuver to steal a good-night kiss because directly in front of her house, on a utility pole, was the brightest of all city street lights. *So it seemed.*

At the end of the first semester it was time to do some serious thinking about college. Joe decided he would petition The United States Coast Guard Academy. Entry to this school was based mainly on one's score on a two-day entrance exam; not on a political appointment as was the case in the other military academies. There were six candidates from Joe's class who sat for the two-day exam. All six received grades exceeding the minimum acceptable grade. However, the appointments were made in order from top score down until all positions were filled. None of the six made it. *An interesting note: all six went on to college elsewhere and the one who scored the highest was the only one who did not complete his college education.*

Joe did not know what career path to follow. Lacking guidance at home and in school he could not make up his mind as to what he wanted to do. His father kept telling him he should be a doctor or a lawyer. This was repeated so many times, Joe tired of it and he would tune out. In his own mind he felt he was not up to such rigorous study and further it would take too many years of schooling.

His American History class provided the opportunity to read a current events publication that featured a different profession every week. It was in one of those publications that he became interested in the field of optometry. At the time, the optometry program was a four year college program leading to a Doctor of Optometry degree. This was great, he thought, now he could be an eye doctor and that would surely please his parents. He began applying to the optometry colleges, of which there were fewer than ten granting the Doctor of Optometry degree, and was accepted to the college of his choice. However, the acceptance was not for the next entering class, it was for the following academic year because returning war veterans were given first priority. Joe decided he would stay close to home and enroll in a junior college, then transfer some of his course work at the end of the first year to the college of optometry. This was an opportunity to live at home and continue to work part time.

The end of his senior year was approaching too quickly. The track season ended and soon after the annual awards day was held on the athletic field. It was a day when the entire student body was required to attend the ceremony and witness the awards for athletic achievement. Approximately three thousand students would assemble on the bleacher seats to watch the award ceremony that would end with a rope pull between the boys of the two upper classes. The local fire company stood by, positioned at the center of a massive rope with a fire hose, and doused the losers as they were dragged under its powerful stream of cold water. The seniors were so confident they would win that they would always dress in their best clothes for this event. They did win despite last minute efforts by several lower classmen who seized an opportunity to come to the aid of the losers -- at the far end of their rope of course.

It was an exciting and proud moment when Joe was called onto the platform in the center of the field and presented with the highly regarded chenille school athletic letter and a 14 kt. gold track shoe. *The miniature gold track shoe was awarded only to seniors on the team who earned a letter and it was designed to function as a decorative piece of jewelry.* This ended high school for him, all that remained was graduation day. No exams to take, it was over. As Joe walked off the field at the end of the ceremony, he suddenly realized four wonderful years had passed.

He walked alone under the arches, connecting two historic buildings on campus and stopped, looked again at his awards. His eyes slowly filled with tears. This was an end to a passing of four wonderful years.

~ THE COLLEGE EXPERIENCE ~

As luck would have it, during Joe's first year in junior college, the optometry colleges added an additional year to their degree program. That did not set well with him. This meant a possible six years of college were ahead for him. He rationalized if he had to spend that many years in college, he might as well enter a dental degree program. He applied to several pre-dental colleges and was accepted at The University of California. He was delighted, but his mother was not. She often cried and begged him not to go so far from home. After all his young years as the family interpreter he was torn with an awful guilt feeling about abandoning his parents. He decided to stay close to home.

He commuted to an area junior college and continued to work part time as a shoe salesman. During his first years in college, he developed a serious interest in boxing. A former Golden Glove boxer, Victor, who had boxed in the famous Madison Square Garden Arena when he was younger and later became a local police officer, convinced Joe he had the makings of a good fighter. Victor had a training gym, often called a boxing stable, converted from a four car garage located behind his house. It had been refurbished with a boxing ring, speed bags, heavy punching bags, weights, jumping ropes, and all the equipment that would normally be used in training fighters. Training sessions were held two and three nights each week.

There were two fighters in training at the time, Joe who was a beginner, and Dempsey (no relation to the great Jack Dempsey) who was about to turn professional. Dempsey was a heavyweight weighing in between 220 and 230 pounds. Joe was training as a welterweight nearer to 140 pounds. Victor decided Joe's speed would serve as a good training experience for his heavyweight who was rather slow and needed to improve his own reaction time. Many sparring sessions pitted Joe against the heavyweight -- obviously a mismatch when considering the enormous weight differential. Although both were equipped with protective head gear and sparring weight gloves, there were times when Joe would land some stinging blows to the face antagonizing Dempsey who reacted with a vengeance. This was especially true when Dempsey's father was there observing a training session. Embarrassed and frustrated with Joe's footwork, coupled with receiving a few stinging blows, he would counter with a savage attack that needed Victor's intervention to stop a barrage of blows that would send Joe reeling about the ring.

Dempsey turned professional and won his first eight fights by knockouts or technical knockouts and was hailed as an up-and-coming heavyweight boxer in the area. Joe would accompany him and Victor to his matches and Victor would often point out the new fighters featured on the undercard that Joe could expect to meet in the ring in the near future. In Joe's mind and Victor's, none of the first half dozen ,or so, fighters would give him much competition and they were thought of as easy wins. After that, the fighters seem to jump into a much more advanced class and Joe had some concerns about fighting them. It would not be long before that worry would end. Dempsey, who also liked to fly small airplanes, was killed when the plane he was piloting crashed. Victor was so distraught about losing his fighter, who he had hoped would become a nationally ranked fighter, decided to close down his training facility for awhile. Months passed, Joe gained enough weight to move him up into the next weight class where he didn't want to be as a fighter. The training stable remained closed for too long a time and Joe eventually lost his desire to fight.

Now he would be free to date his girl friends without the worry about showing up with a fat lip.

BOXERS
Dempsey - 230 lbs. vs   Joe -140 lbs.

Joe decided to change direction and was accepted at the university. Still not knowing what he wanted, he enrolled in the School of Physical Education. The first day of class scheduling was a nightmare. Over two thousand students filing in and out of one of the gyms registered for classes. The required courses he needed were all closed out before he could sign in. Discouraged, Joe contemplated calling it quits and went back to his dorm to pack and return home. Upon advice from some of his friends he went to see the physical education department chairman who quickly arranged for Joe to get into the required classes.

Thinking ahead to the track season, Joe thought it would be a good idea to get himself in shape by running for the university cross country team. This turned out to be a big mistake for him. He hated running long distances, practices were demanding and dull, and the meets were grueling experiences. Not wanting ever to be the last man on his team to cross the finish line in a meet, he always would find enough energy to make it in near the end of the race; thus, avoiding being the last runner in on his team. *You know, the last one in is a rotten egg syndrome.* The season could not end fast enough for him and the only consolation for his efforts would be his team picture would hang in the University's Hall of Fame.

Dormitory life on campus was not easy. It was too easy as a way to have fun but a difficult place to concentrate on studying. Joe was in the first class to move into a new dorm complex, ten, four-story buildings, all connected to each other, that housed an all male population. This huge complex of buildings later became known as the jungle. His roommate was not Joe's type, constantly after him to pledge as a member of his fraternity. Joe was not interested, he had his own circle of friends and enough to do to keep up with his studies. He would spend most of his time studying in the campus library.

Late one night around eleven o'clock, after the rowdy behavior on his dorm floor had subsided, Joe was seated at his desk, clad only in his undershorts, reviewing his notes for the next day classes. His room door was wide open. There was a knock at the door and Joe didn't even bother to look up. He thought it was one of the guys fooling around again. A louder knock came. This time Joe answered, with a nasty remark looking toward the door. There was no response, only a strange silence. Joe turned to look and to his embarrassment there stood a young man dressed in black with a gleaming white collar. It was the campus priest who was making the rounds introducing himself to all the students who had registered themselves as Roman Catholics. Joe, surprised and embarrassed, was fumbling for words to apologize for his nasty remarks. They talked and during the course of their conversation, Father O'Brien asked,

"Joe, when was the last time that you went to confession?" Joe had never been to confession and never made his First Communion and he wasn't about to tell him that, so he replied,

"I really don't know, Father, about ten years I guess." Father quickly stood up, looked Joe in the eye and said,

"Put on some clothes, you're coming with me." Joe looked up at him and said,

"What for?"

Knowing what the answer would be, he got up, got dressed and they both walked over to the chapel. Inside it was pitch black. Father turned on the lights and proceeded to hear Joe's confession in the middle of the night.

That was to be the beginning of a lifelong friendship between them and the events of that memorable night would often be recalled many years later.

Joe's dorm room often was a hangout for some of his home town friends attending the university. They would meet there and decide what to do or where to go whenever idle time was available. Two of his friends, who were attending the university on athletic scholarships, came to his room early one evening and tried to convince him to go along with them for a trip into town for some beer drinking. The university town was legally a dry town in those days which meant you could not sell nor purchase any alcoholic beverages within the town limits. Also, university rules strictly forbade the consumption of alcohol on campus so it was a common practice for students to hitch a ride into the next town in order to drink.

Joe declined the invitation. He was not particularly fond of beer and besides he had to finish a paper due in class the next day. His two friends went to town alone, consumed far too much beer, and late that night on the way back to the campus they decided to take a short cut through a cemetery. Boozer, appropriately named by his friends, and a promising star basketball player, began turning over tomb stones as he staggered among the grave sites. He had the misfortune of turning one of the stone monuments over onto his foot severing several of his toes. Not only did this end his basketball career, it also ended his college education. He was later destined to die at an early age (in his mid-forties) from alcoholism. His companion that evening, a member of the football team, was also expelled from the university for his part in the vandalism.

Joe can thank his guardian angel for not going into town with the boys on that fateful night.

• • •

95

Joe quickly became disenchanted with the physical education program at the university. It was apparent to him the star athletes in the program always seem to fare better when it came to grades. They always seemed to get preferential treatment. He asked to be transferred out of the school of physical education and was discouraged from doing so by the department chairman. On one of his weekends home, he talked with his high school friend, Johnny, who was home for the holidays and was attending college in Pennsylvania on a football scholarship. Johnny convinced Joe to transfer to his college in Pennsylvania at the end of that semester.

So it was off with Johnny to St. Francis College, a thirteen hour train ride. Upon awakening the next morning in his dorm room, Joe could not open his eyes; they were both swollen shut. The next two days would be spent in the college infirmary. He had contracted what the nurse called cat fever. Joe decided he wanted to return home. He spent the next two weeks at home nursing his infected eyes. The next college semester had already begun and Joe was not about to go back to St. Francis or the university. *The University did not realize he was not in school for at least three months, as was evidenced from a letter received from the department chair asking him to come in to see him.* The local pool hall became his hangout and it also served as a hangout for many boys home from college on weekends. On one of those weekends he met Murph, another of his high school friends. Murph's brother, Honey, was the athletic director at American International College at that time and also was a graduate of the same high school as Murph and Joe. Murph called his brother to see if something could be done to get Joe into school there. Honey told him to take him to the college and he would see that Joe would be taken care of. Everything was arranged, from a free room at the Outpost, a converted house standing alone in the middle of an athletic complex serving as a dressing and equipment facility, to any help needed to catch up on past class work.

Living at the Outpost did not last very long. Joe knew that he would never graduate if he stayed there. Late night partying and card games and no supervision made it a fun house with little or no time to study. Joe and another hometown friend, a veteran Marine, moved out and rented a room in a home nearer to the campus. It was a great place to live and study and they both got along fine. The only negative aspect with this arrangement was his roommate's smoking habit. When the alarm clock sounded in the morning, his roommate would reach over to the night stand between the two beds, shut off the alarm and without fail, light up a cigarette and smoke it while remaining in bed. The odor of exhaled smoke, coupled with his morning bad breath, made for a nauseous smell and an awful beginning of a new day.

A few years after his roommate graduated from college he was burned to death in a fire, most likely, caused by his smoking in bed.

~ THE DATING GAME ~

Every weekend Joe would go home to work in Geril's shoe store. He would earn enough money to purchase his cafeteria meals for the coming week and have some spending money. If he couldn't get a ride home with a friend, he would hitchhike the sixty miles home. During his college years he dated several girls during summer and vacation times and rarely dated on weekends when the semester term was in session. There was Annette, Josephine, Celine, Patti, and a few others whose names are now blurred with the passing of so many years.   Joe was careful not to get involved in any serious relationships. He would never date the same girl for more than a few weeks to avoid developing a serious relationship that might affect his studies. His top priority was to be ranked in the top half of his class so he could finish his college education before being subjected to the military draft. The Korean War was underway and college students who ranked in the top half of their class were exempted from the draft so long as they maintained that rank. Dates were plentiful and as soon as one appeared to be headed toward a serious side he would be quick to break off that relationship.

There was one girl in particular who did not want their relationship to end. She somehow knew where to find him even though he tried to avoid her. If the love bug bit anyone it had to have taken a big bite out of her. She would rave to her friends about what a great kisser Joe was.   *About 30 years later he met her married daughter who personally told Joe of her mother's crush on him and, that of all the boys she dated he was remembered as the best kisser.* After a few good night kisses she would start panting leading Joe to believe he was quite the lover. *Sometime later his ego would be deflated when he learned her panting was due to her asthmatic condition and not to his performance.*

Joe preferred dating blondes and rarely would date brunettes. A brunette nearly caused a scene in a local soda shop when she spotted a sizeable red colored blotch on his neck and accused him of two-timing her. She thought some other girl was responsible for the apparent hickey on his neck. Joe had a difficult time explaining the blotch was indeed a birthmark and not the result of some hanky-panky affair. *Through the years the birthmark has been a topic of conversation many times and, even in his old age, continues to draw the attention of some friends who notice it for the first time. He senses when it has been noticed and wonders what they might be thinking.*

~ JOE BUYS HIS FIRST CAR ~

Joe worked several jobs, part of the summer months as a city playground instructor and when that job ended he worked as a laborer on various construction jobs. When college was in session he would be home every weekend so he could sell shoes on Saturdays. He accumulated enough money to pay his college tuition and managed to buy himself a car, a 1936 Plymouth coupe for $75. It had a stick-shift on the floor. He named the car Conswella. Whenever the car was driven up a long hill it would require down shifting of gears and as the car slowed and labored toward the top, Joe would say to the car, as he rocked forward with his upper body,

"Come-on Conswella, just a little more."

This seventy-five dollar car turned out to be the best investment he ever made in a car. It would be driven one hundred and seventy five thousand miles. Several years later it sold for fifty dollars and was converted into a stock car for racing.

It was a fun car, provided reliable transportation, easy for a do-it-your-selfer to fix with a simple wrench and screwdriver, no special tools required. A flashy car it was with its painted white side-wall tires. The windshield could be cranked wide open, straight out, for an open air ride. *On many occasions, night driving with the windshield cranked wide open resulted in a mouthful of bugs.*

Joe mastered the art of shifting gears with his right foot against the shaft of the stick-shift; thus, freeing is right hand. With one hand on the wheel and the other holding a girl snuggled in close to him, Conswella, with her radio tuned on to soft music, made for a romantic ride. *The radio was one salvaged from a friend's car that was junked after it rolled down an embankment and ended up in a brook.*

Conswella provided many miles and years of service carrying Joe through college and his early years of married life. The car was factory designed to be a business coupe with its spare tire stored directly behind the driver's seat. Joe customized the car a bit by removing the spare tire to the trunk and taking out the long shelf behind the seat allowing for more space inside the cab. Whenever Joe's playground kids had a ball game, they would delight in scrambling to pile in to see how many could fit in for the ride. An amazing number of bodies packed themselves in, standing like sardines in a can. If it were not for the baseball equipment carried in the trunk space, the entire team would have most likely been shoe-horned in. Those who made the short ride across town in Conswella always recall this joyful and unforgettable experience. *No seat belts, no padded dashboard, too young to worry about insurance -- just a carefree, fun ride.*

~ *THE COLLEGE SENIOR YEAR* ~

At the beginning of Joe's senior year he met a cute redhead working at a local dairy bar. It was here where many of the boys would go, after a Saturday night movie, for ice cream sundaes and milkshakes. Joe knew many of the girls who worked there and frequently managed to wind up with some extra change when paying for his order. He would put down thirty five cents to pay for a thirty five cent sundae and some of the young girls behind the counter would frequently return him a quarter in change. However, the cute redhead never would treat him in this way, she was strictly a company-girl, as honest as they come.

One particular Saturday evening when Joe and his friend, Gabby, were seated at the bar near where she was scooping ice cream., he commented to Gabby about the dimples showing in back of her knees as she bent over to reach deep down into the freezer. He also commented on her shapely figure as she struggled to fill a sugar cone while bending over with her toes barely touching the floor. When she turned to serve her customer, he noticed that behind her less than flattering eye glasses was a pretty face. It was near the end of her work shift and as she readied to leave, Joe and his friend, who were about to leave also, decided to follow her to find out where she lived. Her heavy foot on the gas pedal left Joe and his Conswella far enough behind as to only give him a general idea as to where she lived.

Near the Christmas season their paths would cross again. Joe was exiting the academy gymnasium when he spotted her leaving the campus to catch a bus to work. He yelled,

"Hey 'Red', need a ride?"
Being called Red was a name she wasn't too fond of. Anyway, she turned, apparently liked what she saw and waited. During that short ride to work he asked her if she would like to go to the traditional Christmas night basketball game. She hesitated and said,

"Yes, but I need to ask my mother first."
It was from that moment on she would steal his heart away. New Year's Eve would be their next date. He fell deeply in love with her.

There was something very special about her, maybe it was her

101

beautiful dark red hair complemented with sparkling eyes and a friendly smile that captured his fascination.

• • •

Returning to his college studies after the semester break became a formidable chore now. He couldn't get her off his mind. Each week in class seemed like an eternity. Fridays couldn't come soon enough for him to get home to see Dottie again. With each date his love for her grew stronger. It seemed like there could be no other love in the world, and as fate would have it, there would never be.

Dottie graduated from high school that June and chose not to accept a full scholarship to further her education. Her father, an Army Captain, was killed during the fighting in France and she, like all war orphans, was entitled to a government paid college education. She had her sights on marriage instead. Joe had an additional semester to complete his degree program and would do so in January. He needed to make up the credits he lost when transferring out of the university physical education program.

Joe's academic efforts in his last year resulted in the honor of being named to the Dean's List. He was also recruited by the Marine Corp to attend Officer's Training School. He was tempted to accept and gave it some serious thought; however, he was easily discouraged by Dottie because of her fear and the tragedy befallen to her own father in the service. Another recruitment effort he seriously considered was an opportunity to join the Teamsters Union as an organizer working the docks of New York City. His life experiences with Italian customs and being able to speak the language apparently made him an attractive fit into an environment heavily populated with Italian dock workers. The high pay was extremely attractive, but the thought of living in New York City and a future of being moved frequently to other cities was not. Of special significance was the thought of being away from the girl he loved so much. So instead, he decided to stay close to home by accepting a job as an investigative social worker in the Department of Old Age Assistance for the State of Connecticut.

~ *A WEDDING DAY DISASTER* ~

During Dottie's last semester in high school, the talk of marriage upon Joe's graduation from college began to take on a serious note. She would be turning eighteen years old in April and, as was common in those days because of the Korean War and the drafting of young men into the service, several of her classmates already had marriage plans in place for weddings shortly after graduation day. That summer, Dottie began to make plans to be married immediately after Joe completed his degree requirements in January 1952. It would be a gross understatement to say the plan was not well received by their parents. Her mother and both of Joe's parents were extremely adamant that this marriage should not take place. Age, religion, and nationality were tossed about as major obstacles to the pending marriage.

Joe's father went so far as to buy a brand new Mercury sedan and offered it as a bribe to his son. If he would not marry "that girl" (*never referred to by name by his parents*) the car would be given to him. Dottie's mother visited Joe's parents and pleaded with them to help her put an end to the planned marriage. She told them their son was a fine boy and she would be justly proud to have a son like him. However, they were too young to marry. His parents could not have agreed more.

At the time, popular singer Nat King Cole had recorded a hit song entitled, Too Young, and it was to become Dottie's and Joe's favorite lifetime reminder of their stormy beginning of more than fifty years ago.

Although Dottie's mother held the trump card that could nix her daughter's wedding, (Connecticut law, at that time, required parental permission for anyone under twenty-one years of age to legally marry), Dottie was prepared to scrap her wedding plans and elope to the State of Maryland where she could legally marry at age eighteen if her mother should decide to carry through on her threat to deny consent.

On the Christmas Day before the planned wedding, Joe had a special surprise gift for Dottie under the Christmas tree. It was the diamond ring she once admired while wishful window shopping a local jewelry store with him a few weeks before. Plans for the wedding were finalized. Dottie, a talented seamstress, designed and made her own wedding gown from parachute satin material obtained through an Uncle. She also made all of her bridesmaid's gowns. Another Uncle would make and arrange for her to have flowers. Joe scrambled to find enough ushers who would be available for the January 26th wedding day because several of his close friends had already been drafted into military service. A church wedding was in their plan. Dottie was an Episcopalian and had promised Joe any children born to their marriage would be raised in the Catholic faith. They decided to be married in both of their churches. However, when Joe talked with his parish priest, he refused to marry them because she was of a Protestant religion and he would not allow a mixed marriage in his church. The old-time priest tried to discourage the marriage and make Joe feel like he was marrying an inferior being. An argument ensued

WEDDING DRESS - 1952
Made from parachute satin by Dottie at age 18.

and they had harsh words between them. The priest abruptly refused any further discussion. Joe decided he would never again talk with him or return to his church. The marriage would then take place in her church only.

The cold, rainy January wedding day was one that would never be fondly remembered. There would be no wedding reception or dinner. Her mother refused to have any part of this wedding and the new hopefuls were without funds. In fact, Dottie paid for the mandatory blood test and the license fee after her mother reluctantly decided to grant her permission. The marriage license was obtained on the very last day of eligibility for the selected wedding date. After the church ceremony, only the wedding party went to Dottie's Aunt's house where she provided them with a wedding cake.

Now the dreaded moment was about to arrive.

They went to Joe's parents home where several of his relatives had gathered. Dottie was greeted by his father with a verbal attack that shocked everyone present. More abusive words could not be imagined. It was a furious, non-stop, insulting personal attack that would forever blacken memories of this day. Relatives eventually interceded to calm him down. A short time later, he looked at Joe and with outstretched arms handed him the keys to his new car and said in Italian,

"Here. Go."

Within the year, his father would begin to cater to Dottie's every wish, for the rest of his life, as if he could never do enough good for her. It appeared he just didn't know how to express in words an apology for his anger and terrible behavior on her wedding day.

The newlyweds received total cash gifts in the amount of ninety dollars which was enough for them to get away for a two night honeymoon at the Mishnook Cabins near Providence, Rhode Island, and have enough money remaining to buy their first week's groceries.

Joe's boss, at the time, would not grant him more than two days off because he had only been in her employ for a few weeks.

~ BACK to WORK ~

Joe started his state job about two weeks before his wedding day. His first paycheck would not arrive until after the wedding. His work supervisor was an old maid who refused to grant him more than two days off for his honeymoon. From the start, their working relationship would always be strained. He was assigned to investigate recipients on the state's old age assistance program who were living in the Groton - Mystic area. He was very uncomfortable with his job because, often, when his clients saw his state marked car come to their home, they would hide behind a curtain and carefully peer out their windows. Sometimes they would not answer the door. Many seemed to live in fear of a state worker who had the power to negatively affect their state benefits. All of Joe's cases appeared to live a meager existence and he soon found himself an advocate of the elderly by recommending, in most of his cases, increases to their monthly benefits. His recommendations were always harshly scrutinized by his supervisor and, more times than not, it was a battle of words before she would consent to any recommended increases.

About four months into his job, he was sent out to investigate a case of and old Indian man named George Big Deer. George had a state appointed conservator. He could not be trusted to handle his own finances because of his affinity for alcoholic beverages. Joe called on him at the listed address only to discover he had a woman conservator who would not allow him to speak for himself whenever Joe asked a question directed to him. After Joe examined George's living accommodations, he left the house, made a few notes as he sat in his car, and then drove away. As he rounded the top of a long hill nearby he couldn't believe his eyes. There was George running out of the woods toward his car waving his arms frantically. Joe stopped. George got in the car and after several minutes of catching his breath, he was able to talk and describe the abusive life he was living. Joe listened in disbelief as he described his real accommodations. This man was living in an old chicken coop in the backyard with cardboard covering a dirt floor and no running water nor toilet. He convinced Joe to drive him back to see for himself. It was worse than he described. It was apparent the woman was using his money for her personal gain. George also told him of some other rather shady goings on in the woman's house. Joe left George and went directly to visit the local police station to inquire if there could be any truth to this story. They were somewhat reluctant to talk about the situation but there was an indication of some talk about town and the police were aware that something was amiss.

Joe returned to his office and wrote a lengthy, detailed report of his findings only to have it rejected by his supervisor. According to her it was "too incriminating and needed to be toned down." This did not set well with Joe and the very next day, while out on the road, he stopped by The Electric Boat Company Employment Office and got himself another job.

~ AN IMPORTANT LESSON LEARNED ~

During the interview process, Joe was unaware of the importance of the job he was interviewing for. He learned later his fate was in the hands of one of Admiral Rickover's administrative team members who were on a mission to hire talented and flexible individuals. The person hired would need to fit a preconceived mold determined by the Admiral himself and would need to pass a security check so as to be trusted with highly classified information. Joe would be working in the Planning Department and would be in charge of expediting all the government furnished equipment to be installed on the *Nautilus*, the world's first atomic powered submarine. He would be hired for an initial six month probationary period while personal security checks were conducted and during that time his performance would be evaluated. Later he was to learn that the F.B.I. did an extensive check on him that included questioning the neighborhood grocer to determine the manner of his driving habits and even went so far as checking his character traits with some of his past girl friends.

It's still a mystery as to how he ever passed that one.

One of the last questions in his interview and one that would be an important lesson that he would carry forward the rest of his life was, "How much do you expect to earn working with us?" It was a question that took him by surprise. He was expecting a pre-determined amount would be offered and then some negotiating might take place. Joe thought for a moment and then sheepishly replied,

"I'd like to make a hundred dollars a week."

He figured in his own mind that was $5,200 a year, about twice the amount beginning teachers were making that year in 1952. At the end of his six month probationary period he sat down with his boss, retired Commander Tex Bryant, to discuss his promotion to the next salary step. Joe was disappointed to learn he was locked into a series of maximum raises based on his starting salary. Tex had taken Joe under his wing and treated him like his own son -- often lecturing him with the worldly wisdom he himself had gathered from his thirty years of service in the navy. He taught Joe all he needed to know about submarines. He was an excellent mentor and a difficult and demanding person to work for, a deeply religious man who never used profanity in any form. It was during one of Joe's evaluation sessions that Tex said to him,

"Son, when you hired on with us, you sold yourself short. Do you remember when you were asked how much you wanted to earn? If you had said a hundred and fifty, you would have gotten it ... and maybe more. You were too quick to lock yourself into a lower salary base."

Joe would never forget that session and vowed he would never again allow himself to be put in a position where he could sell himself short.

• • •

The building of the *Nautilus* was considered to be a top priority government project. All personnel who held key positions in the project were expected to devote their full energies to its successful completion. Work was scheduled around the clock. Thousands of shipyard workers were employed. Three work shifts were in force in order to meet Rickover's demands to stay on his schedule. When orders came down from his office demanding a speed up, many key personnel were *asked* to work overtime. All knew, *asked*, was a polite word for required. No one could refuse any orders from Rickover's office and expect to continue in the same position very long.

For nearly two years, Joe worked without missing a day. The work was demanding with always a deadline to meet. There were times when a seven day work week was the norm. He was making money faster than he could spend it. There was no time to go shopping. It was a great start for a young married couple who started with nothing and were about to start a family. Their first born would arrive eleven months into their marriage. Joe and his expectant wife decided to move into his parents' home to save more money and to have his mother available to help when the new arrival made her appearance.

As work on the *Nautilus* neared time for its sea trials, Joe's responsibilities increased and were subject to pressures of meeting urgent schedules dictated from Rickover's office. This was truly a growing up period for Joe. At weekly progress meetings he would witness old men driven to tears because of the demands made upon them. *These old men had to be in their forties.*

He quickly learned, with Tex's tutelage, how to lie and steal from other ship's contracts to meet deadlines. At times, during periods of seven day work weeks, the morning newspaper would serve as a reminder of what day of the week it was. It was so easy to lose track of the days of the week when there was no weekend to look forward to. There were times when the phone at home would ring at two or three in the morning with urgent requests for critical equipment that required Joe to get dressed immediately and drive to Bayonne, New Jersey, or the Portsmouth Naval Shipyard to bring back critically needed parts.

There was also a light side to Joe's job that added some humor to the workplace. Sometimes "urgent" requisitions would be hand delivered to his desk, by some new and unsuspecting "go-for" (gopher), i.e., two Fallopian tubes urgently needed for UPX sonar unit. Trying hard not to give away the moment, Joe would send the "go-for" back with the requisition to find out what model number was needed; was it for a Model 38-2C or a Model 40-2D? Requisitions for bags of special light-weight concrete to fill in a periscope well were other popular requests. It was not uncommon for a new and uninformed "go-for" to walk the shipyard in search of an item that provided chuckles and laughs to a stressed workplace. Many ingeniously worded requisitions always seem to appear at the right moment.

Another source of amusement could always be found at the requisition window of the storehouse. Joe would visit there frequently and often moved himself out of sight, when a newcomer (easily identified by his serially numbered badge) leaned over and into an opening in the heavy wired cage area waiting for his requisition to be filled. The "go-for" would soon find himself startled out of his skin when a large, furry black spider attached to a fine line, would slowly descend in front of his face and then quickly appear to weave itself back up into obscurity. Joe was a master at picking the right moment to work the spider. The victim, obviously relaxed with other thoughts on his mind, and with no one within his sight on the other side of the counter, would curse and do a sudden, violent jump-back dance that delighted all the observers anxiously awaiting the reaction.

~ DON'T PUT OFF 'TIL TOMORROW WHAT YOU CAN DO TODAY ~

Joe was a very likeable young man who made friends easily,

particularly with older people. He was polite and respectful and always welcomed their advice, never offending or taking issue with what was offered. His father had taught him well. Respect for his elders was ingrained in him at an early age. One of Joe's mentors, early in his career, was a retired undertaker, Mr. Flynn, who had come to work in the shipyard. They got to know each other when they worked together in the shipyard one summer. They became good friends, often enjoying lunch together and discussing what the future could hold for Joe when he graduated from college. Little did either know or suspect at the time that one day Joe would return to be his boss. On Joe's last day at work that summer, Mr. Flynn, called him over and quietly and said to him,

"I think you're a special young man and I got something for you."

He handed him a surprisingly heavy object rolled up in newspaper print,

"Be careful with it," he said, " And don't get caught by the guards on your way out 'cause we'll all be in trouble."

Joe opened it carefully and there was a polished bronze casting of a submarine mounted on a finished wood base, with Joe's full name inscribed on its bronze nameplate,

"I had my friends in the foundry cast it for you, and the boys in the wood shop made the base. It's a piece that's made here for visiting dignitaries. Someday, I know, you'll be one."

Joe, thanked him. They shook hands, embraced and said good-bye.

It was almost a year later that Joe would be back to work there. As soon as Mr. Flynn learned he was back, he sent word to Joe's office that he would like very much to see Joe again and would he please come down to his work station. Joe's position was one that allowed him unlimited access to all buildings in the shipyard; whereas, most other employees, for security reasons, were restricted from roaming about. Two days later, Joe decided he would stop by to see Mr. Flynn only to be saddened by the news that he had died suddenly the evening before. A terrible feeling of guilt came over him. There was no good reason why he could not have gone to see him before he died. He had the chance to see his good friend and missed it. What was it they would have talked about? The next day the hurt would intensify more. Mr. Flynn's family, whom Joe had never met before, sent word that one of his good friend's last wishes was that they were to ask him to be one of his pall bearers. So it came to be.

The bronze submarine sat, as a centerpiece, on Joe's desk for more than forty years as a reminder. If you can do it today, do it, tomorrow may be too late.

IV

From 1952 to 1960

~ *THE FIRST BORN* ~

On December 8, 1952, the first child was about to arrive. Joe was awakened from a sound sleep in the dark, early morning hours by a series of elbow jabs to his ribs and an anxious, sweet voice saying,

"Joe ... Joe, wake up, it's time to go."

"What the hell time is it." he responded.

"I don't know, get up, it's time to go."

All of a sudden he realized it wasn't time to go to work. They both quickly and quietly dressed so as not to awaken his parents and went out into a cold car. As Joe was backing out of the driveway, he turned his head and lifted his right arm onto the back of the seat to gain a better view for backing up. At precisely the same moment, his wife was either having a contraction or just wanting to snuggle up, slid over closer to him on the seat and caught his elbow smack in the eye, breaking her glasses. Joe could not get her to the hospital fast

114

enough. The trip was just a blur in time.

Especially so for Dottie who could not see without her glasses.

Upon arrival at the front door of the hospital. They rushed up the stairs, quickly registered her admission, put her in a wheelchair and a nurse wheeled her to the elevator door. In those days, that was as far as a husband could go. Joe kissed her good-bye and went back home and to bed. The phone finally rang with the news he was the father of a 7 pound 12 ounce baby girl born at 7:30 a.m. Mother and baby, Jacqueline, were doing just fine. Joe was somewhat disappointed the first-born was not a boy but very thankful that mother and daughter were in good health. *Joe hoped the next one would be the boy.*

Living in Joe's parents house after the baby was born would soon became a very stressful ordeal. Old-world customs and a grandmother who was always underfoot just didn't mix with a young, new mother's expectations as to how to care for a newborn. Dottie had a lot of experience caring for babics. She had learned by helping her own grandmother who ran a home for abandoned infants, placed in her home through state agencies. She was far more knowledgeable than most new mothers of the day. Each new day seemed to fuel more concerns as Joe's mother waited for him to arrive home from work to speak to him, always in Italian, about all the things his wife was doing wrong. It appeared to Dottie that the messages she was conveying to him, in a language she did not understand, threatened their marriage.

Visitors who came to see the new family were not kindly received by his mother especially if they were smokers. It was not unlike her to open windows wide, no matter how cold the weather was outside, to air out the house. She even went so far as to make no-smoking signs while visitors were present and post them in their line of vision as they exited the house. Further compounding the living arrangement came with a gift of a puppy dog for the new baby. One of Joe's retired Navy friends at work wanted him to have a beagle pup that he thought would make a good pet for the new baby. The old Chief was so sincere about his gift that Joe could not bring himself to refuse it. The arrival of the pup was not a welcomed event. After much pleading the pup was allowed to enter the house, but restricted to the back hall entry part of the house. The first night the dog could be heard periodically giving out a very low moan that sounded ghostly in the quiet of the night. The pup was then named Spooks. It wasn't very long before Spooks was to be evicted to an outside dog house.

Several months passed and the stressful encounters between wife and mother-in-law became increasingly more frequent. One day, Joe's mother saw Dottie heating the baby's milk in a pan into which she added a pill shaped tablet. Dottie was quickly accused of adding a drug to the baby's milk to make her sleep more. Dottie's explanation that she was merely making a junket pudding that required a junket tablet as a gelling agent was not accepted. That evening Joe's mother waited for him to come home and greeted him, in Italian, with the news she had seen his wife drugging the baby to prompt more sleep. Nothing was said of Dottie's explanation. This event triggered a long discussion between Joe and his wife. She had enough of the conflicting living arrangement and something had to be done. She told Joe his personality was changing, and he wasn't the same man she married. His work schedule with its pressures and demands left her alone to cope with the everyday problems she encountered and his mother was more of a hindrance than a help. The only, and best alternative at this point, seemed to be a move to another home. A move to another home nearby was out of the question. His parents would take such a move as a deep, personal insult. Changing jobs and moving out of state seemed the best solution to their dilemma.

Joe discussed the situation in which he found himself with his boss, Tex. He agreed that a change was badly needed and he was willing to help in any way he could. Joe told him about the possibility of seeking and getting a teaching position out of state. Tex recommended he try that for a year and assured Joe he would have a job waiting for him in the event that things didn't work out. Joe began searching out teaching vacancies in neighboring states.

~ THE BEGINNING TEACHER ~

After several visitations and interviews, Joe was impressed with a school superintendent in Attleboro, Massachusetts, named Dr. Barber. He was looking for a science teacher for placement into a new junior high school building that had received high national reviews for its architectural design. Dr. Barber was convinced that Joe was the one for the job. His background and work on the first nuclear submarine made him a natural fit for the science opening. Joe liked Dr. Barber's views on teaching and the role of the classroom teacher. He told Joe if he had his way in education he would require all teachers to take leave of their position after a five year tenure and obtain work outside of teaching for a year or two before returning to the classroom. He would require this of all his teachers every five years. His teachers would not only be more worldly wise but would come back rejuvenated. *The idea seemed to have a lot of merit then and probably more so now.*

When their talk came to a teaching salary, Dr. Barber seemed prepared to face all of Joe's concerns. After all, Joe would be leaving a position that was paying him about twice what a beginning teacher was earning. He was quick to offer him placement two steps higher on the salary scale for his work experience. When Joe expressed his feelings that was still far too short of what he was earning, Dr. Barber said,

"You know you're only working 180 days. That's 36 weeks a year out of 52."

"Yes I know," Joe replied respectfully, "But my family has to eat every day of that 52 week year."

Joe was thinking about the possibility of summer employment and trying in his mind to factor in a number to make the offer more palatable. Dr. Barber interrupted the silence and said,

"Would some extra work coaching football, basketball, and baseball do it for you? They each pay a small stipend. I can add something more if you can also function as   the audiovisual director for the school."

The grand total of all this still did not come anywhere near what Joe was making, but, now it was within range of what he thought would be a liveable wage.   Joe paused for awhile allowing time in his mind to digest the numbers, then stood up, extended his hand and said,

"Thanks for putting up with me. It's a deal."
They shook hands. Dr. Barber walked him to the door and said,

"I know you're going to like here, I'll be looking forward to seeing you again in September."

Joe arrived in Attleboro, Massachusetts, for the opening of school in September. His arrival was akin somewhat to a hero's welcome. About a week before schools opened that year, the local newspaper gave Joe a headline that read, "SCIENCE TEACHER HELPED EQUIP NAUTILUS." The students were abuzz with the article and were anxious to hear from their new science teacher.

Whoever composed that headline certainly knew it would attract the attention of many readers who knew the Nautilus was the world's first atomic powered submarine.

• • •

For over a month Joe commuted sixty-five miles each way to work because he could not find a suitable rental for his family. He was up at 5a.m. and on the road by six. Football practice did not allow him to leave for the trip home until around six in the evening. Dinner would be waiting and soon after it was time for bed. It was a grueling schedule. Weekends would be spent looking for a place to live. After five weeks of searching, a rental was found within walking distance of the school. Better landlords could not have been found anywhere. The close friendship they developed between landlord and tenant continues to this day.

Joe quickly became a popular teacher with both his students and fellow teachers. His school principal was a veteran, wartime, Marine Colonel, named Oats, who prided himself in running a no nonsense school. Not too far into the school year, one morning, over the intercom system he announced,

"Mr. L, please report to my office immediately."
Joe was taken by surprise by the call and so were the students in his classroom. "Why me, he thought, what did I do wrong?" All the events of that week seemed to flash before his mind. Joe opened the door connecting his classroom with the next and asked the teacher to keep an eye on his class while he went to the office. Upon his arrival in the office, the principal's secretary motioned for him to go right in.

Oats was seated behind his desk and nearby, along the side wall was the public address system console. As he came out from behind his desk he said to Joe,

"Close the door and have a seat."

He must have noticed the bewildered look on Joe's face and said,

"Don't worry, I need to have you here as a witness."

Before Joe was able to ask a question, Oats opened the door and said to one of the students seated outside,

"Billy, get in here."

In entered Billy, a tall and rugged ninth grader who towered over Oats. Oats slam the door closed behind him, walked around in front of him and positioned himself between his desk and the public address system console. He looked Billy square in the eye and said,

"Where were you yesterday?"

"I was home, sick." came the reply.

"Billy, don't you lie to me. I'll ask you one more time. Why didn't you come to school yesterday?"

Billy hesitated as if he were thinking about his answer, and with a silly smirk on his face he looked squarely at Oats and said,

"I told you ... I was home, sick."

Oats, with one quick and continuous motion, reached on top of the P.A. console and grabbed a two foot long, 1X3 piece of wood firing strip, grabbed Billy by one shoulder, spun him around and whacked him with a stinging swing across the butt. He hit Billy so hard, Joe gave a quick jerk in his chair as if he could feel the stinging sensation on his own butt. Tears rolled down Billy's cheeks. Oats spun him around again and said,

"Don't you ever lie to me again, now, get back to class."

Oats closed the door while Joe was still squirming in his seat. He proceeded to his desk, sat down and began to explain to Joe that Billy

120

was a big bully who even bullied his own mother. He was hanging with the wrong crowd in town and she could no longer control him at home. She had asked Oats several times to do whatever was necessary to help keep him in school. She had granted him permission to whack some sense into him. Billy had no father at home. Oats told Joe this kid could be trouble and to keep an eye on him,

"Just remember," he said, "If you ever need to use corporal punishment on this kid it's OK, just don't hit him in the face."

Several times Joe thought about that scene in Oats's office and one day asked Billy to join the football team. He had all the physical attributes that could be molded into a respectable player and maybe Joe could work with him and make something out of him. However, Billy made it clear he wanted no part of football or any sport activity. His interest was with cars.

It was not until the first school dance their paths would cross again. Joe was assigned supervisory duties for the dance and one of his duties was to periodically check the Boy's room for smokers and vandalism. During the evening Joe needed to use the Boy's room so this would be a good time to make his first inspection. Upon entering, it was obvious from the smell of smoke, Billy and a few of his friends, who had congregated in the room, had been smoking. No one, however, was caught holding a cigarette. All butts were timely discarded, either floating in the toilets or urinals. Joe said nothing and went directly to a urinal to relieve himself. As he was zipping his fly, he heard Billy say,

"Let's get him."

The next thing Joe felt a hand placed on his shoulder. This had to be trouble. He turned quickly with one arm knocking the hand off his shoulder and with his other fisted hand sank it deep into the pit of Billy's stomach. The surprise move left Billy doubled over gasping

121

for air. Joe, saying nothing, washed and wiped his hands as the others stood frozen in amazement. He turned and said to them,

"OK, seen enough? Get the hell out."

Joe was feeling badly and somewhat worried about hitting Billy. Billy finally was able to get his breath back and straighten himself out. He slowly walked past Joe and as he did he said,

"I'm sorry. I was only kidding."

Joe was sorry too, but he did not want to say it.

• • •

The next morning Joe reported the incident to Oats who understood Joe's reaction and said,

"I don't think you'll get any trouble from him again. I doubt that he will tell his mother and if he does, don't worry, she'll be on your side."

Nothing but good came from this incident. Joe would never again hit a student again for the rest of his career in education.

Although he would have like to, and came close to, on a few other occasions.

• • •

Billy eventually looked up to Joe as his mentor and was the moving force behind a move to customize Joe's car, Conswella. On an early spring day after school, Billy and one of his friends came to Joe's room to ask if they could work on his car in the school shop. They had a plan as to what they could do to make it into a show car. It sounded good and Joe consented to the plan so long as they understood the car had to be in driveable condition at the end of each day. Several months of work went into the car. Joe would sometimes drive the car to work minus a fender or two being worked on in the shop. Many students walking to school in the morning would delight at the sight of the vehicle. The transformation was slow but steady. Often they would see the car coming in their direction and they playfully would leave the sidewalk and run onto someone's lawn as if to get away from Conswella, the monster. The car's transformation captured the interest of much of the student body. It was almost as if they had adopted a new mascot.

The year in Attleboro was a wonderful experience. Joe's football team had a winning season, his basketball team made the league finals, *they lost in overtime,* and his baseball team won the league championship. Academically, his teaching methods and reputation began to spread to other schools resulting in visitations by other teachers and administrators interested in enhancing their own programs. Joe organized a very well-received science fair, a first for his school. His energy appeared boundless. In the evenings after dinner or on Saturdays he would wheel baby Jacqueline to the school shop where she would watch him work on making furniture for his home and toys for her. The shop became a hangout for many of his team players who would come to help, *sometimes,* watch, or just to talk about sports in general.

• • •

Dottie and Joe lived in a duplex apartment. They occupied one side while the other side housed the owners, Gert and Ed and their family of three young school age girls. The two families lived in harmony always looking out for each other. Dottie and Gert, home all day being full time mothers, became the best of friends. *A friendship that still exists today, nearing fifty years later. As I write this line, in today's mail, Joe and Dottie received an invitation to their 60th wedding anniversary.* Gert was not only a good friend but was also like another mother for Dottie who was expecting her second child.

During the spring school vacation, a second daughter would be born. The scenario for the new arrival would be much like the first. It would never be forgotten. Again, in the dark of the early morning hours, the wake up call was much the same. First the elbow to the ribs and then that sweet voice,

"Joe, Joe, wake up, it's time to go."

"What the hell time is it?"

"Shhhh..., don't wake the baby and your mother."

They both dressed quietly but not quietly enough to escape detection by Joe's mother who had come to stay and care for Jacqueline when the newborn arrived. Joe called,

"Go back to sleep Ma, I gotta go to the hospital with Dottie."

All dressed and ready to go, Dottie sat at the kitchen table waiting for Joe to find the keys to the car,

"Where the hell did I put the keys?"

Still half asleep, he searched his pants pockets, his jacket pockets, and everywhere he thought they might be. Dottie sat there waiting, holding her arms around her mid section,

"Hurry up Honey," she said, "We got to go."

Then she let out a painful moan. By this time Joe was in a panic and sweating. His mind seemed to be racing at the speed of light,

"Where did I leave those G.D. keys?", he thought.

She called out, "Joe, please, we gotta go."

Joe's blood pressure was about to pop the top of his skull. Back and forth, room to room, no keys. He was about ready to call next door for emergency help and headed toward the front door, when, there on a small table by the door he spotted the keys. Joe just plain forgot he had put them there. The ride to the hospital was quick, pedal to the floor, no stopping for stop signs. Conswella never before raced along city streets so fast. Baby Jeannette arrived in less than two hours. Joe came back to see her as soon as he got the call. Dottie was being attended to when he arrived so he turned and went to the nursery to see his new daughter. When he returned to see Dottie she said to him,

"Did you see the baby? Isn't she beautiful?"

"Are you kidding? She's got to be the ugliest kid in the nursery with that thick crop of hair. She's got more hair than I have."

That was not a very nice thing to say, especially to a new mother. Joe's brain just wasn't in gear yet.

· · ·

Living and working in Attleboro was a delight. If it weren't for the struggle to make ends meet, with a take home income sometimes not enough to cover monthly expenses, their stay might have been much longer. Joe had already decided they could no longer keep drawing on their savings and was ready to return to work for Tex at the end of the school year.

Preparation for the move was underway, when Joe received a telegram from his former high school principal, Bulldog George, the last person in the world he ever expected to hear from. The telegram asked him if he would be interested in coming to the academy to teach biology and math and do some coaching. If so, to please call him, collect, at his summer residence. Joe could not have been more surprised. Me of all people, he thought, the kid who sat frightened in his office on the first day of high school, the kid who had to face him to ask for a change in his course of study. He read the telegram over and over again. Could this be real? He was elated and honored and couldn't wait to show the telegram to Dottie. On the way home he wondered how the Bulldog tracked him down. How did he know Joe was teaching in Attleboro? It finally dawned on him that Coach Wills was the one responsible. Coach Wills was the science department chairman and he was the one who was always interested in what Joe was doing. He had to be, *and was,* the one who convinced Bulldog to recruit him.

Joe talked with Dottie about the telegram and the possibility of returning to his Alma Mater. He knew salary would again be the most important issue and teaching salaries could never compete with industry. Already, he had been asked to return to his old job with an offer higher than what he was making when he left. Dottie knew of Joe's great love and admiration for the academy and said to him,

"What have you got to lose? We're moving back that way. Call him and hear what he has to say."

Joe, a bit nervous about calling him, made the call. The academy in those days was not hampered with a set salary scale. Bulldog George was a smooth talker and really buttered Joe up by telling him of all the good things he had heard about him and how much Coach Wills wanted him to teach in his department. He also told Joe he wanted him to start up a freshman football program that had been discontinued for several years. The salary offer was respectable, better than Attleboro, but still not near that of his old job with Tex. A promise of an additional summer job sweetened the offer.

Joe was given a summer job to paint classrooms and learned to detest a paint brush after one summer of painting all rooms the same color.

~ *JOE RETURNS to HIS ALMA MATER* ~

The offer was accepted and he was asked to report to the head football coach two weeks before school started. He would be working with the varsity team to learn their system of play which would be helpful to his new freshman football program. Joe arrived the morning of the first day of football practice driving Conswella. Many of the players, who had already dressed for practice, were waiting outside the dressing facility known as the Clubhouse. The sight of Conswella parking in front of the Clubhouse brought oohs, aahs, and wows from the observers standing by. One could sense their curiosity about what the new coach might be like, especially one who drove a hot-rod car. Soon the players inside the Clubhouse got word of the new arrival and many players, half dressed, scurried out to see Conswella. They swarmed around the car expressing their admiration. *Billy and the boys in Attleboro would have been proud if they could see the reaction to their creation.* The car was finished on the outside but not the inside. It had all of its upholstery removed ready to be trimmed with red vinyl, accented with bamboo wood strips.

It never did get finished because of the move back to his hometown that summer which was a disappointing experience for both the Attleboro mechanics and Joe. Conswella did serve to elevate Joe to instant popularity status on campus.

• • •

The day before school year was to begin, a meeting of the entire faculty was held that served to introduce new faculty and to distribute teaching schedules to all. Two new faculty members were introduced and Joe was pleased to learn the other teacher was a long time friend and a former classmate, Dick Jens. The big surprise was yet to come. Joe read his teaching schedule. Biology and math were on his schedule, as expected, and so were four other different subjects. He must have read and reread the schedule ten different ways. It always came out with six different subjects. He would later learn he got all the leftovers in the scheduling process. It was the practice to load the newcomers with courses left over after the veteran teachers were taken care of. The first year at the academy was to be a true learning experience. Nearly every evening was devoted to study new subject matter just to stay ahead of his students.

He always said he learned more that year than he did in four years of college.

One of his surprise assignments was a new course of study, called industrial science, that had no prescribed textbook nor course outline. He needed to design his own course of study.

Being the youngest faculty member that year made for some interesting situations. Several times Joe's young looks would cause him to be mistaken for a student. He would be reprimanded by some of the older teachers for not being in class or being in an area that was off limits to students. He delighted in listening and letting the reprimand run its course and at the end he would politely remind them, he too was a member of the faculty. An ancient history teacher (*she looked ancient too*) once encountered him in the hall, asked his name and noted it on a piece of paper. She told him to immediately report to the principal's office. She didn't think it was so funny, when at the very end of the encounter, he told her he was also a teacher on free time. She snapped back with a caustic voice,

"Young man, teachers here do not have any free time, unscheduled time is class preparation time."

~ A SHOCKING SITUATION ~

Joe's teaching assignments spanned each of the four grade levels in high school. The industrial science class consisted of senior boys and because there was no prescribed text nor curriculum, Joe designed a course to discuss topics, within reason, that the students wanted to hear about. One such topic was automotive electrical systems. One student in this class would always manage to fall asleep about halfway into the class period. He would sleep so soundly, the only thing that would awaken him was the harsh sound of a bell ringing to signify the end of class period. Unbeknown to Sleepy and with the help of some of his classmates after school, Joe ran two wires from an automotive spark coil on the demonstration counter, down to the floor and embedded the wires in the seams between the shrunken floor boards. The wires were connected to the back of Sleepy's metal frame chair. The class anxiously awaited the big moment. As expected, half way into class period the next day, Sleepy slowly lowered his head and off to slumber land he went. Joe moved over to the spark coil, flipped the switch and sent a jolt of electricity through his chair that produced a jump that would rival that of a high jumper on a track team. Two rows of chairs were tumbled over as the surprised victim moved rapidly away from his resting place.

Needless to say he never fell asleep in that class again. Although the class enjoyed the show, Joe felt badly when he later learned the victim had a full time, second shift, job in a local factory and obviously lacked enough sleep time at home.

This was not to be the end of the spark coil caper. Sleepy wanted to get even. He and some of his friends decided to wire the doorknob and get Joe as he was always the last one into the room before the start of class, always closing the door behind him. The bell rang and Joe started for the door. He thought it was kind of strange the door was partly closed and he could see everyone inside already seated, a rare occurrence for this class. Just as he was about to reach for the doorknob, Coach Wills called to Joe from across the hall. He turned and went over to him and as he did so, a young girl rushed back to the room to retrieve a book she had left behind. She grabbed the doorknob, the books she was carrying went flying in all directions as she let out an ungodly scream that brought out many of the teachers from their rooms along the hallway.

Needless to say, the experience was shocking.

~ GET EVEN TIME ~

Another of Joe's teaching assignments was to teach first aid. It was a course of study that was elected by many students who needed an extra credit to graduate. There was one particular student who, *excuse the expression,* was *a pain in the a--.* Joe was constantly after him to keep quiet and to pay attention in class. One day the class was studying bandaging and Joe decided the Pain would make a good subject. He would use him as a dummy to demonstrate proper bandaging techniques for various injuries. The Pain was laid out on a table and the class proceeded to bandage him for everything from simple pressure bandages to splints and slings and even head and eye injuries. He was bandaged from head to toe. Joe would enjoy wrapping extra adhesive tape to illustrate the importance of immobilizing an injury. *Obviously a sinister motive at work here.* Joe kept an eye on the clock knowing the class was scheduled for lunch near the middle of the class period. By the time lunch time arrived, the Pain was completely wrapped and looked like a mummy just removed from a tomb. Time for lunch, everyone left the room, including Joe. The Pain was left behind struggling to free himself. He was at the end of his struggle when the class began to return for the second half of the period.

Joe got a lot of satisfaction out of this one, and so did the entire class.

~ FRESHMAN FOOTBALL BEGINS ~

The frosh football season opened with a meager showing of candidates. Less than 25 players for a school with an enrollment in excess of 2500 students. For the last game of the season Joe arranged for his freshman team to go on an over-night trip to play the team he had coached the year before in Attleboro. The host school arranged a welcoming dance for the night before the game and a live broadcast on local radio for the next day's game. *Years later one of Joe's players would marry a girl he had met at the welcoming dance.* The players were hyped for the game. Joe's pre-game pep talk really fired up his team so much so that on the opening kick-off Eddy Gee, his star player, ran down the field with such speed and intensity, he hit the ball carrier head-on causing him to fumble the ball and break his own shoulder in the process. From that point on, Joe's team was demoralized and soundly beaten.

Late that night, Joe drove Eddy Gee, who was heavily sedated, home from the Attleboro Hospital. Needless to say, facing his mother was no easy task and the reception was far from cordial.

With the approaching spring of that first year, Bill Kells one of

Joe's former teachers and the varsity baseball coach, asked Joe if he would like to be the frosh baseball coach. The challenge was accepted with delight. The first year at the academy seemed to fly by. It was a hard working year but also a very enjoyable year. Toward the end of the year he got a call from his former shipyard boss with an attractive offer to come back to work for him. It really set him to thinking about his future in education. After much thought he decided to see Mr. George and tell him he would not be back in September. Mr. George questioned the decision. Joe told him his teaching load was too demanding and his salary wasn't worth the effort expended. After hearing Joe out, Mr. George said,

"I can't come close to competing to your sixty-five hundred dollar offer, but I can sweeten your salary a bit and get you a summer job."

He paused awhile, looked Joe in the eye, then said,

"And, I can guarantee you will never again have such a demanding teaching schedule. By the way, you proved to all of us you could handle a near impossible task."

Joe left his office feeling good and went home to ponder a decision. He would eventually return in September with a teaching schedule that included one math class and the rest all honors science classes.

~ OH MY ! NOT AGAIN ~

The first school year at the academy came to a close and Joe and Dorothy were expecting their third child. They both hoped this time it would be a boy. They both were in the midst of remodeling their first house which they were able to purchase only after Mr.

George, who served on the bank board, intervened during the approval process to get their request for a mortgage approved. Joe could not provide any credit references because up to this time he never had the need to finance anything. He was always able to pay cash for all their needs. Mr. George vouched for Joe's stability and credibility without which the mortgage application most likely would have been denied.

True to form, Dorothy would awaken Joe from a sound sleep in the early morning hours with an elbow to the ribs with that familiar saying,

"Wake up Joe, it's time to go."

Quietly, as not to awaken his two sleeping daughters he made his way to the kitchen, in the dark and still half asleep, where he would telephone his next door neighbor to come over and look after the kids while he drove Dorothy to the hospital. The path to the kitchen would take Joe through a new hallway to an opening in the kitchen wall he had cut through the previous day. The hallway was cluttered with tools and building materials and without lighting. Earlier that evening he had moved a large bird cage, that swung on a high floor stand, into the hallway. As he moved carefully through the darkened area he bumped the stand and quickly stopped it from falling over by grabbing onto the stand. The swinging cage came back and hit him smack in the mouth. There he stood holding onto the stand with one hand while the frightened bird screeched and fluttered around in the swinging cage as he tried to nurse, what was soon to become, a fat lip. When the cage stopped swinging and the cursing stopped he made his way to the kitchen lights, called the neighbor, and drove to the hospital, *with his wife of course*. The scene at the hospital was much the same as with previous races to beat the stork. He kissed his wife good-bye at the elevator door and went back home to bed to await the hospital's call. It wasn't long before the call came,

"Congratulations Joe, you did it again, it's a girl."

Baby June arrived to join her two sisters, Jacqueline and Jeannette. The disappointment of another girl would eventually turn out to be a blessing in disguise. She would be his constant companion, a truly Daddy's girl.

~ NEW RECRUITS ~

Before the start of the next football season, Joe began an extensive recruiting program by visiting all the schools with eighth graders who would be coming to the academy. He would speak at student assemblies and, with the aid of his previous year team players would demonstrate some of the basics of football. The result was a tremendous turnout for football that would eventually tax the school's football equipment inventory. Joe did not believe in cutting anyone who tried out for the team. He would work them hard to a point where the uncommitted would cut themselves. Only serious players would survive. His first recruited season would dress a team of fifty-five players. The growing program would soon require the assistance of more than one coach. Coaching at this level was a joy. In those days there were no organized football programs prior to entering high school; thus, no previously learned bad habits to correct. The youngsters didn't even know how to wear their equipment. *At times this made for some interesting laughs.* Coaching at this level would see and savor player progression from start to finish.

The coaching years spawned hundreds of stories that still are remembered and fondly recalled at class reunions several decades later. There was Danny who was hit, spun around and headed for the wrong goal line with his own teammates chasing after him in an effort to stop him.

They did catch him. He never would live this one down.
There was a player whose last name, Usanavich, when yelled out sometimes sounded like the coach was calling him a son-of-a-bitch. In fact, one of the spectator parents, not knowing the player's name, was appalled and criticized Joe when he heard him yell, " Run Usanavich, run."

Joe mastered the art of team pep talks. One time, with his team losing at half time, he gathered them onto their bus as if to take them home, and got them so fired up for the second half that when they exited the bus, the smallest kid on the team tripped and fell. When the dust cleared, there he was lying in the dirt with a twisted helmet on his head, a bewildered look on his face, and cleat marks on his back. His clean white uniform was soiled from the herd that actually ran over him.

Each year Joe's football program enjoyed a winning season; two of which were undefeated seasons. His starting team would be asked to dress for the last varsity game of the season. In fact, in one game they went in as a team and gained more yardage on one special play than the varsity did for the entire game. Often the freshmen would play the junior varsity team late in the season. There was one game where they led the JV team by 18 points at half time nearly driving the JV coach to a nervous breakdown. Joe would soon be moved up to the JV level, a move made against his wishes. He wanted to stay with the frosh program but the head coach wanted him with the Junior Varsity.

~ A TRUE FISH STORY ~

One evening, Joe got a call from one of his fellow football coaches, Jack, baby June's godfather. Jack's neighbor had gone fishing that Saturday and delivered a batch of fish to him and he was too proud to admit he didn't know how to clean fish. His wife suggested he call Joe. He got on the phone,

"Hey Joe, how about coming over and showing me how to clean some stupid fish my neighbor dumped on me."

Joe drove to his house and proceeded to show Jack the art of cleaning and fileting fish. They both stood in front of the kitchen sink with a bucket of fish at their feet. It seemed like Jack needed to have a beer with every fish they cleaned. By the time they got down to the last three fish Jack had enough. *Beer and cleaning fish that is*. Jack turned to Joe and said,

"Do me a favor, on your way home, take these three suckers and dump them someplace. I don't want to leave them in the garbage can until the next collection."

Joe wasn't interested in doing that and replied,

"I got a better idea. Why don't you wrap them up and stick them in the fridge and on Monday morning bring them to school and put them in the teachers' mailboxes."

Jack wrapped the fish individually in newspaper. There was no room for them in the refrigerator so he decided to leave them outside on the back porch for the weekend.

On Monday the three fish came to school and were carefully placed into three selected teacher's mailboxes. Now it was time to sit back and enjoy the show. The fish were moved about in the maze of teacher mailboxes like they were in a game of musical chairs. By the next morning, the fish had disappeared. *Not for long*. Two of the smelly critters found their way into a coach's car. One was placed under the front seat where it could easily be found and the other was tucked in the underside of back seat between its springs. That afternoon, on the way to graduate study classes, the odor was a dead giveaway of fish somewhere in the car. They stopped by the side of the road and made a search for the origin of what was now, undoubtedly, a foul smell. The fish placed under the front seat was easily found and it was discarded by the side of the road. On they went, not knowing there was another sleeping fish tucked in the springs under the back seat yet to be found.

On the way home that evening after class, the fishy smell was the topic of conversation all the way home. The consensus was that the car would need to have a good washing especially under the front seat where the one fish was found. The next morning the floor area got a good scrubbing. An air freshener was used but that did not seem to help. The thought was, maybe the air freshener aggravated the smell. The smell grew worse as the day passed. Two days later the second fish, the one hidden under the back seat, was eventually found.

Meanwhile, fish #3 was making the rounds of the campus. By this time, almost everyone on campus knew enough about the traveling fish to be on their guard and especially to keep their cars locked. During the week of the fish, the school was undergoing an important school accreditation visit. Mr. George was seen several times during the day carefully checking his car because its door locks were inoperable. He wanted to be certain his vehicle would not succumb to a visit by the missing fish. After all, he would be embarrassed if he had to explain that some nut on his staff was a practical joker. This might not set well with the seriousness of an accreditation visit.

At the end of that week, Joe called his wife to come to the campus and take his car to the train station to pick up their guests who were coming for a weekend visit. Dottie hadn't driven more than a block or two when she turned the car around and returned to school,

"Joe, something in this car smells awful," she said. "We can't ask anyone to ride in it."

Joe quickly sensed, that somehow, fish #3 was the culprit. He found it under the hood, in the early stages of cooking on a hot engine. Home it went for the weekend. By this time the fish was really ripe. Its eyes had sunken deep into their sockets. Monday morning Joe arrived at school early enough to get rid of the fish. His classroom was near Mr. Gray's office and he had not yet arrived. The fish was carefully laid out in Mr. Gray's center desk drawer.

During the second class period that day there was a knock on Joe's classroom door. He opened it. There stood Mr. Gray, with a stern look on his face, holding the fish by the tail with one outstretched hand at about eye level, not saying a word. He was studying the expression on Joe's face. Joe had all he could do not to bust out laughing. Finally he couldn't hold it in any longer. The body wrenching attempt to look innocent failed. Mr. Gray then uttered,

"So, you're the one. Here, this belongs to you."
With that said he dropped the fish on Joe's desk, turned and left. The students in class could be heard letting out with, "Phew wee, that stinks." Joe had to get rid of this critter fast. He asked Faith, the teacher next door, to watch his class so he could get rid of the fish. Over to the Clubhouse he went. The Clubhouse was the dressing facility for the football team. It also had a dressing room and a shower reserved for the coaching staff.

The head coach had a habit, at the end of a practice session, of undressing by stepping out of his pants and leaving them in a heap on the floor. They were ready for the next day when he would step into them and simply pull them up. Joe dampened the fish in the sink (*to enhance the smell*) and carefully placed it in the folds of the head coach's pants heaped on the floor. He turned the heating thermostat up to 85 degrees and then returned to class. By the end of the school day, Joe had sent word to the coaching staff of what he had done with fish #3. They all arrived early for practice to await the show. There they sat in a very warm room with the stench of fish that was almost intolerable. Everyone waited for the head coach to arrive and step into his pants. Well, he came in, didn't say a word about the smell or the heat. He kicked aside the pants heaped on the floor, reached into the closet and came out with a clean pair and put them on. With a smirk on his face he said,

"OK guys, let's get the boys on the field."

Everyone had a disappointed look on their faces. The head coach, was enjoying the moment and eventually let on that a student equipment manager had forewarned him.

Fish #3 was finally laid to rest -- in the garbage can.

~ *TROUBLE in FOOTBALL* ~

During his years as a very successful, winning coach in both baseball and football (in his last year as an assistant baseball coach they would win their league title and the State Baseball Championship title in the large school division) the varsity football coach was experiencing just the opposite, a dismal losing season every year. This made for a lot of grumbling by fans and rumors began to surface that Joe would soon be replacing the head football coach. Compounding the rumor situation was an apparent animosity that festered between the head football coach and the school's basketball coaches. The basketball coaches seemed to enjoy needling the head football coach and used every opportunity to spread the word that the football coach needed to be replaced and Joe was the man for the job. This placed Joe in a very uncomfortable position, even though he made it very clear to all who talked to him, he was not interested in the job and absolutely had no aspirations of ever being a head varsity coach. He also made that very clear to the head coach who was disturbed by the rumor mill. Joe would never fuel any negativism about the football program and carefully guarded any comments that could be construed the wrong way. Obviously, it wasn't enough. Joe had to go. This would end his coaching career after seven consecutive years of winning seasons.

~ NUMBER FOUR ARRIVES ~

The end of his football coaching came just as his fourth child was about to be born. By this time, Joe's hopes of having a boy were greatly diminished. After having his third girl in a row and the razzing he was subjected to from his friends about his inability to produce a boy, and all the advice he received as to how to make a boy, he was ready for another barrage of well-intentioned comments should he be blessed with another girl.

Again, in the wee, dark hours of the morning, he was awakened with that familiar nudge to the ribs and an anxious soft voice saying,

"Joe, Joe, it's time to go."

Trying to shake off a sound sleep, Joe's mind was thinking why his wife couldn't for once have a baby at a decent hour. What could possibly happen this time to mar this trip to the hospital? Well, here's what happened. The wake up call came during their first night sleeping in a new bed. Unlike the Hollywood style bed they were accustomed to (a bed without a foot board) the new bed had a foot board. As a sleepy and staggering Joe came around the corner of the bed, he stubbed his toe on the front leg of the bed. Not only did the air turn blue with a barrage of choice words but, Joe performed a dancing pirouette that would rival that of a Russian ballet dancer. The toe was broken.

Lucky for Joe, this was to be the last child to be born to them. Any more and another unthinkable fiasco could have happened.

Joe, painfully limping, escorted his wife to the hospital and then returned home to bed. The pain would soon be forgotten when the call came. He finally got his wish, he became the father of baby Joe, Jr. Needless to say celebration was in the air. Congratulations seemed to come from everywhere. Family and friends were very happy.

Joe's father, Francesco, was especially happy because now he was assured the family name would be carried forth.

~ *TIME for a CHANGE* ~

Now, with a wife and four young children, the monthly paycheck seemed to be shrinking. Joe contemplated a change in careers. A friend who was a state senator at the time, and politically connected to former Governor Ribicoff who had just been appointed to President Kennedy's Cabinet, talked Joe into considering work for the American Embassy in Italy. The wheels were put in motion. First, Joe was required to establish a political alliance by becoming a registered Democrat. Then political connections were made in Washington and the wait began. It wasn't very long before Ribicoff and the President had a falling out and Ribicoff resigned his Cabinet post. That ended Joe's quest for what appeared to be a great opportunity to enter foreign service.

Joe would make another try at negotiating more money for coaching baseball and as a classroom teacher. He went to see Mr. George. *That day will long be remembered*. As Joe entered his office, there sat the Bulldog behind his big desk talking with his assistant administrator, Mr. Gray. They both turned, looked at him and before Joe could say a word, Mr. George said,

"Hey, you're just the guy we're looking for."
Joe was taken by surprise. What did I do wrong, he thought. Before he uttered a word, Mr. George followed with,

"How would you like to work with IBM machines and earn some serious money?"

The term serious money seemed to blot out all of his thoughts for a moment. Joe didn't even know what the letters IBM stood for.

"We'll arrange to have you trained right here on campus." Mr. George added.

This sounded like a great opportunity and Joe, with the sound of "serious money" still ringing in his ears, listened as Mr. George made arrangements for him to meet with training personnel from IBM. Joe was anxious to get home that day to tell his wife the good news.

• • •

The appointed training week arrived and Joe reported ready to begin

142

his new assignment. What a surprise he got when he entered the training room. There were four other staff members sitting there ready to be trained. Mr. George led Joe to believe he was the chosen one. What the hell were these other people doing here he thought? He soon realized the Bulldog most likely had given them the same convincing line. This was indeed a low blow to Joe's ego. Too late now, he felt committed so he sat down for the first day of a week of classes in a course called Functional Wiring. On the third day of classes he was the only one who showed; none of the others came. They chose to drop out.

I guess you can say Joe got the job by default.

~ LOST at SEA ~

Joe quickly adapted to becoming a member of Mr. George's inner circle. During the summer months, Mr. George would invite the chosen few (his inner circle) to his summer home at the shore where they would spend the day on his boat. Little did Joe suspect his first trip out with this gang would be an initiation never to be forgotten. It was a beautiful August day for boating on Long Island Sound. Everyone was enjoying the cruise. There was plenty of beer and hard stuff on board to satisfy anyone's thirst. Captain George was at the wheel. His senior administrator, called PB, had invited his older brother, Herman, to join him for the day. Along with Joe, this was also brother Herman's first trip. PB and his brother sat together on the stern bench seat enjoying the ride as they nibbled on some cheese and crackers. PB began talking about his brother's retirement party and the beautiful gold watch awarded to his brother for forty years of

143

service with the same company. He held up his brother's wrist and said,

"Look at that. Ain't that a beauty? It's got diamonds all over the face."

Everyone focused on the watch as it sparkled in the bright sun. Someone asked if it kept good time. Herman replied,

"Oh yeah, it's the most accurate timepiece on the market." Captain George asked PB to bring the watch to him and he would check it out on the ship's radio for an accurate read. PB removed the watch from his brother's wrist and passed it on to him. After examining the watch and commenting on its beauty he began fussing with the ship's radio. After awhile, Captain George turned and said,

"I can't seem to get thru on this damn radio. I'll check it out later -- here. "

With that comment, and a quick underhand pitch, he threw the watch back in PB's direction. The throw was high and wide over PB's head and into the ocean. The look on brother Herman's face was one of shock and disappointment as he stood in the same spot where he landed after a valiant jump to try to catch the watch that sailed overhead. Everyone stood silent as if frozen with what they saw. Captain George broke the silence,

"Gee, I'm really sorry Herman. Don't worry, I'll replace it with another one."

Someone blurted out,

"Yeah, sure, knowing you it will probably be a top-of-the-line Timex."

Joe couldn't help but feel sorry for PB's brother. What a terrible thing to do to this old man, he thought. The look on the old man's face was the most pathetic look he had ever seen. Captain George went over to Herman and with a big smile on his face handed

144

him the watch thought to be lost forever at the bottom of the ocean. Herman examined the watch carefully. Slowly the color returned to Herman's face as he shook his head in disbelief. A smile of great relief crossed his face. The setup had been executed with perfection. An old, junk watch was substituted for the real one and it was the junk watch that actually got tossed into the ocean. Everyone laughed and drank a beer to toast PB's brother.

• • •

No one on board had thought to bring along a bathing suit and the afternoon was hot. A few individuals were brave enough to strip down and engage in some old time skinny dipping. Joe thought he had seen everything, a bunch of old men with their snow white bottoms bobbing up and down in the ocean waves. *If only he had a camera.* After everyone had their fill of fun in the sun, it was time to head back to the dock.

On the way back, Joe was standing, near the bow, when all of a sudden he was pushed from behind and landed in the ocean, fully clothed. By the time he surfaced, the boat was continuing on its course toward shore with everyone on board at the stern end of the boat waving good-bye to him. Someone yelled,

"See ya back at the dock!"

Joe had all he could do to tread water to stay afloat. These guys are nuts, he thought. No way could he ever swim that far to shore. It was a frightening experience to think these crazy people might lose him at sea. A few minutes seemed like an eternity before the boat turned around and helping hands picked him out of the water.

Joe was now a full fledged member of the inner circle.

V

From 1960 to 1975

~ *A COMPUTER GURU* ~

The year was 1960, a turning point in Joe's career in education. He would soon be one of a handful educators in the entire nation who amassed an expertise in computer applications for school administration. His work with computers in schools was recognized by IBM in an exclusive issue of an IBM Application Brief devoted solely to his work at the academy. The publication was not only distributed nationally, but made available in different languages for international distribution as well. The academy computer center became a model center and Joe became a sought after speaker at several state and national educators' meetings and conventions.

Joe was able to design, write, and implement a variety of computer programs not only for school use but for others as well. He developed computer programs that served as inventory controls for business; analyzed Connecticut Bar Exam candidates' performance; wrote programs serving almost all areas of school administration; computer dating for school dances; counting student election ballots; and, hundreds of other applications.

A most notable challenge came one day when Joe answered a phone call. The State Commissioner of Education was on the other end. When Joe answered the phone and the Commissioner introduced himself, he immediately thought this was another one of his friends joking with him and it took awhile before he realized this was the real thing. Anyway, it served to bond the two in a nice way that has never been forgotten. Joe had a way of handling jokesters and most always got the better end of the play. In this case, after the exchange of some pleasantries the embarrassed computer guru listened to the Commissioner's problem. It should be noted this conversation took place on a Thursday and a target date was set for the following Monday. The Commissioner had a serious problem. He had a $1,865,000 federal grant that had to be allotted to the State's 169 towns by Monday or face returning the grant to the federal government. Apparently, the State Department of Education computer personnel, at that time, did not have the degree of sophistication necessary to develop a computer program in time to meet the deadline date.

The conversation with the Commissioner was long and detailed. A massive amount of data had been collected to be fitted into a mathematical formula within prescribed parameters. This information was to be hand delivered to Joe should he decide to take on the project. Joe explained that the academy computer did not have the storage capacity to handle this job and he would need to solicit the use of a bigger system and hire additional programmers to work the weekend in order to complete the job. He made it clear that because

147

of the limited time constraints he could not promise completion, nor guarantee the success of such an undertaking. The Commissioner stated any expenses incurred to get the job done on time would not be a problem. He was in a desperate situation and Joe was his last hope. He said to Joe,

"I've heard enough about you to know, if anyone can bail us out, you're the one who can do it."

Hearing that, Joe said, "OK, I'll give it shot, but please understand, no promises."

The Commissioner arranged for Joe to be in constant touch with him by letting him know his whereabouts as he moved about that weekend. Joe hired two programmer friends, and obtained the use of an IBM360 computer. They all worked late nights and all day Saturday and Sunday writing and testing programs. As the deadline drew nearer the task seemed almost impossible. Late Sunday afternoon everything came together. They were able to allocate all of the $1,865,000 for all 169 Connecticut towns except for 39 cents. Joe called the Commissioner. He was elated with the news and kept saying,

"Wow ..., thirty-nine cents ..., thirty-nine cents ..., fantastic, how did you ever get to thirty-nine cents?"

Joe replied, "I carried all calculations out to five decimal places."

Needless to say Joe now had a new friend in high places.
The down side to this project was it took the State six months to send Joe his paycheck.

• • •

The following year the Commissioner called again with basically the same problem. This time it was easy money for Joe. Using a

148

modification of the same program he was able to allocate all but 19 cents this time.

Guess what?... another six months wait for a paycheck.

. . .

Another interesting computer application involved his work with The Connecticut Bar Association. Joe wrote a program to process input from eighteen different attorneys. Each attorney was assigned to examine the same two essay questions for each candidate. The results would then be sent to Joe for processing. The input data from the eighteen different sources would be keypunched into cards and then processed by the computer. Each candidate's input would be analyzed for the conditions under which they passed or failed and the questions themselves were analyzed as to their apparent level of difficulty.

The accuracy of the keypunched data entered was of utmost importance. Upwards of five hundred cards had to be checked and rechecked. Joe would personally recheck the data entry and then take the cards home. He asked his two oldest daughters, elementary school age students, if they would like to make some money. They would be paid five dollars for every error found. Unbeknown to them, Joe purposely inserted a few error cards in the file and made note of which cards had the errors. He always placed an error card near the front of the file. The joy of earning five dollars early in the process served to fuel their motivation and kept their interest at a keen level. It also assured a thorough job of spotting any erroneous data, planted or real. *Joe got a lot of mileage out of a twenty dollar bill.*

Some exotic jobs came with a high level of stress. The unexpected was always a challenge. The Bar Exam application ran smoothly, twice a year, for several years until one year when an unsuccessful candidate decided to sue the Bar Examining Committee.

He was suing under the right to know law because he had failed the exam three times. The Committee informed Joe that he should be prepared to defend his program in court should the complainant fail on his fourth try. Joe poured over his program carefully, line by line, looking for a possible bug that could have distorted the end results. He tested the program over and over again, so many times, always wondering what could have possibly gone wrong. It was his program that calculated and printed out a pass or a fail for each candidate. He began to have horrible thoughts of a bug that may have affected the results of years past. He could not find any bugs.

The next exam processing day arrived. This time the entire Bar Examining Committee wanted to be present when Joe ran the program. All eyes were glued to the computer printer as the results began to print. Everyone was focused on the name of the complainant. *Here he comes.* Joe stopped the printer and said,

" Look at that. Wouldn't you know, ... the son-of-a-gun passed by one point."

All that work and worry and Joe didn't get his day in court.

~ A FABULOUS JOB OFFER ~

From 1960 to 1968, computers and the development of computer programs for school use occupied most of Joe's workday. He became active in professional data processing organizations -- state, local, and national. He was elected and served every office from President to International Director. The internationally known Data Processing Management Association (DPMA) recognized his service and dedication to the profession with several of their highest awards. He was a much sought after speaker and also a consultant for many school systems. IBM would fly him, in their corporate jet, to Florida for lunch and home for supper on the same day just to get his thoughts on a new computer system they were about to market to educators.

• • •

As he sat in his office one fall day three men paid him a surprise visit. They had heard of Joe's accomplishments and decided to stop by his office hoping to catch him and arrange a meeting. They were from the Board of Cooperative Educational Services in New York State (BOCES). They were looking for someone to establish a model computer center for their state's BOCES operations and Joe was their target. They arranged to wine and dine him and his wife in New York. They offered to double his present salary. This was an offer that needed serious consideration.

By this time, Mr. George had retired and a new headmaster was in place. Joe discussed his future at the academy with him and the best he could do was to elevate Joe's position to that of a part-time assistant administrator. The increase in pay however, would not come close to the New York offer. Joe really did not want to leave the academy. His love for his Alma Mater was very strong and a decision to leave would not be easy. After many sleepless nights, Joe decided what would be best for his family's future. *New York here we come.*

Because Joe would be entering the New York educational system at an assistant superintendent level pay level, the offer was not without a caveat. He would need to meet their State certification requirements within a five year period. He was assured this would be no problem. (One of the three BOCES visitors was a professor at Columbia). They would arrange for him to take the necessary courses at Columbia University. Joe tendered his resignation effective the end of the 1967 school year.

~ *A NEW BEGINNING* ~

During the time between the decision to leave the academy and the effective date of his resignation, the leadership of the academy was on shaky ground. The headmaster, also called the principal, resigned in the middle of the school year and the Associate Principal, Mr. Hammar, was elevated to the vacant position. It was a bittersweet promotion for him because he had been passed over three years earlier during the search for Mr. George's successor and the token position of Associate Principal was created just for him. Now, the trustees finally realized he was the man they should have chosen in the first place.

Shortly after Mr. Hammar's appointment he visited Joe at his home late one Sunday morning. Joe was taken by surprise when he answered the door and saw him standing there,

"Good morning Joe, I hope you can take a few minutes to talk. I need to discuss some important business with you."

Joe, wondering what this was all about, invited him in. Mr. Hammar, always a kind and considerate gentleman, delivered friendly greetings to Joe's wife and children. After a few minutes of pleasantries they both went into the living room to talk,

"Joe, I know you have accepted another position and I'm hoping there's a chance you will reconsider and stay on with me. I could use your help and I've been thinking about creating a new position of Vice-Principal for you."

This took Joe completely by surprise. The academy had never a position of Vice-Principal before. He was completely flattered and speechless for a moment. He bowed his head and stared at the floor,

" I don't know what to say, you really threw me a curve. I really do appreciate your confidence in me. Thanks. Can I sleep on this for awhile?"

Joe needed some time to clear his head and Mr. Hammar was willing to give him whatever time he needed. After a couple of sleepless nights, he went to see Mr. Hammar to discuss a way to honorably bow out of his commitment to the BOCES people.

Joe had lost his father a few months before all this and his grieving mother was further upset with his decision to leave town. *He played this card nicely.* He explained, to the BOCES people, the need to be near his grieving mother and the unexpected opportunity offered at his Alma Mater. They understood Joe's plight. A disappointed and amiable release was agreed to.

Joe would become the first Catholic person appointed to an administrative post at the academy in the school's one hundred thirteen year history, dating back to 1856.

~ *TIME to START GRADUATE STUDIES* ~

The New York offer awakened Joe to the fact that he could be locked into the academy forever with little or no chance of moving up to an administrative post in another school system without proper certification credentials. As luck would have it, he received a visit from a nationally known university professor, Dr. Bill Gren, who heard about his work with computers. Impressed with what he saw, he took Joe to dinner and they talked about the opportunities the future might hold for someone with his computer talent. Dr. Gren stressed the value of having an advanced degree. Joe was very interested in getting an advanced degree in computer science and had already begun to explore that possibility. A national search of several large universities in the mid '60's yielded not one advanced degree program in computer science.

Dr. Gren convinced Joe he should start at the university even though they could not offer him much help in the area of computer science. In 1968 Joe began a masters' program in school administration at the university with Dr. Gren as his major advisor. Joe, as a part-time student, was awarded his master's degree within one calendar year.

Working all day as an administrator while attending graduate school three nights a week was no easy task. The experience he had gained working for Mr. Hammar, at the academy, was the best training in administration anyone could ever hope for where he was allowed to handle almost every aspect of administrative problems that seemed to surface on a daily basis. Mr. Hammar served as a great mentor and Joe was an ambitious learner. He soon became a very capable and popular administrator who earned the respect of students, teachers, and staff. A strict and fair disciplinarian, everyone knew where Joe stood and where he was coming from on any issue. He knew when to be serious and when to have fun. The administrative load did not diminish his flair for seizing an opportunity for some hilarity.

~ HALLOWEEN NIGHT SECURITY ~

Many Halloween night pranks are remembered, especially by those who fell victims to Joe's antics. On this night, the school always took special precautions to prevent vandalic damage to its campus buildings. The headmaster's home, adjacent to the campus, was especially secured because of its proximity to the street and its attraction for student pranksters. The maintenance crew was assigned the task of guarding the properties.

One Halloween night, Joe and his friend, Big Rob, decided to test the security of the headmaster's residence. The residence was guarded by one of the workers who sat in his car parked at the entrance to the driveway. This position allowed him to have full view of the front door and traffic along the street. Joe and his friend dressed for the occasion. Joe donned a long-haired wig over a face distorted with a sheer stocking and wore ragged clothing. He also carried a guitar. Big Rob, who stood over six feet tall, was dressed in an army jacket worn over a set of shoulder pads, an old army hat, and a mask. He carried a wooden toy rifle. The shoulder pads added to the already large size frame of this man in such a manner as to make his appearance very threatening. They parked their car on a corner street; then marched toward the headmaster's house; Joe strumming his guitar and singing <u>We Shall Overcome</u> and Big Rob marching alongside with his rifle held in a present-arms position.

As they approached the so-called "guard" seated in his car in the driveway they expected to be challenged by him. It was apparent the guard didn't want any part of what he saw coming toward him. Slowly, he slid down his seat and positioned himself, out of sight, under the dashboard. It was an hilarious sight and the perpetrators had all they could do to maintain their composure. They marched on to the front door. The "guard" never exited his car. He didn't even chance raising his head to peek out !

Big Rob knocked on the door with the butt end of his rifle while Joe continued to sing. The door opened. There stood Mr. Hammar's son, about thirty years old at the time, in an apparent state of shock. Before he could say a word the two "visitors" pushed him aside and stepped inside and said,

"Hey you, where's your father?"
Without thinking, he answered with a nervous stutter and pointed to the stairs,

"He-e-e, he's a-a-up there ... in his den."
Quickly they went upstairs and confronted Mr. Hammar who stood among papers strewn about the floor. He was working on a school report. Big Rob and Joe took one look at his eyes, which were about to pop out of his head, and they busted out laughing. They all enjoyed a good laugh. Mr. Hammar, being a good natured guy, decided to join them when he asked about their next stop. He grabbed a shawl and draped it over his head and around his neck and off they went to seek another victim. Mr. Hammar's thin body frame, hunched beneath the shawl, made him look like a little old lady.

● ● ●

On many Halloween nights Joe and Big Rob would team up, disguise and mask themselves, to test their skills on unsuspecting neighbors and friends. One of their best performances came one time when they wanted to test the security crew assigned to watch over the campus buildings. On this night they managed to sneak on campus from the rear. They found the security crew, four men on this night, enjoying a coffee break sitting in a car between two of the buildings. Joe carried a long-handled ax and Big Rob a large plastic bucket.

They climbed to the top row of the bleacher seats along the football field within earshot and view of the car. Joe began pounding on the bottom of the bucket with the butt end of the ax and Big Rob started stomping on the bleacher boards. The booming sounds were soon heard by the guards and they spotted the two figures on the bleachers. Thinking that someone was vandalizing the bleacher seats they quickly exited the car with flashlights in hand and headed toward them. *Now the fun starts.* Joe and Rob ran down the bleacher seats and onto a running track that was at the base of the bleachers. As they ran along the track, two of the guards gave chase along the backside of the bleachers, paralleling the track, hoping to head them off at the end. The pursuers were totally surprised when Joe suddenly turned midway along the bleachers into a large opening, separating the two sets of bleacher seating, meeting the pursuers head on with his ax held high. Joe stood motionless in a semi-crouched position and watched his pursuers come to a grinding halt. There they were, two brave souls, actually one brave soul, the other backed behind the lead person. With flashlights quivering in their hands one said,

"OK guys. P-p-put it down. D-d-d don't get crazy now." The flashlight continued to quiver. Joe made a sudden move by moving the ax upward to get a better grip lower on its handle. This apparent threatening maneuver caused the guards to jump backward. One of them moved back so quickly he backed himself hard into a brick building causing him to drop his flashlight,

"C'mon now. P-p-put it down."

By this time, Joe and Rob couldn't hold it any longer and their laughter gave them away. That brought a sigh of relief from the guards ... followed by a few choice words. Off came the masks. Rob wanted to check the brick wall of the building to see if brave Pierre left his imprint there.

"You'd better check his underwear too, he may need a change," replied Deluke, the other guard.

The following day during the maintenance crew's coffee break, appropriate trophies were awarded to these men of courage. The Golden Sneaker Award, made especially for Deluke, was presented along with clean undershorts for Pierre.

Halloween nights for many years to come became a very special event at the academy. It kept the security people on their toes.

~ ELMER'S FOLLY ~

Elmer was a retired plumber who came to work part time at the academy. He was a small man nearing his eighties and when on a job he was always accompanied by a helper. Deluke was assigned to help him and the two of them often tended many of the daily plumbing needs of a large school campus. Elmer was always a good-natured gentleman and the maintenance crew took delight at every opportunity to exploit some of Elmer's wit and work experiences on some of his campus projects. His best-known project was the installation of a large, beautiful white cast iron fountain on the front lawn of the administration building. The fountain was donated from the estate of a former alumnus. Elmer worked for days putting it together and connecting a water pipe to it. The day came when he would turn on the water -- obviously a proud moment for him. He had invited Joe, the maintenance crew, and many of the occupants of the administration building to witness the spray as it exited the ornamental top of the fountain. With everyone gathered around the fountain and many onlookers gazing out the windows, he was ready to turn on the water. Elmer signaled his helper to turn on the valve. All watched intently as the hissing sound of air being moved by a column of water in the pipes made its way to the top of the fountain.

"Here it comes," said Elmer with some excitement in his voice.

Then came a few sputtering sounds with a few droplets of water. That soon ended and a steady stream of water, about four inches high, flowed from the top of the magnificent fountain. Oohs and aahs and cheers came from the crew, each one looking at the other. Elmer took it in stride and laughed along with everyone. Elmer checked to see if the valve was wide open. It was. From that day forward the fountain was referred to as Elmer's Folly.

• • •

Joe's office was the stage for another encounter with Elmer and his helper They were trying to run a pipe up through a closet in his office up into a vacant area on the next floor. Deluke and Elmer took several measurements in Joe's office. After several trips up and down the stairs, and much discussion, they agreed on their measurements.   They were ready to drill a pilot hole down into the closet.   Joe heard the drilling and thought the sound was awfully close to his desk area. He looked up just in time to see the pilot drill come through the ceiling far from its intended mark. Joe jumped from his chair, went out into hall and yelled up the stairway,

"What the hell are you guys doing? You just put a hole through my nice ceiling."

Down they came to see their drill bit hanging about three feet away from where they wanted to be. The blame for this blunder began to be tossed back and forth. Each accusing the other of not being able to read a ruler. After they cooled down a bit, Joe said to them,

ELMER'S FOLLY

"Hey, where are your brains? If you want to go through my closet ceiling why don't you drill up from here instead of down?"

They looked at each other and Elmer and Deluke commented on why they hadn't thought of that. Up they went to get their drill and a ladder to begin their drilling upwards. Joe in the meantime left his office, hurried upstairs, filled a cup with water and waited for the drill bit to come through the floor. As soon as they drilled through the floorboards they pulled the drill bit back down; Joe was upstairs waiting. He slowly poured the water through the hole. Deluke was still standing on the ladder when the water began to flow through the hole and onto his head. Joe heard him blurt out a few expletives and tell Elmer he thought they had hit a sewer pipe. He told Elmer the water smelled like sewer water. They both ran up the stairs only to find Joe still holding onto his side, in pain, trying to control his laughter.

Joe would not allow them to patch the hole in his ceiling. Instead he hung a red flag from it and it was to become a conversation piece whenever someone saw the flag and asked, "What's that?"

. . .

One of Elmer's best moments came one day when he was dispatched to replace a broken toilet in one of the stalls in a Boy's room. Elmer removed the broken toilet and had it carted to a dumpster. He then proceeded to remove the new toilet bowl from its carton and was about to remove the tank portion from its carton when he decided to go to lunch, leaving the toilet bowl and the unopened toilet tank in the hall area leading to the toilet stalls. Shortly after he returned from lunch, Joe got a call to come over to where Elmer was working because there was a problem. When Joe arrived he found Elmer visibly upset, shaking his head and mumbling. While he was

160

out to lunch, a prankster decided to make an unwelcome deposit in the new toilet before it could be assembled and connected. It was still in a wide open space far from its intended stall. Elmer lost all his respect for the younger generation that day. He told that story for many years to come and each time he would shake his head in amazement, or was it disgust?

This was to be the first of many related incidents to follow on campus. The unknown perpetrator would be labeled The Phantom. He must have had a warped sense of humor. He would make his unwelcomed deposit in the most inappropriate places in several of the campus buildings, always in the Boys' toilet area. He even went so far as to load the paper towel dispensers. The search for The Phantom became a daily chore. In one toilet area that was serviced by a large venting system, one of the smaller bodied maintenance workers was actually hidden in the ventilating shaft in an attempt to catch the culprit. It didn't work. The Phantom eluded every attempt to catch him. After two years of these sporadic cat and mouse games, the incidents ceased.

"The Phantom" must have graduated leaving behind his unforgettable and smelly legacy.

~ BEING an ADMINISTRATOR HAS ITS UPS and DOWNS ~

Joe regrets he did not keep notes on all his experiences during his long career as an administrator and teacher. Some experiences still remain as cherished memories while others he'd like to forget about. Back in the late sixties, school campuses were in a state of turmoil.

Rebellious youth movements seemed to be everywhere. The academy was not immune and student sentiment on worldly issues often surfaced.

One of the fads of that era was a rash of streaking incidents that attracted a lot of publicity. (In case you forgot, "streaking" was the exposure of a naked body running by at public gatherings.) During lunch time, whenever weather permitted, students would gather outside and sit on the bleacher seats surrounding the football field. On this particular day an exceptionally large crowd had gathered. The word had gotten out that streakers would make their debut across the football field. This well-planned event apparently was flawed. Both ends of the campus were bordered by side streets and the streakers disrobed in a friend's car at one end and the friend was to drive to the other end street and wait for the streakers to reclaim their clothes.

The streakers, clad only in sneakers, began their run and were about to cross the length of the football field among the cheers and howls of an excited crowd. They were spotted by Ed, one of the security officers, and a chase began. Although Ed was in his forties, at the time, he was in great physical shape . Both he and Joe were on the same track team in high school and through the years managed to stay in good shape. Seeing the security officer gaining in pursuit, the streakers diverted from their planned course and headed for the woods. This proved to be a big mistake on their part, especially for one of them. Ed caught up to one as he was trying to run through a briar patch. The other streaker made his way to the other street. In the meantime, the driver friend, seeing other security people closing in on the field, drove away from the scene with both streakers' clothes. *Apparently, he didn't want any part of this situation. The streaker who got away was from another high school and was of little concern in this case.*

An embarrassed streaker, trying to keep his private parts covered with both hands, was escorted back across the field to the laughter, cheers, and boos of his classmates. Joe would soon be surprised to see Ed walk into his office escorting a young man who was completely naked, except for the sneakers he was wearing, with a body covered with bleeding scratches. The door was quickly closed. There stood the streaker with both hands crossed covering his private parts. He was about to sit down in one of the office chairs when Joe quickly stopped him,.

"Wait a minute, you don't sit down until I tell you to. What the hell is this all about?"

Ed proceeded to explain as the streaker, obviously embarrassed, stood listening. Joe, glared at the young man as he listened to Ed's explanation. Then, followed by a moment of dead silence, Joe rose from behind his desk and said,

"What are you, some kind of a nut? What's your name?" The streaker nervously stuttered his name and fumbling for words tried to explain he did this stunt for charity. *An unlikely story ... he couldn't come up with a charity name without a fumbling hesitation.*

"I think I know your father."

With an astonished looked he answered,

"I know you do."

Joe returned to his seat behind his desk, picked up the phone and said,

"I'll give him a call. I'm sure he'll be pleased to hear about your charitable endeavors."

"Oh no! Please."

Joe got the father on the phone,

"Frank, how are things with you? We haven't talked in quite awhile. I need to ask you a favor. I have your son here in my office and I think you'd want to come and take him home. By the way, bring him some clothes. He's standing here bare-ass."

Came a long silence on the father's end. Then the father responded,

"Joe, are you kidding me ... am I hearing you right?"

"You got it right. Your son got caught on campus seeking fame as a streaker. Maybe he thinks he's another Adonis, the Greek God."

Came another long silence. The father tells Joe he's on his way and "can't wait to get him home and kick his stupid a--."

The streaker was suspended from school for a week. Joe knew full-well the week off would not be a vacation. There would be hell to pay at home and his father would duly sentence him to hard physical labor on one of his construction jobs.

~ STUDENTS ARE NOT ALWAYS the PROBLEM ~

Problems with students, coupled with those of some teachers, can make for interesting and perplexing days. An unexpected teaching vacancy developed in the English department and because it came in the middle of the school year it became a difficult position to fill. Mr. Hammar, in his haste to fill the position, because he was scheduled to leave in a few weeks for the annual national meeting of school principals, hired a young man who came highly recommended by one of Hammar's academic colleagues. This had to be one of those get-even jokes that was sometimes used by administrators on each other, particularly when they were looking forward to ridding themselves of an undesirable teacher.

It wasn't long before reports of the new teacher's weird behavior began to filter through Joe's office. The kids were talking and the teachers' room was abuzz with bizarre stories. Several attempts to talk some sense into this individual proved futile. The showdown came one day while Hammar was attending a national conference some three thousand miles away. Joe got a call from one of the building administrators telling him he should get over to his building because during passing time between class periods that day, Mr. Wierdo could be seen brushing his teeth in the hallway drinking fountain. That was it. Joe had enough of this guy. He hurried over to Mr. Wierdo's room and escorted him back to his office. After a lengthy session Joe thought he had convinced him it was the appropriate time to seek professional help. Joe would not allow him to return to his classroom and arranged for security personnel to see that he left the campus. In the meantime, he called the teacher's father to tell him what had transpired and that his son was on his way home.

Two days later, Joe was warned that Mr. Wierdo was planning to pay him a visit and it was rumored he was coming in with a friend who was carrying a gun. Before Joe had much time to think about this situation, Mr. Hammar's secretary came into his office to tell him Mr. Wierdo and another gentleman were in the hall waiting to see him. An adrenaline rush seemed to take over. He knew he would need to act quickly to avert a scene. He told the secretary to seat them in Mr. Hammar's office, which was vacant that week, and he would be in shortly to speak to them. He also instructed her to alert security and to leave the door connecting her office and Mr. Hammar's ajar so she could listen to what transpired and keep the security people, who would be standing by, informed just in case he needed help.

After a few minutes, Joe entered Hammar's office. He tried very hard to keep to keep a calm air about him. Surely his blood pressure and heart beat must have gone off the scale. He politely greeted his visitors and asked them to be seated. He then walked over to the fireplace in the office which was located next to where the visitors were seated. Wierdo's friend was seated closest to the fireplace. Joe would not go behind the desk, but strategically located himself next to the fireplace and stood with his right arm resting on the mantle as he faced both of them. Wierdo's friend made Joe very nervous because he sat there looking at Joe and not saying a word, both hands tucked inside the side pockets of his jacket. During the entire conversation, Joe had his hand positioned next to the base of one of the many trophies sitting on the mantle and an eye fixed on the jacket pockets. He was confident he could grab onto a trophy and strike a devastating blow, if need be, to the head of the visitor seated below him and within arm's reach. If a hand had come out of that jacket pocket holding any metallic looking object, the resulting action might have produced a major headache, particularly for the victim and maybe a different kind of headache for Joe too.

Joe was a fairly smooth talker in tight situations. He was able to convince the teacher and his visitor friend that it was in everyone's best interest to take his advice and get some professional help for an obviously disturbed young man. The finishing touch was a comment made by Joe when he said he would welcome talking about a return to the classroom when the doctors were able to give him a clean bill of health. In Joe's mind, he knew it would be a cold day in hell for him to ever talk to this guy again.

When Hammar returned and learned of what had happened during his absence. He commended Joe and at the same time let him know he should not have taken such a risk.

Knowing Joe, he knew it couldn't be any other way.

~ *A SHOOTING in the CAFETERIA* ~

It seemed that every time the boss was away attending a conference, something would happen and Joe would find himself in the middle of an unexpected situation. Such was the case one day, during lunch time in a cafeteria packed with students. He was passing through on his way to the faculty lunch room when a loud bang was heard. The school nurse was walking just ahead of him and she turned to Joe and commented on kids and their use of fireworks. She entered the lunch room and Joe was about to follow when he noticed that in the doorway leading out of the cafeteria, the student monitor stationed in that doorway, seated in a chair leaning back on its hind legs, did not extend his usual friendly greeting. He had a painful look on his face. Joe noticed blood dripping from the side of his shoe down onto the floor,

"Hey, what's wrong with you?"
Looking up he replied,

" A kid just shot me".
Someone called for the nurse a few feet away and she came over and then she heard this was a shooting. Obviously shaken, she responded with,

"Oh no ... what do we do now?"

"Hey, you're the nurse, fo' Christ sake, stop the bleeding. I'll get an ambulance."

The boy was transported to the local hospital and treated. Luckily, the bullet did not damage any vital organs and a few weeks later he was released to resume normal activities. The surgeons decided it would be too risky to remove the bullet and; therefore, abandoned any effort to do so.

An investigation revealed the happenings of that eventful day.

A student had brought a loaded hand gun to school and was showing it to the student monitor as he was seated tilted back in his chair against the wall. The student monitor grabbed for the gun and when he did, he pulled it toward him causing the trigger finger holding the gun to fire the weapon. The bullet entered the upper leg, which was angled upward in the chair, traveled along the bone, and lodged itself dangerously close to the base of the spine. The boy who fired the gun panicked and ran home. On the way home, as he crossed over a bridge he threw the gun into the river.

Many years later, Joe happened to meet the young man who had been shot. He was surprised to see him dressed in a U.S. Navy uniform. Joe asked if he ever had the bullet removed and was told "no."

"How did you manage to get in the Navy with the slug still inside you?"

The reply with a big smile was,

"I didn't tell them I was ever in the hospital, and besides, during my physical exam, they only x-rayed me from the waist up."

~ ATTENDANCE RECORDS ARE IMPORTANT ~

Teachers were constantly reminded it was an important duty and an obligation that they keep accurate class attendance records. Joe would always cite his embarrassing experiences with derelictions to new teachers during their orientation sessions at the beginning of each school year. The police always came to his office whenever investigating a crime which may have involved a student enrolled in

168

his school. Two cases, both causing some embarrassment for teachers and administrators would never be forgotten.

One particular student came to school, knowing whom of his teachers were less than diligent when it came to recording absences, and tried to use this to his advantage. He would cut class and burglarize homes in the vicinity of the school, load the loot into his car and return to school in time for the next class. The system worked well for him until the long arm of the law finally reached him. During the ensuing investigation, police detectives were gathering evidence to make their case and needed to prove he was not in school when the homes were burglarized. Needless to say, there was one angry administrator and some reddened teachers' faces when all the pieces were put together.

In another case, a student cut class and went home to get his step mother's car. Her refusal to let him take the car led to an argument and he killed her. Some of his embarrassed teachers were unable to give testimony as to whether or not he was in their class at the time of the murder.

It soon became apparent there were enough flaws in the school attendance system that something had to be done. The absentee rate climbed to ever increasing heights. In a school with over 3,000 students with a loose attendance accounting system it was not uncommon on some days for over 1,000 students to cut school on a given day. Joe took it upon himself to look for a remedy to improve school attendance. It came sooner than expected with the unfortunate death of a model student who was killed in a car accident on the way home from a "cut day" at the beach. Joe was bothered by this loss and felt strongly that, had a strict attendance policy been in place, this tragedy most likely would have been averted.

Joe designed and implemented an attendance policy based on

a "no-work, no-pay" philosophy. If you weren't in school and the absence was not excused, your pay (your grade) would suffer a deduction. It was a controversial policy that proved to be very effective in dramatically reducing school absenteeism. It was adopted by many school systems and in some instances it was challenged in court and successfully defended. The key phrase in its defense was the published policy statement "class attendance is considered an *integral part* of the course of study."

~ *A RIOT in the LUNCH ROOM* ~

You can expect the unexpected when you're dealing with teenagers in a school of three thousand students. The word student is used loosely here. Not all students are students. It would appear that some come to school for purposes other than learning. Some are marking time until they are old enough to quit school and others seek to be with their peers as a social entity often seen as a small group or gang.

A call came into the office one day that a big fight had erupted in the lunch room and it was quickly developing into a bad scene. Mr. Hammar called in the police and they responded by sending several police officers to the school. Joe hurried over to lunch room and soon found himself in the middle of an ugly situation. One of the building administrators who arrived just before him had been pushed down a flight of stairs and luckily sustained only a few bruises. Both he and Joe entered the lunch room and were confronted with flying chairs and a melee of people. The police were struggling with two groups of black students fighting each other over an apparent turf war. In their attempt to quell the disturbance they too were attacked. A black police sergeant was on the floor being pummeled by several black youth. Joe knew the sergeant as one of his former football players he coached many years ago and they had since developed a fond respect for each other. Without hesitation, he began pulling and wrestling his attackers off him. As he rolled on the floor, during the struggle, Joe suddenly experienced a sharp pain to his back. During an ensuing roll over he saw the attacker coming at him about to swing another blow at him with a wide leather belt. The belt had a large metal buckle attached. As the belt came down, Joe was able to grab hold of it. With a forcible yank he pulled the attacker, who had the other end of the belt wound around his hand, down and over his head crashing him into the wall behind. By the time Joe was able to break free and get up, the stunned attacker staggered into the crowd leaving Joe holding onto the belt. *To this day, that infamous belt hangs in his workshop as a souvenir of the good 'ol days. No one ever dared to claim ownership of that belt.* The identity of the attacker is but a blur in memory. In the heat of battle, the preoccupation with self preservation made it doubtful he could ever positively identify the culprit; however, he did have a suspect in mind.

The next day, appearing in the local news media, the news article made mention of the disturbance but no mention of any arrest. This was somewhat disturbing to Joe. He immediately called his friend, the police chief, to question why no arrest had been filed,

"John, what's this in the morning paper; no arrest were made?"

"No, Joe, you know how it is."

"No, I don't. Didn't Sarge tell you what happened, he was getting the sh-- kicked out of him?"

171

"Yeah, he told me you saved his a--. He appreciated your help. He's gonna tell you so himself."

"John, I don't get it, why didn't he press charges?"

"Joe, he refused to. He thought it would be better not to. He thought it would hinder his working relations with his black brothers in the community."

"Bull----, I don't buy that crap. You can bet that'll be the last time I put my a-- on the line. I'm sitting here hurting because, I tried to help one of your guys."

Chief John was sympathetic with Joe's feelings. They understood each other perfectly. Having grown up together in a tough section of the town, they had a lot of respect for one another. Both had made it to highly respectable positions in the community. Both had experienced the hardships that came with being discriminated against during their early school years. Joe often called John a "big, dumb Polack" and he in return would refer to Joe as the "Top Wop." Never, in public company, however, would they address each other this way.

Chief John was big and Polish, but he surely wasn't dumb by any means.

After a day of hurting, Joe decided he would call a surgeon friend of his to take a look at his back. The next morning he met Dr. Tony at his hospital office and it was determined he was suffering from a pulled muscle. Joe returned to work wondering whether or not he should tell Mr. Hammar about his visit to the hospital. He decided to tell him because if Mr. Hammar should find out about the visit he most likely would be upset at not being informed.

He went into Mr. Hammar's office and carefully eased himself into a chair as the principal watched,

"What happened to you, Joe?"

Joe told him the entire story as Mr. Hammar sat looking at him without saying a word. When he finished he expected to hear some sympathetic remarks, but, instead he got a good old fashioned tongue lashing.

"Why do you think I called the police for? That was a police matter and it was not your place to get involved."

"But, I couldn't stand by and let a friend get beat on while I watched."

Mr. Hammar, with both hands folded together placed far forward on his desk, stared at him. It didn't matter to him, he made it very clear that school personnel had no business involving themselves in dangerous police matters.

Mr. Hammar was right again, Joe did have a lot to learn, but in his heart he still felt he had done the right thing.

~ *EARNED STUDENT RESPECT* ~

Joe was especially fond of students who participated in school sponsored activities. He often said if he could, he would mandate every student be involved in some after school activity. To him, this was almost as important an educational experience as academic performance. He encouraged this of his own children.

It would be indeed a rare occurrence for Joe to turn down an invitation to any student sponsored activity. He made it a point to be seen at virtually every home athletic contest, cheering on the participants, and always complimenting them for their efforts, win or lose. His sincere interest in sports and all school activities helped create a special bonding between him and many of the students. Whenever he felt they could use his help, he was there to lend a helping hand. He helped student organizations on campus with their school-wide elections by designing a computerized system for counting ballots. The selection of a homecoming queen by punch-card ballots was a notable first. He helped with their fund raising activities by designing and implementing another first, a computer dating dance. It turned out to be a huge success. Or was it?

It was a sellout even though the system proved to be somewhat flawed. Before a ticket could be purchased, the student was required to fill out a questionnaire concerning likes and dislikes. During the information processing phase each multiple choice item was assigned a numeric code along with a distinct numeric code identifying the participant. The information was punched into a card and processed by the computer. The computer would match those with like interests and print out on a punch card the identifying number/s of those who best matched the information gleaned from the questionnaires.

When the students arrived at the dance they would be issued their card with their personal identification number clearly displayed, followed by all the numbers that best matched that persons own interests. They were instructed to pin the card on their lapels so it could be easily read by another seeking to match their identification number with a person of the opposite sex. The girls played according to the rules. They proudly displayed their card and sort-out to find their matching number/s on a boy's card. However, many of the boys decided to play it cagey. They would hold their cards in hand and seek out their match. If their match for some reason did not meet their visual expectations they would not divulge their matching number and moved on to seek another. When and if they found a

174

matching number of a girl to their liking, only then would they introduce themselves.

This resulted in many of the girls not being able to find their match. Therefore, it caused some girls to sit out many of the dances.

Leave it to the boys to screw things up. Anyway, it was the talk of the campus and Joe refused to run another "computer dance." As Joe often said, "Ya just can't trust biology."

• • •

Joe always tried to plan his work schedule so as to accommodate some involvement with students. The weight training room was a regular stop for him. Twice a week after school he would walk over to the gym and join several boys who were in a weight training program. They would delight in challenging him to better their own weight prowess. These kids were strong and Joe tried hard to beat them. Most of the time youth would prevail.

The very few times he was able to beat someone the win would be met with plenty of cheering and the clapping of hands.

The kids looked forward to the days when Joe was scheduled to join them. Whenever they met him elsewhere on campus during the day, they would remind him by saying,

"See ya this afternoon, Mr. L."

Many times after school, some of the boys would stop by his office and wait to walk over to the gym with him. It was a great feeling of camaraderie without compromising his respected status as a school administrator, and it kept him in excellent physical condition.

The word seemed to spread about the campus that this man was a "regular Joe, but, don't mess with him 'cause he could break you in two." The image cast upon him was one that would served him well as an educator. Many students, mostly boys, would confide their most personal concerns and seek his advice for many of their teenage problems. His reputation as a no-nonsense strict disciplinarian, who was always fair and friendly, would follow him throughout his career.

He always listened first and when he spoke, they listened ... students and teachers alike. His words were always to the point, never fancy nor of long duration.

~ *A DUAL LIFE and MORE* ~

Although the educational field was to occupy the major portion of Joe's life, his energetic make-up, coupled with the necessities of raising a family and a desire to provide his children with a full-time mother, moved him to look at other opportunities. The business world provided another outlet in which he would involve himself. He wanted something more than just the basic existence on an educator's income. *Teaching salaries in those days were lower than low ... less than three thousand dollars a year to start.* The real estate business in both sales and construction seemed to hold a lot of promise for earning some serious money. Joe wanted more than just a salesman's license; instead, he studied for and passed a State Real Estate Broker's exam and began to sell real estate on a part-time basis. Within the first two weeks after receiving his license he sold two houses. Twelve hundred dollars in commissions seemed like heaven on earth. Christmas this year was to be very special. He was going to buy his wife a gift he knew she would love.

Early morning the day before Christmas, Joe called his friend, Brun, to ask if he wanted to take a ride to Providence with him. Brun asked what time they could expect to be back home and was assured

176

it would be in plenty of time for Christmas eve. Off they went in Joe's station wagon, fifty-five miles to Providence. This wagon was ready for the junk pile, it had a personality of its own and was as reliable as the weather. They made it into downtown Providence only to run out of gas in the middle of one of its busiest streets. The gas gauge didn't always tell the truth. On this particular day, the needle did not drop below the half tank mark. Joe and Brun exited the car and pushed it over to the side,

"Brun, you stay with the car and I'll go for gas. Make sure we don't get towed. I'll be right back."

Did you ever try to find a gas station in the middle of a big city?

It would be some time before he would return with ample fuel to get them to a gas station. This was not an easy task. It seems nobody wanted to trust Joe with a gas can for fear he wouldn't return it. However, he was able to convince a trusting soul of his honesty and he was able to return the can after driving to a station to fill the wagon's tank and refill the gas can. Back into the city they went looking for a place to park near a Hammond organ store. It was mid-afternoon before they were able to enter the store. Joe couldn't decide on which organ he wanted to buy. Finally, a decision was reached and negotiations over the sale price began. Now the owner of the store enters the picture. They agree on a price and the owner asks Joe when he could take delivery. Joe responded with,

"I was hoping to give it to my wife for Christmas."

"That's tomorrow." the owner replied. "We don't deliver on holidays."

"That's OK, no problem, I can take it home in my wagon." The store people readied the organ to be loaded into the station wagon only to find it wouldn't fit in. Joe looked the owner straight in the eye and said,

"Damn it, I guess it's no deal today."
The owner quickly responded with an offer to deliver the day after Christmas. That was unacceptable. As Joe and Brun headed for the door the owner, fearing a lost sale, offers to deliver the organ first thing early Christmas morning if Joe would be willing to provide him with an ample deposit that would cover the store's delivery expense. A deal is agreed to and the shoppers head for home. Both are concerned with the lateness of the hour and facing their spouses on Christmas eve.

Just outside the city limits, a tire goes flat and guess what? They have no spare to replace it. Off comes the flat, Joe standing by it trying to hitch a ride with a passing motorist. Brun stays with the wagon and Joe eventually gets a ride with a good Samaritan who takes him and his tire to the nearest service garage. By the time they got home that night they knew they would be facing a couple of irate wives. Arriving at Brun's house that night, he begged Joe to come in with him to verify the events of the day that had befallen them. After all, it would be very doubtful she would believe her husband's story,

"Brun, look at the time. You know if I go in I'll never get home. She'll want to shoot me. Besides, I'm not looking forward to the fireworks waiting for me at my house."

Isn't it amazing the fear these little women can instill in a grown man?

When Joe got home he explained, to his wife, the gas and tire problem but not the nature of the gift he had purchased for her. He had aroused her curiosity. He remembered a lesson taught to him by one of his grammar school teachers who told him you could always keep a women interested if you could arouse her curiosity. She

178

would have to wait until morning for the surprise.

Early Christmas morning a delivery van pulled into their driveway. Dorothy was excited and they both went out to the van. The store owner opened the two side doors of the van as Dorothy anxiously waited. There before her was a beautiful Hammond organ wrapped in a big red bow,

"Oh, no." she exclaimed, "It's beautiful. You shouldn't have done that," while slowly shaking her head no.

Obviously she was thrilled with the surprise. Holding Joe's arm she looked up at Joe and said in a sobering voice,

"I love it. I'm sorry. You've got to send it back. We just can't afford it."

Joe was stunned and disappointed. The owner quickly stepped in and said,

" Let me bring it inside and I'll play it for you."
She insisted he not take it out of the van as she stood there admiring it with a longing look on her face. The owner handed Joe a long extension cord and asked if he could plug it in somewhere. He sat at the organ and began to play. The rich musical tones filled the van and the morning neighborhood air. After a few selections, he turned to her and ask how she liked the sound,

"It's beautiful and something I've always wanted. I'm sorry, please, take it back. We just can't afford it now."

Sadly, and with some disgust, the owner secured the organ to the van wall and drove away. Dorothy, saddened and with tears in her eyes, stood and watched the van drive away until it was out of sight. She looked like she was about to yell out to bring it back. For about two weeks after, she felt badly for refusing delivery of a gift her husband was so intent on giving her, so, Joe took her shopping and they purchased a Lowrey organ that made her very happy.

The price was right on this one. She never did ask the price of the Hammond and Joe never did get his deposit refunded.

~ REAL ESTATE BUSINESS WAS GOOD ~

The part-time real estate business was so good, Joe was able to earn more money in one month during his first year than he earned for teaching that entire year. He seriously considered leaving the educational field to pursue real estate as a full-time profession. His father was adamantly opposed to this thought and convinced him not to.

His energy, coupled with his real estate earnings, allowed him to build a home of their dreams in an exclusive area of town. He personally drew the detailed blueprints for a four bedroom, three bathroom, four fireplace, southern colonial style home with impressive columns that spanned the face of the two story home. The circular driveway gave it a touch of class that caused many who knew him as teacher to wonder as to where and how he got the money to build such a fine home. This was Joe's first experience as a general contractor and doing much of the work himself.

He often said he could afford to build a house with his building skills; however, the taxes on it would be so high he could not afford to keep it.

• • •

Joe's real estate world put him in touch with many individuals who were well-seasoned business people who took a fond interest in him because he was just a youngster trying to make big money. One such person who motivated him was a dentist who saw a need for housing for married college students and proceeded to build housing for them near a university campus. Campuses at that time did not provide dormitory housing for married couples and there were many of them, especially war veterans, returning to school. After completing a building project the dentist would sell it. His profits were enormous and soon he was able to give up his practice and retire at an early age of forty-five. The dentist proved to be a clever man. He gave Joe a tour of his home and showed him an impressive in-house swimming pool he had constructed in his basement.

He purchased a forty-foot used steel tank, ten feet in diameter and had it trucked to his home. It was rolled into an excavation next to his foundation so that one end of the tank rested against the foundation wall. Prior to rolling the tank into the hole, several old car tires were positioned inside the hole so as not to damage the tank as it rolled in. Once in position, he cut away a half slice section of the tank end against the foundation wall leaving a depth of five feet remaining in the ten-foot diameter tank with room above that depth to dive in. The tank was cleaned and a concrete cover built over the top of the opened end. Next, a doorway was cut through the basement wall in line with the end of the tank. The tank was then covered with earth and planted with lawn seed. No one would ever suspect that under his lawn was a forty-foot long swimming pool. Only two small venting pipes would show above ground hidden in a clump of shrubbery. It was heated by an ordinary household water heater and when the long string of fluorescent lighting, attached to the ceiling of the tank, was turned on the reflection in the water made the tank appear endless.

Each day, all year long, the dentist was able to get his swimming exercise by swimming forty feet each way, back and forth, the length of the tank.

He was able to beat the tax collector with this arrangement. Only a few of his friends knew there was a swimming pool buried under his lawn.

• • •

He convinced Joe the demand for rental apartments was growing and the time was right to invest in building rental units. It sounded like a very promising opportunity. Joe convinced one of his contractor friends to form a Limited Liability Corporation and they ventured into building a housing complex. Joe would use the "sweat equity" in his home to good advantage. He refinanced his home, borrowing an additional ten thousand dollars and invested in the venture. This was not done without some serious reservation, he rationalized by thinking if he were going to lose money it should be at a young age. Many years later, after they finished building one hundred seventy-six units Joe sold them turning his ten thousand dollar original investment into a 496,000 dollar profit. He thought he was on "easy street." *Not for long.* He invested all of it in another massive real estate venture that would end as the largest real estate fraud case in the state and he lost all of his money along with hundreds of other investors. This was to be a devastating blow to Joe and his wife's retirement plans.

~ *ON the WAY to a DOCTORATE* ~

By now, Joe had nearly finished his studies at the university for his Sixth Year Professional Diploma. Dr. Gren, his major adviser up to this point, convinced him he would be an excellent candidate to enter the doctoral studies program. He advised Joe it would be in his best interest to select another major advisor because he was planning to retire and the retirement would hinder seeing Joe through to the completion of the program. However, he offered to serve as one of the members on his doctoral committee. All along, Dr. Gren seemed to be grooming Joe toward the doctoral program. All the courses he took for his Sixth Year Program were doctorate level courses and the credits earned could easily be transferred toward the course requirements of a Ph.D. degree.

Joe had some reservations about going for a Ph.D. degree. He would need to go through an acceptance process and be required to spend a year in full-time residency on the university campus. This would not be an easy task. He had two of his daughters attending college at the same time and he would need to apply for a sabbatical leave from his job to meet the residency requirement. That meant he would be on half pay for a school year. His family most likely would eat a lot of spaghetti for a year with his salary cut in half.

Administrative personnel normally would not be eligible for a year's sabbatical. He talked with Principal Hammar about applying for a sabbatical and he was willing to take Joe's request to the Board if he would agree to return in the springtime to schedule students for the next school year. He also reminded Joe, if a sabbatical were granted he would be committed to return to work for a period of at least two years. At this point, Joe planned on fulfilling the two year commitment and moving on to work for either IBM or Honeywell. Both companies, previously, had expressed an interest in hiring him.

The sabbatical was granted with the caveat that he return in time for scheduling students for the next school year. Joe accepted a university graduate internship position which meant he would have a few extra dollars of income to supplement his reduced salary. Before starting his sabbatical, Joe had completed all his course work requirements for the doctorate, gathered most of his research data, and prepared a research proposal for his dissertation. All that remained was, getting his research proposal approved, writing the dissertation, and the capability to defend his findings before a gathering of university professors.

That doesn't sound like much, but, anyone who has gone through this process will attest to the fact that this is a mammoth task and could take several years of work.

Joe was ready for anything the university internship would throw at him. His mind-set was one where he would do anything that was asked of him even if he had to sweep floors. Nothing would be beneath his pride. The first week on campus he was assigned to be the telephone switchboard operator for the Education Department. He found it to be a fun job trying to keep some of the old, crabby professors happy. Sometimes Joe would embark on a humorous introduction of incoming calls. It didn't take long before the entire faculty knew the character manning the switchboard. He was asked if he would be interested in working with a couple of professors on a textbook they hoped to publish.

Maybe this was their way of getting him away from that switchboard.

This project would occupy the rest of his internship days with plenty of time left for him to do his own work.

Joe had submitted his proposal for approval in time for the first meeting of the graduate school committee that acted on dissertation proposals. His proposal had to wait its turn and was not acted on and approved until early December. During the three month wait, his advisors urged him to start writing. He could not do that knowing the

184

experiences of other doctoral candidates who started before receiving an approval, only to have their proposal rejected and all the writing done beforehand was for naught.

Writing the dissertation was a grueling experience. The typing requirements alone were a tremendous chore. There were no word processing programs nor computers to ease the task. Each time a correction or revision was made it required the re-typing of all the pages that followed. It took Joe's wife four full months to complete the necessary typing. She would send the kids off to school in the morning and type until they came home. Most Saturdays and Sundays were devoted to typing. The pages had to be perfect. The margins were specified by regulations, erasures were unacceptable, and erasable paper was not acceptable, only twenty-weight bond paper would be accepted.

Joe's work in helping to put together a textbook for publication made for some interesting experiences. He was able to develop a close relationship with many of the faculty members. He was privy to many of their problems and concerns. Often, the older faculty members would call him into their office to chat. Joe was one of the oldest, if not the oldest, graduate student enrolled at the time and his opinions were of interest and respected.

One such conversation would long be remembered. One of his professors wanted to talk. It was apparent he was in a disturbed state of mind. Joe sat down in front of the professor's desk and as he did, the old professor stood up, threw down a one inch thick stack of papers in front of him and blurted out,

"Look at this thesis. It's full of plagiarized material ... from a graduate student who should know better."

Joe reached over and thumbed through the pages to take a look as if he were reading, but made no attempt to absorb any meaning from what was scanned,

"What would you do if you were I and your advisee presented you with this?"

"Are you sure it was plagiarized?" asked Joe.

"Without a doubt," came the answer.

"Then, I'd kick his a--, or her a--, out of here," Joe replied. With a feeble laugh the professor sat down and looked at Joe, then broke into a forced smile,

"I'd like to do that, but I don't think I can. This person is black."

"So. What's the difference?"

"I guess I'm getting too old for this crap. It's not worth the aggravation I'll have to go through on this one."

Joe thought awhile thinking about another similar situation he knew about, only that person was white and was asked to withdraw from school, or else.

"I wish I could be of help on this one ... I know if it were my work, this Italian boy would probably be long gone. No second chance for me. Is that what you're thinking, a second chance for this bird. Cheez, I hope not? "

The professor sat motionless and quiet for awhile, then thanked Joe for listening and told him he planned to discuss the matter with some of his colleagues.

It would be a few years later, and with disappointment, that Joe learned this person did get a second chance and was awarded a graduate degree. Joe still believes, in fairness to all, there can be no exceptions to the rule and the decision made in this case was wrong.

In April of the sabbatical year Joe was ready to defend his findings before an audience of university professors. The date for the defense was scheduled for the thirteenth day of the month which just happened to be a Friday. The Friday the 13th syndrome seemed to kick in with a few superstitious people, particularly Joe's major advisor. He and a few others asked Joe if he might want to change the date. The answer was, "no." He was not to be intimidated by any such superstitious date.

More than the usual number of professors attended the defense hearing and Joe started to show a little nervousness. Was it the topic that interested them or were they going to crucify him with difficult questions? The dissertation was entitled, *The Identification And Analysis Of Factors Related To Secondary School Absenteeism.* Joe made his presentation and was comfortable fielding questions from the audience. After approximately three hours on the hot seat, Joe's major advisor stepped in and halted the proceedings. He directed Joe to go to his office and wait for him. The wait seemed like an eternity as he sat waiting for word on his fate. Finally, he heard the familiar footsteps approaching and looked up to see a somber look on his major advisor's face. Joe could feel the nervous perspiration trickling down his back under his shirt,

"What's your wife's phone number?" his advisor asked with a scowled look on his face.

Joe was really worried and all kinds of crazy thoughts were racing through his head and he was having difficulty trying to recall his own telephone number.

"Hello Dottie, this is Richard here. I think Dr. Joe would like to talk with you, and, I know you certainly would like to talk to Dr. Joe."

With a huge smile and a hearty hand shake he handed the phone over to Joe. With that maneuver the weight of the world was lifted off his shoulders. Joe does not remember one word of the conversation he had with his wife. Many of the professors who attended the defense hearing came in to congratulate and shake his hand as he was trying to talk to his wife.

As he drove home alone that afternoon, his life seemed to flash before his eyes. He thought of his childhood struggle with school and how far he had come from those early days. He thought of his father who had died and would have been the proudest man in the world if he could only be with his son on this day, and his eyes began to well with tears. He thought of Mrs. Geril whose caring, kindness, and faith in him, steered him onto the right road while in high school, and he sobbed as his eyes filled with tears again. The ride home alone allowed his thoughts and all his emotions to flow freely. He felt a need to make one stop on the way home.

Mrs. Geril was in her late eighties by now and confined to a nursing home. He wanted her to be the first to know of his achievement on this day and he was determined to thank her knowing she would be happy to see him and happier to know the results of her efforts of long ago. Joe introduced himself and asked the nurse at the front desk of the nursing home if Mrs. Geril were still there and could he see her.

"Yes, she's still with us, but, I'm sorry she doesn't know anyone."

Joe asked to see her anyway. She pointed in the direction of her room and reminded him Mrs. Geril would not know who he was. He entered her darkened room, with the window shade drawn, and found a frail, old woman propped part way up in bed, her shriveled, bony arms hanging motionless at her side, her eyes partially closed and a blank stare on her face,

"Hello Mrs. Geril, do you remember me? I'm Joe, the boy who cut your lawn when I was in high school during the war years. Remember?"

No response. Joe, saddened by her appearance and the lack of response, pulled up the window shade and tried again,

"Hello Mrs. Geril. It's Joe ... remember me?"

This time, her eyes opened a bit more. He proceeded to tell her that just a few hours ago he was awarded a Ph.D. degree and he wanted her to be the first to know the good news. Joe was certain she heard him. A slight smile came on her face, a momentary gleam in her eyes, then movement of her lips as if she were trying to say, "Joe," and a feeble attempt to move her hand toward him was enough to convince him she heard and remembered. The smile quickly faded. She closed her eyes. Joe took her hand and thanked her for the last time and left the room.

Not long after that visit, Mrs. Geril died and Joe felt good that he was able to tell her the good news and thank her before she left this world.

~ LAUNCHING a Ph.D. ~

The news article in the local paper announcing the awarding of the Ph.D. attracted the attention of the Italian community. One of Joe's cousins decided this called for a celebration. Through his efforts, a testimonial dinner was arranged. Tickets were sold; the local Masonic Hall was rented; and a speakers' program featuring the local State Senator was held. Approximately two hundred people attended, including family, friends, local educators and politicians, and prominent local professionals and, of course, lots of Italians.

Joe wondered whether they all came to honor him or just to rub elbows with the politicians, or maybe the full course Italian

dinner was the attraction.

Joe was well-known by local politicians and admired for his willingness to help his community whenever he was asked. He was never a volunteer but did serve when asked. His latest community endeavor had been acceptance of the City Manager's request that he chair a Blue Ribbon Committee composed of several high profile citizens. This committee's charge was to make recommendations to the City Manager relative to the financial administration of the city. He found himself to be the youngest member of the committee that was comprised of a strong-willed bank president, other bankers, and some very knowledgeable citizens. He had some reservations at first about his ability to handle this group but soon found he could match wits with the best of them. He would later receive a letter of commendation from the City Manager citing his leadership and a job well-done.

Joe's political connections would serve him well in the years ahead. This became apparent when the academy became embroiled in a dispute with the local board of education over tuition payments. The academy threatened the town with closing its school to town residents if the tuition were not duly paid. Behind the scenes Joe played masterfully the role of mediator, manipulating the personalities involved. He had mastered the art of a good listener and was able to sympathize with the other side's rationale, without compromising his own position.

He often surprised himself with what he was able to accomplish by smoothing things out, and so was Mr. Hammar, his boss.

His skills were called into play one evening at a public hearing. The hearing had to be held in a school gymnasium because the issue at hand had captured the interest of an unusually large number of people. The town wanted to educate its own ninth grade students within its own school system. That would mean the academy's four year high school program would be reduced to a three year program. Mr. Hammar asked him if he would like to speak on the issue. A very nervous Joe made his pitch extolling the benefits of a four year high school asking for renewed cooperation to end the hostility between the two warring entities. When he ended his talk, he was soundly applauded for his message.

Overwhelmingly, it was later decided to allow the academy to continue to serve the town with its four year high school program, and the tuition bill was paid in full.

VI

From 1975 to 1988

~ A CHANGE in COMMAND ~

After an eight year tenure as principal of the state's largest high school, Mr. Hammar was ready to retire. He summoned Joe to his office to tell him, along with the other assistant administrators, that he wanted his administrative team to be the first to know he would retire at the end of the current school year. This came as a complete surprise to all of them. Even Joe, who had become a close friend during his tenure, both socially and professionally, did not have any indication of his planned retirement. Not one of the assistant administrators was approached by any of the trustees as to any possible interest in filling the pending vacancy ... not even Joe, who was the vice-principal at the time. No one was encouraged to apply. In talks with one another, none of the administrators, including Joe, was interested in the position. Joe was committed to meet his obligation of serving two more years, as a condition of his sabbatical leave. He was then planning a career change into computer technology.

The trustees decided on a national search for Mr. Hammar's successor. When Joe learned the names of some of the applicants, and he knew some of them personally, he was disturbed to think he could be working for one of them for the next two years. Mr. Hammar had entrusted Joe with many of the responsibilities of running the school and he shuddered at the thought of doing it for *one* of the applicants in particular. So he decided he would test the waters.

Joe requested the application packet that was being distributed to interested applicants and made it known he was interested in applying for the job. He would not divulge why the change of heart that caused him to change his mind and apply. Several trustees, learning of his sudden interest, came forth and encouraged his application. However, there were several people in the community who felt he "didn't have a chance in hell" of landing this job. In fact, one high profile community citizen said to him when he learned Joe would be an applicant,

"You know Joe ... you are the man for the job and you deserve it, but you'll never get it."

"How's that?" he replied.

"I hate to tell you this, but you know how it is. You're a Catholic and to make matters worse, you're an Italian Catholic. If I were you, I wouldn't get my hopes up."

Joe had heard similar comments before and this one hurt a little more than the others because of the person who made the comment; a well-known and respected member of the community. In its own peculiar way, this comment coming from this man, made Joe more determined than ever to complete the application process.

The national search was narrowed to forty applicants and then to ten and finally to three who would be the three recommended to the full board for interview. Joe and one other made it to the final interview. The local press was notified as to the day the announcement would be made. At two in the morning of that day Joe's phone rang. It was the publisher of local newspaper who called and awakened him from a sound sleep. He told Joe he was going to run a story that morning on the new principal because he had heard from reliable sources that Joe was the front runner. This was very disturbing to Joe because he felt he was on thin ice and the ice would surely crack if he made any comments to the press. A misquote about his feelings might scuttle his chances. The publisher did a lot of talking and tried his best to get him to comment. All Joe would say was,

"Look Dan, apparently you know more than I do, I can't comment. I still have one final interview this afternoon and I don't want you to screw things up for me with a story that is premature. Please back-off and give me a chance."

Joe tossed and turned the rest of the night wondering what would appear in print that morning. His heart jumped when he saw his name on the front page. He read the article slowly, studying every word. He was able to breathe a sigh of relief. Dan had done him no harm.

Late that afternoon, Joe would have his last interview alone with Mr. Roy, the Board President-Elect, who was to bring a final recommendation to the full board. In that interview, somehow the often heard term of WASP (white Anglo-Saxon Protestant) control of the academy came up. Joe had heard enough of this stuff in the past and this set him off. He came on strong with his displeasure of the comments he had been subjected too. Everything turned quiet. The interview ended with Joe's parting words that he tried hard to convey in a respectful manner,

194

"Mr. Roy, you know what I am and what I can do. What you see is what you get."

Joe drove home to get a bite to eat and await a phone call announcing the board's decision. When he arrived home his wife asked how his interview went. The reply would be short,

"I blew it, I really blew it and I don't care. I don't want to talk about it."

The awaited call did not come. They had plenty of time to decide, he thought. In his mind he wanted to forget about the whole thing. He had his chance and he lost it.

He needed to return to school that evening at six-thirty to teach a graduate computer course for the university. During the drive to class, the local six o'clock news station was usually tuned on his radio. This time he was deep in thought about the events of that afternoon and did not have the radio on. When he pulled his car into the parking lot he spotted Mr. Richard, the Board President, nervously pacing back and forth anxiously awaiting Joe's arrival. As Joe opened the car door he greeted him with,

"I called your house and your wife told me I would find you here. Congratulations Joe, the board voted you the new principal."

Needless to say, Joe was stunned with the news. He waited a moment and said,

"Thank you, but we haven't discussed a salary or whether or not I will accept your offer, yet."

"Don't worry about that, Mr. Roy will take care of everything tomorrow."

Wow, Joe thought, what a way to do business and this guy's a lawyer ... nothing in writing?

As Joe opened the door to his classroom, the class stood up and cheered. How did they know? He hadn't yet said a word. He soon would be told they heard it on the six o'clock news on their way to class.

How about that? It was on the radio and the world knew before he did.

There would be no class that night. Joe called his wife and told her his students wouldn't let him teach. They were all headed for the Sheraton Hotel to celebrate and she should come along. After a few rounds of drinks the party moved to Joe's house. It was to be a most memorable evening for all.

The next morning's front page of the local news said it all. Congratulatory calls began to arrive early in the morning. The first of many congratulatory calls came from the local Catholic clergy. Joe was the first Catholic elevated to the principalship of the very prestigious academy in its 119 year old history at that time.

There was great joy in the Catholic community. A barrier had fallen.

One call, not to be forgotten, came from an old Italian friend who asked, "Joe, what the hell am I going to do with all the gasoline stored in my garage?"

"What gasoline? I don't know what you're talking about?"

"I was gonna burn the place down if you didn't get the job." They both enjoyed a good laugh. The congratulatory calls continued for several days. One that he recalls fondly came from a nice old lady who called and told him he was a lucky guy being appointed on Saint Patrick's Day and to be canonized two days later on Saint Joseph's Day.

Joe would always remember this comment and thought of it as a good omen.

~ THE MANSION ~

The job specifications for the academy principalship clearly stated the new principal would be required to live in a mansion provided by the academy adjacent to the school campus. Joe was not too happy about being required to live there. He always thought of the majestic looking building as more of a mausoleum than a home. It was a three-story brick structure, built in 1786, approximately six thousand square feet of living space, and with a ballroom on the third floor. It was originally named the Teel Hotel -- Sign of George Washington. It was said by some that the house was haunted by the ghost of a woman, dressed in colonial garb, who roamed about the house and was last seen, by a prospective buyer interested in the property, standing in the basement.

Joe had a workshop in the basement for fourteen years and during the many hours he worked there he never met up with the lady.

• • •

Within a few weeks after his appointment to his new position he and his wife arranged for a cocktail reception at their home located in a rather exclusive section of town. They invited the entire board of trustees and their wives to meet the family. It was Joe's plan to show off his southern colonial style home, that he had designed and built some thirteen years earlier, with the hope they would allow him to stay by waiving the residency requirement stated in the job specifications. All the trustees and their wives attended and everyone seemed to be impressed with their ten-room house with four bedrooms, a large sunken living room that opened into a raised dining room, and with several floor to ceiling brick and stone walls accented with four fireplaces. The quiet rural setting was impressive.

197

After a few days, Joe talked with the president and vice-president of the board and tried once again to get them to waive the residency requirement. It was a futile attempt. They were adamant about where their principal should reside. Joe remembers a comment made during that conversation when he was told that someday his children would marry and the mansion would see the feet of his grandchildren running about in its mammoth sized rooms. They also told him his wife could decorate the house to her liking and they would take care of all the expenses.

Years later, the prophesy of marriages and grandchildren running about in the mansion would come true.

Joe's salary with the all-expense paid perks that came with the mansion made him one of the highest, if not the highest, paid school official in the state. It was not what Joe really wanted. He knew that this arrangement would be to his disadvantage when he retired. Several times he asked the trustees to set a figure as to what the house perk was worth and add that number to his salary amount and he would pay it back to the school as rent. He knew if they would do that, his retirement would be enhanced upward between fifteen and twenty thousand dollars annually. Years later at his retirement, former members of the executive committee admitted to him it was a mistake on their part. They should have taken his suggestion to help with his retirement benefit.

• • •

Dorothy's decorating skills turned the mausoleum into a beautiful home. It would be the site for many social functions. Faculty and staff along with other community functions would share the fruits of her labor. She would become a true first lady of the academy. She would host the monthly board meetings and always

198

THE MANSION
(*The Teel Hotel - Sign of George Washinton*)
Top - front view. *Bottom* - rear and side view.

provide the trustees with freshly baked delicacies. The aroma of these freshly baked goodies seemed to put everyone in a relaxed and friendly mood.

It most certainly made board meetings an enjoyable event to look forward to, and most likely enhanced the attendance rate.

Joe's first official board meeting was a meeting of the full board comprised of twelve trustees, five of whom were members elected to serve as the executive committee. The executive committee would meet monthly and the full board would meet quarterly. At the start of Joe's first board meeting Trustee Dr. Loo, a highly respected physician in the community, requested permission to address the board. He stood up and looked directly at Joe and delivered an eloquent congratulatory message which was applauded by all the trustees. After the applause ended he turned to the board and said,

"Now gentlemen, what I have to say is important to the prestigious nature of this fine institution. We all have known this young man for years as Joe. From this day on, all of us should address him as Doctor."

It did not take very long for his word to spread and most everyone would address him formally as Doctor. The students would be among the first to call him Dr. Joe.

Dr. Loo then turned to Joe and said, "Doctor, I want you to know you and your family need not ever worry about medical care. We'll see to it that they will be taken good care of, and it's on us."

Joe also learned at this first meeting he had been elected on an 11 to 1 vote. The one trustee who cast his vote for the other candidate stepped forward and apologized saying he felt obligated to cast his vote for the other candidate because he was not only a long time friend but his classmate as well. He hoped Joe would understand.

~ *THE HONEYMOON IS OVER* ~

Dr. Joe would soon be tested. The secretary he inherited served three prior principals for more than thirty years. The power she had assumed during her tenure intimidated faculty and staff and they often questioned who was running the school ... she or the principal? For the first few months Dr. Joe wondered too. Complaints seemed to come more frequently as the months passed and several faculty members and even trustees would tell Dr. Joe he'd better do something soon because the situation was going from bad to worse. Several times she seemed to completely ignore his directives and proceed to do most everything her way. They were on a collision course. Her actions increasingly bordered on insubordination. Several attempts to talk out the problem proved futile. Dr. Joe felt it was time for her to take a month's sick leave, with full pay, get some help and if she needed more time he would arrange that for her. When she felt ready she could come back to work. Reluctantly, she took the offer. The alternative was clearly spelled out to her.

A month later she returned. Things were worse than ever. Dr. Joe tried to relieve her of some of the load she had put on herself. That didn't work either. He tried changing her job to one with lesser responsibility but continuing her at the same pay. She refused to accept. By this time he surmised there had to be something physically wrong with her. There was. She was suffering with a progressive diabetic condition that caused her great mental anguish. She refused to take a medical leave. There was nothing left but to terminate her employment. Dr. Joe wrestled with this decision for days and many nights.

How do you rid yourself of someone who has served so long and who puts her job above everything else?

Her job was her life. Her loyalty was without equal. The work load coupled with her ailment had affected her state of mind. She had never married, had no family left, and no one at home to care for her. Soon, she was to spend the rest of her life in a nursing home.

Dr. Joe would never feel right about letting her go and he would live on with a haunting memory that he had not been able to give her a happier ending for all those years of service and devotion to "her school."

~ PRINCIPAL and BUILDER ~

The academy was woefully lacking when it came to providing adequate athletic facilities for what was now the state's largest high school. An earlier attempt to build a four million dollar field house and natatorium, in partnership with the town, failed at a special referendum to garner the minimum number of votes . Dr. Joe felt this defeat was a blessing in disguise. If it had passed, the academy would have provided the town with a ninety-nine year lease allowing the town to be a partner in the operation of the proposed facility.

Since its incorporation in 1854, and its opening in 1856, the academy managed its own affairs without political intervention. If Dr. Joe were to have his way, the same would continue. The academy founding fathers wanted it to be a school far removed from any political controls. The founding fathers' mission strove to provide an education of a "higher order" than could be found in any public school system. Dr. Joe committed himself to those ideals and would continue to move the academy along the same visionary path during his tenure.

Dr. Joe had a plan that would allow the academy to upgrade its physical plant to provide for the needs of a burgeoning enrollment. He had sketched out a plan to build a field house on campus. He would need to convince a reluctant board that his plan was the way to go. At the time, The academy was not willing, or able, to be burdened by any massive debt ... certainly not the likes of the four million dollar price tag that had been put on the recently defeated project. Dr. Joe scaled out his drawings and priced his plan at one million dollars. He also detailed how the project would be paid for. The board found his presentation very interesting; however, they lacked full confidence in his ability and needed to check it out with the head of a local architectural firm that happened to be well-known to several board members. The architect was impressed and, at the next board meeting, several members of the board suddenly lost their initial skepticism and were ready to hear more. With renewed confidence, they allowed Dr. Joe to move forward with his detailed plan. They allowed him to engage an architect to answer and help with any technical engineering problems he might encounter. Dr. Joe would personally supervise the construction and serve as the "clerk of the works."

Who ever heard of a school principal who would burden himself with such a mammoth building project?

There would be no building committee to report to -- only monthly progress reports to the board. Dr. Joe was given complete control of the project. He would be ready to break ground as soon as the school year ended. Before any new construction could begin, an old brick building would need to be demolished or moved out of the way. This building, known as the Clubhouse, was used as a dressing and meeting facility for boys' football, baseball, and track teams. It was a gift from a wealthy alumnus; a building rich in traditions and memories. Dr. Joe wanted to save it and he found a place on campus for it. He needed to find someone experienced in moving a brick building. The search led him to a contractor some fifty miles away. When the contractor came to price the move he brought along his father who had many years of experience in moving masonry buildings. What a surprise this project was to be for Dr. Joe and the contractor. They both learned the contractor's father was the one who had moved this same building over forty-five years earlier to where it was now standing. They agreed to move it again.

It took one week to get the Clubhouse up onto a wheeled rig and another two weeks to move it to its new resting place about one hundred yards away. The wheels on the rig turned so slowly it required a prolonged stare to detect any movement. The move was made without so much as a hairline crack in any of its masonry construction. The move was a $12,000 investment to save a building worth in excess of $250,000. Not only did it continue with its glorious past but for many former athletes, who passed through its doors, the efforts to save their Clubhouse were greatly appreciated.

(It would be several years after Dr. Joe's retirement that he would learn that an insensitive board had voted to demolish the popular Clubhouse, the generous gift of an alumnus. When this fact became general knowledge, Dr. Joe began receiving telephone calls from former athletes who were upset with their decision. They begged him to do something and many offered to provide labor and money to restore the building to its former glory. The calls were upsetting to Dr. Joe, so much so, that one night one of the calls caused him to awaken at three o'clock in the morning and prompted him to write the board president a rather caustic letter. He did not answer. Instead he forwarded the letter to the current principal who called him and said she was sorry but it was a "done deal" and it was scheduled for demolition in a couple of weeks. Dr. Joe met with the Alumni Association and they also made their displeasure known, in writing, to the board).

A perfectly sound and valuable building was demolished, the bricks were offered for sale as mementos hoping to raise funds -- the board was never aware of the ill-will they caused with their decision. Not many bricks were sold; however, they did get eight additional parking places. Wonderful !

Immediately after the Clubhouse was up on wheels and out of the way, construction began on the new gymnasium. A design-construct method of construction was adopted because there were no detailed architectural drawings. A heavy burden fell squarely on Dr. Joe's shoulders. The next twelve months would require in excess of two thousand hours of his time. Daily site visits and weekly meeting with the various building trades were needed to move the project along. Arguments were unavoidable. Some bordered on near violent behavior. The construction office housed in a trailer would often rock when heavy fists hit the drawing tables and vulgar language blued the air. Dr. Joe could dish it out as well as they did. He earned their respect. No one expected the demands and the toughness that came from this man who always wore a white shirt and tie. There was no pulling the wool over his eyes.

Fifteen months after the ground breaking, the building was ready for dedication. Total cost came in at 1.1 million dollars, just slightly over the one million dollar estimated figure quoted to the board in the first proposal. There were a few trustees who knew and appreciated the yeoman effort expended to make this gymnasium one of the best basketball facilities in the state. A name for the new facility was in order and some suggested it should be named after Dr. Joe. However, his modesty got in the way and when he was asked what he thought of the idea, he thought it would be too much too soon and, he suggested it be called "Alumni Hall." It was so voted.

Joe would live to regret the day he did not jump at the chance to have this monument named for him. A second opportunity would come soon after his retirement, ending thirty-five years at the academy, when a move by some of his friends to name the gymnasium for him was inconsiderately quashed, along with his pride.

Alumni Hall, for many years after would be publicly acclaimed by basketball officials as one of the three best basketball gyms in the state.

~ *A YEAR'S SALARY EARNED in ONE DAY* ~

As principal of a large high school one soon learns to expect the unexpected. Not a day passes without some interesting turn of events that makes one wonder what will come next. On this particular day, Dr. Joe stood by the window in his office watching the school buses arriving at the end of day. His secretary interrupted his thoughts by coming into his office. She had that look of concern on her face and informed him one of his building administrators, then called housemasters, needed to talk with him immediately. What now, was his thought, maybe an after school fight? He picked up the phone,

"What's happening Hank?"

"You better get over here, we need you here in my office."

"What the hells wrong?"

"I can't tell you on the phone, get your a-- over here, quick."

"OK, OK, I'm on my way."

As he hung up the phone he sensed something was drastically wrong. Hank never talked to him like that, ever. Never would he dare to utter a command to Dr. Joe.

As he entered Hank's building he was met by him at the door. They both entered his office and there sat a young girl sobbing. Hank quickly closed the door behind them, turned and said in a quiet voice as not to disturb the sobbing girl,

"She told me she's just been raped."

"What ! When? Where?

"During the last period, in the Tower."

Dr. Joe knelt down in front of the girl and with both hands gently pulled both of her hands away from her face. Her face was wet with tears, she looked up at him. He asked in a consoling voice if this were true. She nodded yes and began to cry hysterically. He rose slowly, turned to Hank and said,

"Drive her to the hospital right now. I'll call ahead. I'll get her parents and the police."

The hospital was less than a mile from the school. Hank would be back soon to fill in some of the details the young girl had told him. Dr. Joe hastened to his office to notify the police. Then he sat motionless thinking how in the world was he going to tell the girl's father. All he could think of at this moment was his own three daughters and what if this had happened to one of them. He felt a real urge to kill the bastard responsible. He could feel a hair raising sensation on the back of his neck. He called the father and asked him to come to his office to pick up his daughter because she got herself involved in something she shouldn't have. He did not tell him what really happened. He told the father he couldn't talk on the phone and would explain when he got there.

It was an agonizing wait but not a long one. How would he tell the father?   How would he react to the news that his daughter was raped? Again, his own personal feelings surfaced. All he could think of was if he were in the father's shoes he could possibly explode into a violent rage. The father arrived at Dr. Joe's office within fifteen minutes. Dr. Joe, fumbling for words, nervously confessed he didn't really know how to say what he had to say. By this time he noticed the bewildered father moving towards the edge of his seat. Dr. Joe took in a deep breath and said,

"I'm sorry. Cindy was raped here in school this afternoon. I had her taken to the hospital."

"My Cindy? No, it can't be. She's only thirteen."
Dr. Joe nodded his head yes it was his daughter. Complete silence overtook the room. No reaction, not a word was spoken, only a long, cold piercing stare. It was like someone hit the father over the head with a hammer -- no body movement whatsoever, just that long piercing stare.   Joe felt an explosive reaction was about to happen. Instead, the father slowly rose from his chair and headed for the door. He stopped and turned with a strange expression on his face that Joe will never forget, in a voice just above a whisper, he said slowly and clearly,

"You need to come to my house and tell my wife, she'll be coming home around five o'clock."

The two men stared at each other ... a long silence.

"OK, I'll be there."
The father quickly left for the hospital and Hank returned to tell all he knew from what he was able to get from Cindy.   Police detectives had been dispatched to the hospital and to the crime scene. The crime

scene was sealed off while pictures were taken and semen specimens were removed from the floor. The assault and rape took place in a building tower high above a room where the school band was practicing. The attacker took advantage of the loud music that served to cover her screams for help. She had been accosted as she entered the building to deliver a note to the band room and instead was lured to the tower. Cindy had no scheduled last period classes that day and was running errands for the office.

Cindy knew her attacker's first name (no one in the entire school had that same unique name). He was a senior. He was quickly apprehended and arrested. When it was learned the attacker was black, Dr. Joe knew this could further complicate an existing situation on campus where race relations had been deteriorating for some time. He could picture the front page headlines in the morning news instigating a full scale race riot on campus. He immediately called his board president informing him of the situation and the need to somehow dampen any news article that could inflame a very dangerous situation. They both went to visit the newspaper publisher, who was well-known to both of them, to plead their case. The publisher understood and was sympathetic to their efforts; however, he made it clear he could not suppress the story. Dr. Joe feared the worst was yet to come. He returned to his office to ponder the five o'clock meeting with Cindy's mother.

That afternoon he arrived at Cindy's home promptly at five o'clock and was cordially invited in. It was obvious upon entering the house that these people were a highly religious family. Religious artifacts were plentiful. Cindy's mother had arrived home shortly before Dr. Joe arrived and her husband had already told her that Cindy would be home soon but was at the hospital for some kind of a check-up the school had arranged, but did not tell her what for. That would be up to Dr. Joe to explain. This time the explanation seemed to flow a bit more smoothly; however, not without some anxious moments. Cindy's mother seemed to have a bewildered look on her face. She kept looking at her husband and her bewildered expression slowly turned cold and angry, as if to say, why didn't you tell me this? She kept moving her hands, clenched in a prayer like position, up and down, as the tears slowly trickled down her face. Dr. Joe went home that evening completely exhausted, wondering what the next day would bring. He felt like he had earned a year's salary in just one day. Apparently the local rape crisis center didn't think so. They criticized him for not contacting them immediately. There was no room in his mind on that day to think of them.

The next morning, after a night of tossing and turning, he dreaded the thought of reading the morning newspaper. He could envision a headline on the front page, "Academy Student Raped In School." No, it was not on the front page. He scanned each page and couldn't find the story, not on the first try. The second time around he found it -- a small headline buried in the inside pages -- "Student Charged With Sexual Assault."

The publisher did listen and did have a heart. He had played the story down as best he could.

The rapist was sentenced to prison. Cindy was withdrawn from school and went to live with an aunt in another country where she finished high school and went on to college. The rapist, within two weeks after serving several years of his sentence and released from prison, was killed when his car raced by the school and went out of control. It hit a tree within sight of the building tower.

To this day, Cindy's parents still hold Dr. Joe in high regard. They have since met on several occasions and often have conveyed their sincere gratitude to him and his wife. Over the years, the wives

209

became good friends.

~ *A TRICK for a TRACK* ~

The academy's running track had become one of the worst high school tracks in the state. It was a cinder track that had deteriorated to a point where competing high schools refused to run on it. For several years there were no home track meets scheduled on it because of its deplorable condition. At the end of a track season, Dr. Joe was approached by a parent whose children had been members of the track team; the last of whom would be graduating in a few weeks. They met to discuss the sad conditions the track program was subjected to. The parent and his father before him, and all of his children were academy alums. Something had to be done about the running track. He wanted the academy to have a new track. He asked what the cost might be for building a new all-weather track and Dr. Joe responded with a one hundred thousand dollar price tag. This number sounded reasonable to him, however, at the time it was a bit more than he could afford with some children still in college and another about to start.

He was willing to write out a check immediately for $25,000 toward a new track. Dr. Joe thought about the generous offer for awhile and said,

" I gotta an idea, I'll accept your offer if you will allow me to use it as a challenge gift to the student body."

"What do you mean by a challenge gift?"

"We have three thousand kids here. I know they can be a powerful force when it comes to raising money. I would like to resort to a little white lie and tell them that I have someone who willgive us $25,000 if they can match it. Will you go along with that?"

"Interesting, I like it. It's yours anyway even if they don't make it. I have a good feeling that somehow you'll get a lot of mileage out of this."

At the beginning of the new school year, Dr. Joe asked if he could address the student council's first meeting. His well-prepared presentation of the "challenge" without a doubt piqued their interest and they enthusiastically accepted. This, to them, would be the fund raiser to top all those of previous years. Within the next few weeks they formulated their own plan to meet the challenge. They decided the first fund raising activity would be a twenty mile walk-a-thon. The council leaders came to Dr. Joe's office and asked that he lead the walk.

"Whoa," he said, "I'm in no shape to walk twenty miles.

"Will you lead us part of the way ... please?"

"How 'bout me walking the lead from here downtown ... that would be a start I can handle?"

In his mind he thought this activity would be just one of those run of the mill walk-a-thons raising just a few dollars. He would get himself a couple of sponsors and do his part by walking a mile or so downtown and calling it a day. Right? Wrong. The local newspaper gave the kids some great publicity and in the article it mentioned that Dr. Joe would lead the upcoming twenty mile walk. Before he could solicit any sponsors on his own, a phone call came in from a local business man who doubted he was up to walking that far and volunteered ten dollars a mile for every mile walked. Dr. Joe thanked him and thought he was off to a good start. He would walk a couple of miles and make his friend pay for the needling comments he was subjected to. Soon after another call came through. This time, a

211

local surgeon friend, started in on him with the same tact doubting he would be able to make twenty miles,

"Hey Joe, what makes you think you can walk twenty miles? I'm willing to bet you'll never make it."

"I just got off the phone with Sol and he's willing to sponsor me for ten bucks a mile. So, top that if you can. Put up, or shut up."

"I know Sol, and if he offered you ten, he's betting on no more than a mile for you. I'll give you a hundred."

"Tony, that's a hundred dollars for every mile, right?

"You got it, maybe it will get you to walk an extra mile."

"You S.O.B. You're making me walk twenty miles and you're gonna pay. You'd better be there with your check book."

By the time that day ended Dr. Joe, without ever seeking solicitations, had amassed sponsors for an amount totaling over two hundred dollars a mile for his walk. The news spread rapidly. One trustee went so far as to sponsor a wheelbarrow to accompany him on his walk, just in case. The pressure was mounting. The students and the community were waiting for the big day. His wife prepared their station wagon as a first-aid wagon with several red crosses pasted on its side. She had a change of white socks for him at every five mile interval to prevent blisters developing on his feet.

The big Sunday arrived and so did hundreds of students. One student in particular, Danny, would always be remembered. He was a special education student who, in his own simple way, was a very loveable kid. On campus he would always go out of his way to be seen by and say hello to Dr. Joe. He eagerly awaited a response. Upon hearing his name, he would radiate a glow of importance to those around him because the Principal knew him by name. Danny wanted to walk alongside Dr. Joe. *He* was his hero. The weather that day was ideal for walking. It turned out to be a parade moreso than a walk. The kids were singing and dancing and having a lot of fun. Several placards and banners reading "Go -- Go -- Dr. Joe" were bandied about. Spectators lined some of the streets on the route. Several times people would come out onto the street and stuff money into Dr. Joe's pockets as he walked by. Some would come out to shake his hand. These were emotionally touching moments for him. The miles at first seemed to fly by -- at least the first five. After the first change of socks, the pace began to slow down. Many of the students who were behind him at the start began to pass him and take the lead. At the next change of socks, at ten miles, most of the students that passed him earlier were now out of sight. The wheelbarrow and Danny were still at his side. The pace at the fifteen mile mark slowed considerably. At this point, Dr. Joe thought a change of shoes along with the change of socks would be helpful. *Definitely a wrong move.* At first it felt good, but after about a mile his feet began to ache. Only a dozen or so students were walking with him now. Danny and the wheelbarrow were still at his side. Several of the students who had finished their twenty miles backtracked and, with chalk in hand, wrote messages on the pavement as an encouragement to Dr. Joe. "You can do it." "Don't quit now, only 3 miles to go." "You're almost there, 2 miles left." "We're waiting for you, one mile more."

These messages seemed to take the pain away. These kids had mastered some motivational skills they most likely didn't know they had. The chalked messages erased the temptation to ride the wheelbarrow to the finish line.

The last hundred yards were across a grassy green to the finish line. Nearly five and a half hours from the start, Dr. Joe walked across the green with his faithful entourage, with Danny cheering at his side and the empty wheelbarrow. Hundreds stood by clapping and cheering. The first congratulatory hugs and kisses came from his wife. Before she could let go of him he said to her,

"Get Tony on the phone and tell him we're here waiting for his two thousand dollar check."

Within a few minutes Tony arrived, "I don't believe you did it."

"Ask the kids. They were with me all the way."

The kids cheered and told Tony to pay-up. He took out his check book, placed it on the hood of his car, and wrote out a check for $2,000. That walk-a-thon kicked off the fund raising to the tune of over $8,000. Just over half that amount came from pledges made to Dr. Joe. He never thought a walk-a-thon could ever raise that amount of money. The students and their zeal for fund raising were not only able to match the twenty five thousand dollar challenge during the first three months, but raised in excess of $40,000 before the school year ended. The track would be installed and operational before the end of that school year, thanks to the dedicated efforts of some of Dr. Joe's contractor friends, and the students.

The dedication ceremony would turn out to be a bittersweet occasion. Danny couldn't be there to stand next to Dr. Joe. He died after an epileptic seizure a few weeks after the walk-a-thon.

~ THE BIG FIRE ~

A fire in a school is probably an administrator's most dreaded fear. Fire drills, no matter how frequent, do little to arrest the fear. Smoke and the ensuing panic that comes when an evacuation route is unexpectedly cut off can raise havoc with the best of planning. The

214

academy would lose the use of twenty-two classrooms in a spectacular fire that erupted one weekend. This particular weekend was not an ordinary one. Snow began falling as school let out on Friday and gradually intensified into a major storm that evening and for the next two days. It was to be a blizzard that would long be remembered. The state declared a state of emergency. Visibility during the storm was non-existent. Many roads and major highways were closed awaiting snow removal equipment. Drifting snow, in many cases, reached a depth of six feet or more.

Directly across the street from a fire station, within seventy-five feet, stood one of the academy's classroom buildings. Dr. Joe's phone rang. It was the fire station calling to inform him they spotted a fire in the building and that they were unable to drive their fire trucks onto the campus because of the deep snow. Dr. Joe quickly got dressed and hurried over to the building which was about a hundred yards away from his residence. In the meantime someone had commandeered a passing bucket loader to begin clearing a path for the fire apparatus to approach the burning building. When he reached the building, the entire top floor was engulfed in flames. Windows were popping and the howling wind seemed to suck the flames out of the building and upward toward the night sky. There was no smell of smoke, it was absorbed by the wind and carried upward and away. Conditions for burning could not have been better -- plenty of oxygen feeding this fire.

The next day, upon entering the building, it was apparent the fire must have started in the stair well just inside the entry on the first floor of the building and traveled upward along the stair well, eventually igniting the top floor. Insurance investigators and the state police crime squad were quickly able to agree this was an apparent case of arson. There was evidence that an accelerant had been used to start the fire. At this point in time, Dr. Joe had to scramble to find room to house the students who would be returning to school. Remarkably, he was able to identify enough spaces for makeshift classrooms. Physical education classes were canceled and that space alone made for six classrooms. Building foyers, basement rooms, the cafeteria, equipment rooms, and every space capable of accommodating twenty-five students was used. All academic classes, with a minimum of disruption, would resume the day the students returned after the storm. Not one class period was lost because of the fire.

Almost everyone marveled at this feat. It was disaster planning at its best. The students were disappointed at not having a few vacation days.

Building cleanup and rebuilding began at once. A million dollars worth of damage was repaired and the school would resume normal operation by the end of the same school year. The arson investigation primarily was the focus of the insurance investigators. It yielded nothing. Who had a reason or motive to set this fire? Dr. Joe had his suspicions. He studied the suspension records of those suspended in the days immediately preceding the fire. He found a likely candidate. No, it couldn't be he. This kid often visited his home and hung around with several of the football players who made it a practice to use up some idle time before a scheduled practice session. He was always polite and respectful; however, no one ever messed with him. He had a volatile temper. He was super strong and known to have picked up a student over his head during a fight hurling him down a flight of stairs. It would be several years after his graduation, Dr. Joe would learn, via his grapevine, a girl who had spent some time, bar hopping with the suspect during a college spring break talked about the fire. An alcohol loosened tongue bragged about his past exploits -- the big fire was one of them. Apparently it was a get even act against the building administrator who suspended him from school the day before the fire. This information was given to the appropriate authorities. For the longest time Dr. Joe heard no more until he called to find out the status of the investigation only to learn the insurance company decided to give up on him. They learned he was on death row, awaiting execution, in a Texas prison.

~ SNOWBALLS SNOWBALLING ~

A large triangular grassy green, called the Parade Grounds, was a favorite place for students to congregate in the mornings before the start of the school day. It also served as an area where buses would disembark academy students and wait for transfer students to board and be taken to other area high schools. It actually served as a bus terminal for four area high schools and eight area towns. Often this area would prove troublesome to police and school officials. It was sort of a no man's land because it was not considered part of the school campus, but public property instead. It came under local police jurisdiction. Efforts in the past to find another bus terminal location proved futile. The bus companies always ruled this was the best and most efficient location for transferring students. The masses of humanity that gathered here shielded many drug deals and other clandestine activities.

After an evening snowfall, the snow was wet enough to be easily packed into snowballs. Friendly snowball fights were common on the green. After all this was an activity that met with suspension from school if it should happen on school grounds. On this morning, like every other morning, a group of black students would walk to school on the sidewalk across the street where the buses were parked. Suddenly, a barrage of snowballs came over the top of the parked buses and found their mark. Not being able to see who threw the snowballs, the black students retaliated with their own indiscriminate barrage and soon the entire area erupted into an ugly scene. A fist fight, with racial overtones, became the center attraction. During the altercation, a black student freed himself from his coat and threw it on the ground. As they continued fighting, a group of white students grabbed the black student's coat and set it afire. This act infuriated the black students and now a full scale riot was underway. The police patrolling the area called in for back-up. They responded in force to quell the disturbance. The bitter feelings harbored that morning carried over onto the campus and several fights erupted during the school day.

The news media quickly jumped on the band wagon attracting the attention of a few who sought to exploit the situation by adding more fuel to a simmering fire. The exploiters, self-acclaimed black leaders of the community, called into the area TV stations and tried to play-up their role as heroes of the moment while trying to enhance their cause by alleging flagrant discriminatory practices by the school. They would arrive in the morning with vans and entice black students not to attend their normal classes but to go with them to a safer haven, (a local black community center). Dr. Joe knew he had the support of many black parents and worked diligently to restore the campus to a sense of normalcy. Amid threats of personal bodily harm to himself and his family he would volunteer to address black groups throughout the city. He was very well-received and appreciated. He especially remembers a speaking engagement at a black church service where his talk was interspersed by several Amens from the audience and at the end he was roundly applauded and presented with a collection plate overflowing with money. He could not and would not accept their generosity. He did accept an invitation to address parents at the community center from which, much, if not all, of the hostility was being generated. He did not fear to face the lion, even in his own den. All would end well when the lion and his den were found to be operating an apparent fraudulent endeavor and the city moved to withhold all further funding for the center. It was closed and the principal player resigned. He moved from the area to reside in another state. *Dr. Joe felt that this was a lonely battle he had to win. It appeared that those who could have helped him shied away from any encounter. It takes something like this to find out who has the courage and is willing to step up to the plate.*

~ *A PICNIC on the GREEN – EATING CROW* ~

The public green bordering the front of the academy complements the beauty of its campus. People driving by, who are not familiar with the area, often think the academy campus is that of a small college. The green can easily, and does, become an attractive nuisance particularly in good spring weather. Even though it is not part of the campus proper, students are not permitted to loiter there; especially students who are free the last periods of the day. Often when a crowd begins to congregate, campus security are asked to move students away. On one of those nice spring days when Dr. Joe was holding a meeting in his office, that looks out onto the green, he noticed a large group of students having a good time for themselves. This time was different -- not the usual lounging on the grass and absorbing the sun's rays. Someone had set up a gas grill in the center of the green and was grilling hamburgs and hot dogs. It attracted a lot of attention with lots of smoke. At the end of the meeting, Dr. Joe instructed two of his administrators to go over to the green and get rid of that grill and the congregation gathered there. They did so and dispersed the crowd. Back to his office they came and reported mission accomplished. He noticed a smirk on one of the administrator's face and asked him if they got rid of the grill,

"Oh yeah. We had it taken to your house."

"What did you do that for?"

"Because it's yours?"

"What do you mean it's mine?"

"Those were your kid's friends who were cooking out there on your grill. Now what?"

"!*~*@*^#*." Everyone had a good laugh.

~ BEES but NO BIRDS ~

After the episode on the green, Dr. Joe was anxious to get home and read the "riot act" to his son, Joe, Jr., and his friends. His son was in the kitchen with several friends feasting on left-overs that were in the refrigerator. A common practice among growing young boys, especially football players, who always seem to be hungry. In fact, his mother attempting to keep them away from some of the left-overs would resort to labeling them with a note that read, "do not eat -- poison." The effectiveness of this tactfulness soon wore off and an empty plate with the poison sign on the plate was all that was left.

As soon as Dr. Joe walked in he was greeted by Paul, a former neighbor, who often played with Joe, Jr. when he was a neighbor.

They had not seen each other for several years. It wasn't long before they started reminiscing. Paul shook hands and said,

"Hey, do you remember the time we had the battle of the bees?"

How could they forget? This experience would be etched in their memories forever. When the two boys were about twelve years old they wanted to learn how to shoot. At that time, Dr. Joe lectured them,

"OK, I'll teach you. Here's the deal. This is serious stuff and you need to pay attention to everything I tell you. I'll teach you the way my father taught me. Guns are not toys and need to be respected. I'm not going to repeat myself and if you make a mistake handling the gun you'll be punished. I'll slap your face and believe me when I tell you *that slap* will get your attention. That's the way I was taught."

The boys looked at each other and nodded, "OK." A target, a flat sided can, was attached to a small tree in a hollow at the end of the property that was bordered by a heavily wooded area. After some instruction on handling a 22 caliber rifle, the boys were ready to shoot. They would take turns shooting about ten rounds and then they would all walk down to the target to check the number of hits. They did that several times without incident until the last time when one of the boys strayed a bit off the pathway leading to the target. A bees' nest that was in the ground was disturbed and out they came. It was like what one would see in a cartoon show. Hundreds of bees came out in a funnel shaped formation and began attacking the two boys. They screamed as the relentless stinging began. Dr. Joe took off the baseball hat he was wearing and began to swat, furiously, the swarming bees away from the boys and began yelling,

"Quick, run, run for the house."

As they ran screaming toward the house, the bees continued to follow them in their funnel shape formation. Dr. Joe continued to try to fight the bees off with his hat as he chased after the boys. Not one bee ever stung him. It seemed the bees were only interested in stinging the young boys. The screams attracted the attention of neighbors who must of thought the worst of Dr. Joe for chasing after the two little boys and beating them in the process. By the time they arrived at the back door, the bee attack had subsided and Dr. Joe and his wife furiously stripped the clothes off the boys. Some bees were trapped under their loose clothing and were continuing to sting. Again not one bee stung anyone else.

Luckily, Paul's father was a pharmacist and his wife was at home. She quickly administered a healthy dose of Benadryl to the boys. The boys were a mess. Young Joe had twenty-six stings in the face alone and soon would swell to a point where his facial features were completely distorted. For the next two days, neither of the boys were recognizable.

• • •

About two weeks later, another encounter with bees would occur. This time they were white-faced hornets that constructed a beehive between two spotlights attached high on a back corner of the house. They had been there for some time and high enough where they didn't appear to be a menace to anyone. White-faced hornets can be a nasty lot. When they attack, their stingers are curled forward so when they hit their prey, they immediately insert their stinger. Not like the ordinary hornet who must land and then curl their stinger downward to insert their venom.

Below the spotlights was a swimming pool and on this particular day one of those hornets came down and stung young Joe between the eyes. That was it. Dr. Joe had enough with bees. That night he would be ready to do battle with them. He waited until dark when all the hornets were in their hive. He then started a roaring fire in an old steel barrel -- *to fry the nasty critters.* He put on a bee keeper's head and face protector, wore leather gloves, put on a rubberized shirt and pants with elastic fittings around his wrist and legs. High work boots completed the protective gear. Now, a ladder was carefully placed beneath the hive. He took a large black plastic garbage bag and with a kitchen knife between his teeth he was ready to take on the hive.

Carefully he climbed the ladder. When he reached the hive, he gently slipped the garbage bag over the hive and quickly gathered the end of the bag as to seal it. *So far so good.* Now comes the delicate part of this operation. With his knife he begins to cut away the hive from the spotlights. The hornets are now in a frenzy. The bag is humming and vibrating with activity. Dr. Joe looks at the pool below and his thoughts are to jump into the pool if the bag doesn't hold. The sweating inside the rubberized clothing is compounded by nervous sweat. Carefully, he descends the ladder and makes his way over to the barrel with flames licking out the top. Everyone is watching from inside the house. In goes the bag into the fire -- got 'em all. *Nope, one got out and stung him when he let go of the bag. Of all places, the only skin available between the glove and elastic closing on his sleeve. Revenge, sometimes, can be sweet?*

~ *A NIGHTMARISH DAY* ~

Dr. Joe got an urgent call that a terrible accident has just occurred at the Mechanics Building at the far end of the campus and an ambulance is on its way. He rushes out the door and runs across campus to find a terrifying scene. There, outside the building lies a student with the top of his head severed with part of his brain exposed. He lays in a pool of blood and is being tended to by a few teachers. The sight is sickening. Nearby are two other students who appeared to have been injured sitting dazed on the pavement. The ambulance and a team of medics quickly take over and transport the victim to the nearby hospital. The other two students are examined and it is determined that one most likely has a broken arm and the other is suffering from shock. Both are taken to the hospital. What could have happened?

It was a beautiful spring day and both bay doors to the automotive repair section of the building were wide open. Two instructors were preoccupied inside when a student who had his car parked outside decided to remove a spare tire from his trunk and inflate the tire. The tire was not the full size type but, the smaller, space saver kind found in many of the later model vehicles. Without heeding the warning instructions on the tire, he proceeded to put the tire on the pavement and ask his friend to hand him the air hose. He began filling the tire when suddenly the tire exploded sending the steel rim high into the air; but not before striking him in the head on its way up. He was bending over the tire during the process of filling it with air. Nearby students who witnessed the accident said the tire and rim traveled to a height above a neighboring three story building. When it came crashing down, it bounced upward hitting and breaking another student's arm. Because of this accident, many people would be involved in the lawsuit that would follow -- the academy, the two instructors, the car dealer who sold the car, the tire manufacturer, and any other person who could have had any connection with the incident.

Luckily the accident victim survived some very serious brain operations and was able to finish his education. The insurance companies settled for a large undisclosed amount of money even though there appeared to be ample warnings by the tire manufacturer and educational opportunities to learn proper inflation techniques for space saver tires.

The next car that Dr. Joe bought came with a space saver tire; he would not accept delivery of the car until the auto dealer agreed to remove it and replace it with a full sized tire. Wonder why?

~ *POLICE ARE ALWAYS at YOUR DOOR* ~

A large diverse student population brings with it many problems. Obviously there is a direct correlation between the number of students and the number of encounters with the police. Dr. Joe always had an excellent working relationship with the local police. Many of them were former students and former athletes who knew him well. They knew what he stood for and they knew and respected him as a friend.

It was late one afternoon and Dr. Joe was preparing to go home when his secretary came in to inform him a police officer was out in the hall and wanted to see him,

"Sure, tell him to come in."

As the door opened and quickly closed behind the entering officer he thought he recognized a teacher pacing the hall and thought nothing of it at the moment. The officer came over to his desk with extended hand. Dr. Joe rose and they shook hands,

"Have a seat.....What brings you here so late in the day?"

225

"Doc, you're not gonna like this. I got one of your teachers out in the hall."

"Oh. What's going on?"

"I was patrolling the Dump Hill area when I noticed the back end of a car sticking out of the bushes so I stopped to take a look. Your teacher had his arms around a young chick. They were kinda cozy."

"Are you kidding?"

"Hell no. They weren't doing anything at the time. He told me she was one of his students who needed counseling. When she told me her name I told her to get in the cruiser and I would take her home. Then I told "Romeo" I'd meet him here in your office."

"Who's the girl?"

"You know her father, we all know him. Jake Proot."

"Oh sh--. He's apt to kill him and her, when he finds out."

"That's why I wanted to get her home to her mother before he gets home. She most likely won't tell the ol' man what happened. I hope."

Everyone who knew Jake knew he could turn from a nice guy into a raging maniac at the drop of a hat. Nobody was too big for him, and he had an established reputation for settling an issue with his fist, and if need be, a baseball bat. The police officer left the office and on the way out he glanced at the teacher and sarcastically wished him luck. Dr. Joe motioned the teacher to come in and slammed the door behind him,

"What the hell is wrong with you? You stupid ---hole. Do you know who the girl's father is? Do you know what he's going to do when he finds out you've been messing with his kid? You'll be lucky if you still have a face left when he finishes with you."

By this time, the barrage of words began to show on the

226

already nervous teacher's face and his skin color was about as white as could be. All the teacher could do was look up at him with a frightened stare and with his mouth drooped open. Dr. Joe never did like this teacher and never trusted him. His behavior seemed weird to him and he seized on this opportunity to get rid of him. He knew he had him reeling on the ropes and continued his relentless verbal attack.

"Dr. Joe, I was only trying to help her. What can I do?"

"Help her? That's bull---- and you know it. I'll tell you what, if I were you, I'd get my a-- out of town, fast, before her father finds you. If he catches up with you, you'll be dead meat."

The teacher sat there trembling and whiter than ever. He began fidgeting with a ring on his finger. After awhile he looked up.

"Can I get some of my personal things from my room?"

"Yeah. You better get moving."

Dr. Joe watched out his office window as he scurried across campus. Several months passed during which several more indiscretions surfaced. This teacher had developed a habit of playing psychologist to young girls. Dr. Joe felt good about ridding the school of this bad apple. Almost a year later, a call came from another school superintendent who knew Dr. Joe. He was calling about the same teacher who had applied for a teaching job in his school district. Upon hearing his name he laughed and said,

"Didn't he tell you why he left here?"

" Yeah -- he said your teaching philosophy didn't agree with his."

That comment triggered a long and hearty laughed. Still laughing,

"Truer words were never spoken ... that S.O.B."

More laughter -- nothing more needed to be said. The laughter said it all. He never did get the job.

To this day, Dr. Joe never did find out where the teacher went from there and never received another inquiry about him. It's doubtful that anyone would ever hire him without checking him out. Most superintendents are savvy people when it comes to hiring a teacher.

~ *I GOT a DISEASE* ~

Dr. Joe was truly a students' principal. He always seized the opportunity to mix with the students. Often he would join them for lunch in the cafeteria, a practice shunned by the faculty who would rather eat in the teachers' lunch room. To have "the man" sit at their table was looked upon as a special honor by the students sitting with him. *After being with the students all day, lunch time for teachers was a welcomed break away from them -- understandably so.* He would make an extra effort to attend as many student activities as possible, including home athletic contests where he often could be found sitting on the bench with the football team or in the dugout with a baseball team. On many occasions he would be asked by the coaches to give the kids a pep talk before an important athletic contest. Never would he miss an opportunity to help fire-up a team. He always seemed to convey the tough guy image coupled with a sincere caring for his students. It was this relationship that made him a popular and well-respected person on campus. It also allowed the student to feel that here was a person, who was not untouchable, but would welcome a conversation with them. That opportunity would surface many times.

One time comes to mind when a black male student made an

appointment to see him,

"Dr. Joe, I think I have a problem."

"What do you mean, you *think* you have a problem?

"There's this girl ... and a ... I think I got a disease."

"You mean you've been fooling around with her and you caught something from her?"

"Yup. That's it."

"How do you know ... and how do you know you got it from her?"

"She's the only one I ever did it with and I got this awful itchy rash ... want me show you?"

"No. I think we'd better go downstairs and have Dr. Loo take a look at it."

Dr. Joe escorted him down the stairs to the health center and introduced him to Dr. Loo. About two weeks later, the young man came back to the principal's office. This time he had a big grin on his face showing his pearly white teeth that seemed to sparkle whenever he smiled.

"Dr. Joe, I wanna thank you for helping me. The Doctor said I don't have a disease. He gave me some stuff to put on and it went away."

"That's good news. You even had me scared for awhile. You better stop fooling around before you do catch a disease and that thing might shrivel up and fall off."

"Yeah ?"

The big grin disappeared and was quickly replaced with a look of concern. The big grin was now on Dr. Joe's face as he escorted him to the door.

During the years that followed this young man would distinguish himself on the football field and would become a sought after player by several small colleges. There were times his mother could not afford to take time off from work to drive him to the airport for a flight to an interested college. Dr. Joe would arrange for his own wife to drive him to the airport -- a favor she had done many times before for others under similar circumstances.

During his graduation ceremony when Dr. Joe handed him his diploma and shook his hand, the hand shake transmitted a friendly feeling of appreciation and, this time, they both had big grins on their faces.

~ *THE "GODFATHER" IMAGE* ~

Many faculty and staff members confided their very private feelings and problems to Dr. Joe. He had developed a reputation as a truly caring administrator who always was willing to help anyone who came to him with problems. He was an excellent and compassionate listener. They all knew he could be trusted with whatever it was they wished to share with him. He would listen to problems developing between spouses, to those who had drinking problems, to those who had developed serious illnesses, to those who were at their wits end with their own problem kids, to those who recently lost loved ones and, those who were worried about their pregnancies and those with a myriad of other problems. Often he would ask himself, why me? Why do these people tell me these things? Often he would go home at night and his wife would ask what kind of a day he had at work and the reply would be,

"It was another Dr. Anthony day."

Dr. Anthony was a well known, popular radio talk show back

in the late thirties and early forties. Dr. Anthony would discuss and advise people who would write in with some of their problems.

Most of the time, just the opportunity to talk to someone they trusted was comforting enough to get them through trying times. Many times, Dr. Joe would arrange a few days off for some of them, giving them time to sort out their problems and seek out the help they really needed. If they asked for his advice, it was given in such a manner as not to convey any expertise. He would always preface his remarks with,

"Please understand, I don't profess to have all the answers to your problem, or for that matter any answers, but this is what I think." His thoughts were always well-received and appreciated. He always made an effort to follow up on his conversations by personally visiting that person, several days later, at their work station to ask how things were going. This caring touch earned him the respect of many faculty and staff members. However, there were those who did not share this admiration and respect for him. He could be tough and demanding and have little patience with those who shirked their duties and took personal advantage of the trust he placed in them. Everyone seemed to know what this man stood for and where they stood in his eyes. He could be your friend or a formidable opponent. This was very evident during teacher contract negotiation times. These were trying times for him and to those negotiating for the teachers' union. He would fight all demands deemed unreasonable often reminding them the school did not exist for them -- the teachers; he firmly believed, first and foremost, the school belonged to the students and they were his most important concern. All of his contract talks eventually would end up in the arbitration process. There were many marathon mediation and arbitration sessions that would end at three or four o'clock in the morning.

Because the Board chose not to participate in contract negotiations, this responsibility was placed squarely on his shoulders. It put him in an adversarial position with many of the teachers. Although he knew he had been put in an unfair position, and so did his teachers, time would eventually heal all wounds. This was one part of his job that he definitely would not miss when he retired.

~ A REWARDING PROFESSION ~

Being in the education profession can, at times, be a very rewarding experience. *Everything but money that is.* Dr. Joe's tenure as a school principal was laced with several experiences that gave him much satisfaction and pride. Under his leadership, several transformations took place at the academy. He was able to sell a building that was off the main campus that he considered a safety hazard for students who had to access it by walking across a busy intersection. The building housed the home economics program which was subsequently relocated to the main campus.

He established a student operated TV station that was considered a first in the state. It served the town and area communities with interesting programs while providing students with broadcasting experience and courses of study for credit. After a few years of successful programming he negotiated a deal with the state's largest TV station where the school was able to upgrade its facility with state of the art equipment.

A mother of one of Dr. Joe's science students of years' past, and at that time a math teacher at the academy, came to see him. It was she and her husband's desire to reward the academy for the inspiration their son received there during his formative years. He went on to earn a doctorate in science from M.I.T. and became a well-known scientist. She gave Dr. Joe a check for $10,000 to buy a telescope to be used in the teaching of astronomy. It was her wish to keep the donation a private matter and to avoid any publicity. Dr. Joe then purchased a ten-inch reflective telescope, and with the aid of his maintenance people, designed an observatory and placed the telescope in a moveable dome on the rooftop of one of the campus buildings. A year later he built a room in the attic space below the observatory which functioned as a planetarium. Although the math teacher and spouse did not want any publicity recognizing their generous gift, Dr. Joe did have a bronze plaque made and affixed to the wall recognizing their generous contribution to the school's science department.

Over forty years later the former science student still stays in touch with Dr. Joe, his former science teacher, a cherished reward to a proud teacher whose influence was able to positively affect the life of one of his students.

Academy alumni proved to be very generous people. Never did Dr. Joe openly solicit any money for his school. Nevertheless, he seemed to cultivate a spirit of giving without ever asking. During his tenure, more awards, prizes, and scholarships were established than in the previous history of the school. Donations exceeding several hundred thousand dollars were not uncommon. One, in particular, stands out. It was given to recognize the most proficient speller in each of the four classes. Up until this time, spelling bees had become a thing of the past. Dr. Joe could think of no better way to recognize the most proficient speller than to bring back the good old fashioned spelling bee. The winners in each of the four classes would take home better than $800 each. The first year the income earned from the established fund made more than $3,200 available for distribution to the winners. Needless to say, this amount of money attracted a lot of attention and spelling bees suddenly sprang back into vogue in many area schools.

Another alum and a friend, who will always be remembered, came in to talk one day. Dr. Joe, in retrospect, thought he was acting strangely but did not think much of it at the time. Randy was always the quiet type who tended to keep to himself. He devoted all of his adult life to caring for his aging parents. Now that they were gone, there was a big void in his life. He was devoted to his work as a machine operator in the computer section of a large company and was always available to work extra hours to help anyone. Several times he helped Dr. Joe. Always soft-spoken and kind he was an individual who merited respect of those who knew him. He entered the office on this day, his first and only visit there, wanting to give a "little something" to his school. Before he left that day, he wrote a check for ten-thousand dollars. *What a surprise from a hard working man who never held a high paying job.*

"Randy, what's this for?"

"Joe, you can use it for whatever you want."

Randy shook Dr. Joe's hand. It was one of those handshakes that conveyed a special meaning. A few weeks later, a local news story detailed his stopping on a bridge and jumping into a river to drown.

Later, when his will was probated more would be added to an established memorial award to help a deserving student.

· · ·

With living alumni numbering nearly 25,000, Dr. Joe convinced his board they should dedicate a recently purchased building to alumni affairs. Before his retirement he had planted the seeds for a future development office. Many years later the building would be dedicated and named after him in recognition of his early vision of the importance of strong alumni support. He was an individual who radiated a true love for his Alma Mater; his visionary talent followed him beyond his retirement. He planned for a new library, a college of art to supplement an award winning art program, a theater for the arts, and a swimming pool -- all of which were to service both school and community. He also envisioned a day care center for faculty children. Many of his visions were to elude him. There was not enough time left in his career to accomplish what he had contemplated. Several years before his retirement he would suffer a health warning that had a profound effect on his plans. This event led him to inform his executive board he planned to retire a few years later when he would reach thirty-five years of service in education.

Not only did this event curtail many of his ambitions, his involvement concerning some pending major problems with personnel requiring years of legal wrangling were already underway and consumed a great portion of his time.

~ FIVE YEARS in and OUT of COURT ~

For Dr. Joe, a real sexual revolution was about to begin. The next five years would find him occupied with cases involving sexual contacts between teachers and students, one of which, would lead him all the way to the U.S. Supreme Court.

It was a nice spring day when a building administrator came in to report a disturbance in the gym between two teachers. Apparently, several students witnessed a nasty confrontation between the two -- one of whom was a football coach and, the other, Bonnie, a popular, female basketball coach. Dr. Joe was told he'd better look into the situation because of the bad blood that had developed between the two. The first thing he did was to call in the football coach. He knew the coach well and the two could sit down to have a man to man talk,

"John -- tell me what the ruckus was all about in the gym the other day."

"You really want to know?"

"Yeah, I do."

A long pause ... John looked down at the floor as if he were debating in his own mind as to whether to continue. Then he looked up and said,

"I've told that bitch many times to stay away from one of my best players ... she's going to ruin him."

"That's pretty strong talk, John. What's happening?"

"She's been taking him out of school and covering his absences from class and this winter she has been taking him on weekend ski trips. I don't like what I'm hearing."

"What could that be?"

"I know she has been feeding him alcohol."

"Whoa. Are you sure of that?"

" Oh yeah, my players know it and so do a lot of other kids on campus. The kid works at her husband's store and she feeds him beer."

"How old is this kid?"

"I don't know ... maybe fifteen or sixteen. You'd better talk to him."

By now Dr. Joe was on the edge of his chair. John tells him the boy's name and the next day the boy is called into the office.

The young man appears to be much older than he is. A handsome, rugged young man who could easily pass for someone in

236

his twenties.   He appears nervous and scared as he enters the principal's office,

"Hello Sam. Have a seat."

Sam sits down on the edge of his chair, resting both arms on the front part of the arm rests. Dr. Joe tries to put him at ease by talking about the past football season. Eventually he leads up to his relationship with Coach Bonnie and his football coach's concern about him.

" Tell me Sam, what's going on between you two?"

"Nothing, Dr. Joe."

"That's not what I've been hearing. I heard you've been out drinking with her. Is that so?"

"Well, yeah. Sometimes."

"When was the last time?"

"Aaaah, last week, at the night baseball game."

"Anybody else involved?"

"Just the three of us -- me and my friend and her, we were drinking beer and wine in the car on the way up."

"Where did you get the booze?

"She had it in her car when she picked us up."

The interrogation continued for more than an hour. Sam was talking freely and made no attempt to duck any of his questions. Before the session ended, Dr. Joe learned about the weekend ski trips and how the relationship started with a seemingly friendly kiss and eventually led to torrid sexual encounters. Not one, but several affairs over a span of several months. He would also learn that several other underage students, male and female, were involved in drinking alcohol provided by Coach Bonnie.

It was time to call in Coach Bonnie and get her version of the relationship. There would be no warm and fuzzy introductions at this meeting. It was Dr. Joe's style to come straight on with his guns a blazing when he was certain he had all his ducks lined up in a row,

"Bonnie, you're in big trouble."

"What! What are you talking about?"

"I talked with Coach John and with Sam. Sam told me everything and I mean everything. The kid is only fifteen and how old are you? This is real serious stuff."

The color quickly drained from her face as she sat motionless staring at him and not speaking a word. Tears welled up in her eyes,

"I don't understand. What did I do wrong?"

"C'mon ... do I have to spell out all the details. Providing liquor to under-aged kids ... ski trips ... drinking on the way to the ball game ... do you understand the mess your in?"

"I wasn't the only teacher who had kids drinking in the car. Melinda had a bunch of kids drinking in her car too."

Dr. Joe was stunned by her comment about Melinda. Melinda was a first year teacher and one of his daughter's good friends. He was speechless as he pondered his next move. Bonnie broke the silence by asking if she could call her husband. Dr. Joe pointed to the phone located on a low shelf next to his desk,

"Be my guest."

Her conversation was brief. She told him what had just transpired in the office and asked him what she should do. She hung up the phone, turned and said her husband told her it would be best for her to resign. Dr. Joe quickly seized the moment. He reached into his desk, pulled out a sheet of paper and pen and pushed it in her direction. She was having difficulty structuring the letter and Dr. Joe helped her with the wording. He suggested she make the resignation effective the end of the school year which was a few weeks away. He was thinking this would be least disruptive to the students and the school and with the summer coming it would make for a nice clean break.

In the days that followed Dr. Joe was feeling good about his ability to get rid of this teacher quietly. That was to be short-lived. A week later, Dr. Joe received a call from his school's law firm,

"Hey Joe, what's going on with Coach Bonnie down there?"

"How did you hear about it?"

"We got a call from her attorney informing us they are going to contest her resignation."

"Why, how come?"

"They're saying it was taken under duress and they are going to fight it."

"That's bull----, she offered it."

Dr. Joe proceeded to explain what had transpired and was told not to worry. With what he had on her, he could give her a hearing before the board and after they heard the evidence against her they would surely fire her. Dr. Joe didn't like the idea because he knew this could turn into a real circus; however, he didn't have any choice in the matter. She was legally entitled to a hearing before the board.

Apparently, she was advised by some of her friends to seek legal counsel. She first sought help from her teachers' union. When they learned more about the case they refused to get involved and advised her to seek out her own private attorney.

Soon the word spread that Dr. Joe had fired her and she was going to fight him. Here was a well-known girls' basketball coach who recently was recognized statewide as Woman Coach of The Year. Her team members quickly came to Dr. Joe's office, some in tears, some indignant, demanding an explanation. No explanation was forthcoming because this was now a legal matter and he was not free to share his findings or reasons with them. He was not to be most popular person on campus now. Being a top administrator can indeed be a lonely job.

To complicate matters, he was now not only forced to face Melinda but also disappointment and anger this could bring to his daughter. He called Melinda to his office for her side of the story hoping to get her off easy with a reprimand for allowing students to drink in her car. She was a very young first year teacher who was naive and unable to control students a few years younger than she. At the time she was also serving as secretary for the teachers' union. *Nobody wanted that job and the union was happy to lure a rookie teacher into taking this assignment.* She felt she could not offer any explanation until she consulted with her union first. They advised her to seek her own attorney as they did with Bonnie. That left Dr. Joe with no choice other than to proceed with charges against her too. He felt badly about this situation, not being able to share his thoughts with her. He eventually learned that she was unaware that the students in the back seat of her car had managed to sneak beer into her car. She was well on her way to the ball game when she saw them drinking in the back seat. She did tell them to stop several times but they would continue to drink when they thought she wasn't watching.

Melinda's demeanor and personality was anything but stern. It never occurred to her to turn back, and tell the drinkers to get out. She wanted to be everybody's friend.

• • •

Up to this point in time, very few people knew any of the details of what really happened and the charges that would be forthcoming. Only the individuals who were directly involved knew the seriousness of the situation. There was much speculation and all kinds of rumors being spread about. Even Bonnie would lull herself into thinking the drinking problem was the major issue and that Dr. Joe wouldn't dare pursue any sexual charges because Sam would certainly be on her side and never admit to it. She was unaware that Dr. Joe carefully cultivated the support of Sam's mother, a single mom, who in turn worked to sway her son over.

The date of the hearing was set and the executive board would serve as the hearing panel. Subpoenas were served and arrangements for a hearing room were made. The day before the scheduled hearing he received a call from his attorney,

"Joe, guess what? Our friend has requested the hearing be open to the public. You'd better be prepared to house a lot of spectators. I've been through these open hearings before and they can turn out to be real spectacles."

"Oh yeah! I think it's time to play hardball. Tell her stupid lawyer we're going to pull all stops and hit her with the sex charge too. She's probably thinking I don't have any sex related stuff on her."

"Are you sure you want to go down that road?"

"I'm ready. I got enough support now to hang her."

Dr. Joe proceeded to explain and just in case she still insisted in going through with a public hearing he would be prepared with extra police to control the expected crowd. Dr. Joe dreaded the thought of what might happen that evening.

The evening of the hearing began with Bonnie's team members lining both sides of the sidewalk leading to the library building. There they were in full uniform, each with a long-stemmed rose in hand, waiting to present their queen with a rose as she passed before them. Dr. Joe watched from inside as Bonnie arrived.

The sight gave him a sickening feeling to his stomach that quickly turned to anger. He couldn't help but think these kids who once considered him a friend, now despised him.

He turned to his lawyer and said,

"Did you tell her lawyer we're gonna hit them with the everything *and* the kitchen sink?"

"I did, but they weren't impressed. We're going to caucus before we start the hearing and maybe they'll change their minds."

The building halls and hearing room were quickly filling with people. The lawyers met to caucus in an adjacent room. After about a twenty minute caucus, the door opened and the lawyers announced the hearing would be a closed hearing (private) and all those who were there on subpoenas or testifying were to remain out in the hall and all others were to leave.

The hearing was called to order and the charges against Bonnie, made by Dr. Joe and recorded by the board at an earlier meeting, were read aloud to both parties. More than a dozen witnesses were called in to testify during the hearings that were continued during the course of two, long evening periods. Most witnesses were subjected to examination and cross-examination by attorneys as they would be in any regular court trial.

Damaging testimony by students attesting to several drinking incidents of alcoholic beverages provided by Coach Bonnie was heard. The most damaging testimony came from Sam who openly admitted to drinking and sexual encounters with Coach Bonnie. Because this was a closed hearing, each testifying witness was not permitted to hear the testimony given by the other witnesses. Coach Bonnie's lawyer called to the stand several character witnesses who would sing her praises. These witnesses were creditable people in the community who apparently were unaware of all the allegations in this case.

Dr. Joe sat in disgust as he had to listen to all the flowery testimony on her behalf. He silently wished they could have sat with him in his office and listened to what really happened. They surely would never have agreed to take the stand, had they known.

At the conclusion of the hearings, the board announced they would meet the following week and render a decision. They did. The decision was unanimous. She was terminated.

Dr. Joe's ordeal was finally over. Wrong -- it was just the beginning. The board's decision was to be appealed to the civil courts. The appeal would be based on a technicality and not the alcohol nor the sex charges. *It should be noted here, the sex and alcohol charges which led to her firing were never an issue from here on.* Two members of the hearing panel were attorneys employed by the same law firm that, in the distant past, had prepared a land deed for the academy. The land transfer was a donation to the school made several years prior to the hearing. The cost of drawing the deed was billed and paid by the school. Considering the time and effort involved in the legal transfer of the property, a minuscule amount of sixty dollars was charged -- most likely, only a secretarial and paper expense. The argument here was the two attorneys in question were accused of a "conflict of interest" situation and they should have disqualified themselves because their law firm had been engaged and paid for by the school. This situation along with an accusation that the Freedom of Information Regulations Act was violated because the hearing date for the decision meeting time and place was not posted became the issues to be litigated.

The appeal would be heard before the Superior Court. Once this process was initiated, all the documents and recorded testimony from the hearings, previously held in private, became public property open to the public. Needless to say, a hungry news media had a feast with this story. The news quickly spread statewide and then some. Bonnie's secret life became open to the public.

What a circus this turned out to be. The cat really got let out of the bag this time. A barrage of telephone calls came into Dr.

Joe's office. Many of the rumors that had been circulated were put to rest.

After the case was tried before Superior Court, the court ruled in the school's favor. Obviously, this decision did not satisfy the losers. They would appeal again, this time to next level which was the Appellate Court system where three judges would sit to hear the case. Here, the judges ruled, two to one, in favor of Coach Bonnie. The dissenting judge's opinion was so strong and well-written it drew the attention of several attorneys statewide. Dr. Joe began receiving calls from several of them, many unknown to him, who read about the case in a weekly published law journal that reviews and presents cases tried in the state each week. Of particular interest to all of them was the published *dissenting* opinion. All who called encouraged him to take the case to the next level -- the State Supreme Court.

This was to be the big fight. A decision was made to hire a well-known attorney with experience trying and winning cases before the state's highest court. He would prepare and try the case as the lead attorney for the school. The day in court finally came and Dr. Joe traveled to the state capitol. This was to be an uncomfortable day for him. He was known to some of the justices sitting on the bench that day and was careful not to give the appearance of a friend. He did manage to get a quick smile out of one of them. The court over-ruled the Appellate Court decision and ruled in favor of the school.

Not satisfied with The State Supreme Court decision, Coach Bonnie's lawyers took the next step. The case was now headed for the highest court in the land, The United States Supreme Court.

Something more for Dr. Joe to worry about; what if, after all these years of legal wrangling, she should win? The school might be forced to pay her back wages and give her job back to her -- what a horrible thought.

What transpired during this five year saga, from the first hearing to its finality with the U.S. Supreme Court, could fill the pages of a sizeable text. To complicate matters along the way, Dr. Joe found himself in the middle of a lawsuit where he had to defend Coach Bonnie because the school was sued for a questionable training practice that injured one of her former students . The student claimed a carpal tunnel syndrome injury because Coach Bonnie had tied her hands together during a volleyball class. Again, Dr. Joe's lips would be sealed because of the ongoing litigation and no reference could be made to what was transpiring in Bonnie's case because it was considered, in legal terms, to be irrelevant and inadmissable in this court case.

He really wanted to express his opinion as to her real character, but couldn't; his duty was to protect the school's interest. The school eventually lost this case and fifteen thousand dollars was awarded to the student -- paid through the school's insurance policy.

Getting back to The U.S. Supreme Court, several months after receiving the case, they elected not to hear the case and let the state's Supreme Court decision stand. Finally, this court case was officially ended.

While all of this was going on, and in conjunction with Coach Bonnie's first hearing, Dr. Joe was occupied with another hearing -- that of Melinda. This was a closed hearing resulting only in a reprimand issued by the Board.

The reprimand was all that Dr. Joe wanted to do in the first place but the circumstances at the time would not permit it. Legal expenses, in both cases, were staggering for all parties involved.

Another serious problem arose during this infamous five year period. A recent graduate came in to see Dr. Joe during one of her college breaks. She was, at the time, a junior year college student who was undergoing personal psychological counseling at her college because of sexual encounters with one of her teachers during her senior year in high school. Her college counselor recommended that she tell her story to her former high school principal,

"Dr. Joe, I know you're busy and I hate to burden you with my problems. I had to build up my courage to come to see you today, but I know you would want to hear what I have to say."

"I hope it's something I can help with."

"Thank You. Let me catch my breath."

Dr. Joe's mind was wondering what could this be about. The young lady had a disturbed look on her face and he sensed some bad news was on its way.

Lately, it seemed there would be no end to the crisis situations that would cross his desk. He had talked with so many people with so many problems, what was said to him sometimes became difficult to recall in its entirety a few days later. To pencil notes during a conversation, he considered a display of rudeness and a definite inhibition to a free flow of conversation. He was intent on listening for, and making mental note of, key words he could recall after the conversation ended. Then, he would immediately detail on paper what was said to him. He would review the detailed papers several times before taking any action.

The young college junior began with,

"During my senior year here, I was having an affair with a teacher and I think he's still teaching here."

"Wait a minute, why are you telling me this now?"

She began to spill out all her inner feelings and how it had adversely

246

affected her life when she went away to college, so much so, she could no longer sleep and began to fall behind in her studies. Dr. Joe was taken back when he learned the name of the teacher. Never would he suspect this individual. He appeared to be happily married to a very lovely girl. He was a very personable and a dedicated young teacher. To make matters worse, his in-laws were well-known to Dr. Joe and he knew they were elderly and not in the best of health. They seemed to worship the young man who came into their family. He was the son they always wish for, but never had. To them this was a marriage made in heaven.

Dr. Joe carefully reviewed his notes, for several days after their meeting. Over and over again until all the details were clearly fixed in his mind. *Sex Education 101 was never like this.* Now he was armed and ready to call in the young teacher. Dr. Joe put him at ease with conversation capitalizing on their mutual interest in sailing boats and then, abruptly, jumped into the real purpose of their meeting. The element of surprise was very evident when the name of the young college junior surfaced. Before he could respond, Dr. Joe said,

" Hold on. Just hear me out. I'll tell you what I heard. Then you can tell me your side of the story."

Dr. Joe recited nearly all the intimate details he had gleaned from his detailed notes and then asked for an explanation,

"I, aa-, I guess, I really don't have one. I knew it was wrong when I got involved."

Dr. Joe then expressed his disappointment with him and lectured him on the trust that was violated and demanded his resignation effective the end of that school year.

He handed in his resignation the next day and at the end of the school year he left the teaching profession. Whether his wife or

247

family ever knew what really happened is still a mystery to this day.

• • •

A few weeks passed and as Dr. Joe was home enjoying dinner with his wife, the phone rang. As usual, his wife would always answer the phone at dinner time and if the call were for him she would ask the caller to call back a little later. This time, her attempt to put the caller off did not work. The caller pleaded to talk with him as she asked if it couldn't wait until dinner was finished. She turned with phone in hand and said,

"It's Sam, and he says he needs to talk with you, right now." Dr. Joe took the phone and asked what was wrong. He and Sam had become close over the time of their ordeal and Sam looked upon him as a father image always seeking his advice. Sam said he needed to talk but couldn't talk on the phone and it couldn't wait,

"O K. When can you get here?"

" I'll be at your house in about ten minutes. Thanks Doc." Sam arrived within ten minutes. He was shaking and obviously distraught. They went into the den and sat. Sam started sobbing. He tried to control himself and looked up with eyes full of tears and said,

"My brother just killed himself."

"WHAT! What happened?

Sam collected himself and began to tell Dr. Joe his brother Amos went to a nearby cliff top, took off his shoes and left a hand-written note tucked in one shoe, and then jumped to his death off the high cliff into the rocks and river below. The police had just left his house where they came to inform him and his mother of the tragedy and that they were holding onto the note as evidence. By this time Sam was bordering on hysteria and Dr. Joe knew he was in need of special help. He left the room to call in a psychiatrist friend who was not

248

home at the time.   He called his own Catholic priest who came immediately to the house. They talked for several hours. The hurt that was evident that evening was more than words could ever explain. Sam's hurting was felt deep within the priest and Dr. Joe ... never to be forgotten.

Amos, Sam's older brother idealized his younger brother. He also, on occasion, ran errands for the school office when he had free time. Like his brother, he was a handsome boy who looked like a big football player but lacked the motivation to be a participant in any sport. He seemed to be content to follow his kid brother and take great pride in basking in his glory.

The police detective who investigated the suicide was a former athlete who had been coached in high school by Dr. Joe. He would confide the contents of the suicide note to him. It was a sad commentary on the feelings of a young man who had been deeply disturbed by the break-up in his family and now, the recent taunts by his peers, relative to his idol Sam, may have proved too much for him.

• • •

After all the litigation of this period in time finally ended (five years), Dr. Joe called in Melinda to explain why he had no choice but to bring charges against her. He expressed his sorrow for having put her through a very troublesome and expensive experience. She fully understood why he could not risk prosecuting Coach Bonnie alone and not letting her off the hook she unknowingly was snagged onto. Melinda, an excellent teacher, was a very likeable and trusting person whose kindness to others could turn on her. This was an admirable quality she had that may have put her through a most terrifying experience in the months to come.

One weekend, Melinda was accosted in a shopping mall

parking lot and forced into a car. She actually was kidnaped at knife point and driven out of town to a remote trucking terminal parking lot. Here, she was forcibly pushed over a locked chain-link fence, dragged into an empty trailer and sexually assaulted. She was then locked in the trailer and left there for the weekend. It was not until Monday morning when drivers arrived to connect and haul away their rigs that her cries for help were heard. This unfortunate, traumatic experience caused her to look at her life in a different perspective. As a young teacher, in her mid- twenties, she wanted to forget about the past and begin life anew. She resigned her position as a teacher and sought employment in another field in another state.

Melinda, to this day, wherever and whenever she meets up with Dr. Joe, always greets him with a hug and a kiss.

~ *THE END of a THIRTY-FIVE YEAR CAREER* ~

Once Dr. Joe reached the thirty-year mark in his career he began thinking about retirement. He envisioned his retirement as a time in his life when he would be at the top of his career. He wanted things to be running smoothly with no hanging controversial issue for a successor to contend with. It was to be a time to be remembered as a good administrator and to be held in high esteem. Too many times he had seen other administrators retire when it seemed like everyone was throwing rocks at them. This was not for him. If need be, he would stay until all was well and running smoothly..

It was now time to put into place all the unfinished dreams he had for the future of the school. At this point in his career he got a bad scare. One weekend, after a long day working on remodeling his lake front cottage, he came home, showered, changed into clean clothes and sat down to watch television. During the course of the viewing he had occasion to remove his glasses and rub one eye. In doing so, he noticed the TV set he was focused on was gone -- no longer visible to him. Strangely enough, as he kept the eye he was rubbing shut and the other eye open, whatever he focused on was gone. He looked up at a picture that hung on the wall above the TV. Now the picture was gone but he could see the TV set. He had clear vision of all objects above and below the focus area. The first thing that entered his mind was, maybe he had suffered a detached retina. He banged his head quite hard that day while working in a crawl space underneath his cottage. To make a long story short, it turned out it was not caused by a detached retina but by a tiny piece of cholesterol plaque that became lodged in the keen vision area of the retina. One of the tiny capillaries was blocked by the tiny piece of plaque rendering him with a permanent banana-shaped blind spot in one eye. This was a signal to him of the possibility of a dreaded stroke, in the near future, should another piece of plaque break free and lodge in his brain. This frightening experience made him rethink his future plans. He decided, definitely, to retire if and when he reached thirty-five years of service. This was to be a personal secret shared only with his wife. He planned to give his board three years notice before his retirement date. In the meantime it was business as usual. However, the future of the school would always be foremost in his mind. So much so, he designed a corporate restructuring plan that was accepted by his board and voted pro by the corporators. The school's endowment was grown rapidly by several million dollars during his tenure and he was fearful the next superintendent, seeing all this wealth, might be tempted to squander it, especially if that person were allowed the broad range of authority enjoyed by Dr. Joe. He had

251

earned the ultimate faith and trust of his board. He had become a model influential leader for the board to follow. He enjoyed a level of power and authority that other school administrators could only dream about. At times, he could easily assume the role of a benevolent dictator -- *sometimes he did behave like one.* The corporate restructuring plan was designed to throw cold water on that ever happening again. He did not want any successor to wield the power afforded him, especially those relating to investments and other financial matters. It was too much power to be trusted in one person. The corporate restructuring was designed to diversify a variety of functions among newly-formed corporations all of which would come under the umbrella of one holding corporation. The school was to be only one of four distinct corporations, serving as the "flagship" corporation, under the parental control of a holding company.

The years nearing the end of his tenure would see Dr. Joe cited many times with several distinguished service awards. He was named Italian Man of the Year, not once but twice, within a span of seventeen years, an unprecedented occurrence in the Italian community. He was also named Man of the Year and received several awards recognizing his work in the computer field. He received U.S. Congressional recognition for community volunteer service. Awards were available and plentiful for a man who was always willing to help wherever he was needed. It can be said he was not one to seek out opportunities to volunteer; however, when asked he would put his best foot forward.

• • •

There would be one more significant encounter with the state department of education which would come two years before he retired. Each year, Dr. Joe would carefully read all the new laws concerning education passed by the legislators in their last legislative session. What a surprise? Written into one of the laws called "The Teachers' Enhancement Act" was the name of his school, (named separately because the state considered it to be a "quasi-public" school). Several million dollars would be available during the next three years for distribution to school systems, state wide, to enhance teachers' salaries. When Dr. Joe saw this he immediately called the state education commissioner's office,

"Jason, what's this with this enhancement act? I never asked for our school to be written into the act."

"What's the matter? Don't you want more money for your teachers?"

"Sure I do. That money shouldn't come directly to us, it belongs to the eight towns we service. It's tax money that's rightfully theirs. Furthermore, what's going to happen at the end of three years when the money runs out -- who's going to fund the salary account?"

"What are you worried about? The state has plenty of plenty of money."

"Yeah, sure. I've heard that song before."

" Look Joe, you need to decide whether or not you're going accept the money. If you don't, the money will be allocated elsewhere. I'm going to transfer this call to Willie. Talk to him."

Obviously, the commissioner was in no mood to continue the conversation. Willie was his associate commissioner. Dr. Joe gave him the same line and it wasn't long before they would lock horns.

"Yes Willie, my teachers deserve more money and you can bet our salaries will always be competitive with the area schools. If town X pays their teachers fifty thousand a year, you can bet your a-- we'll do the same."

"Joe, I'm not going to argue with you. You've got two weeks

to the deadline to decide if you want the money. If you don't, I'm sure someone else will be happy to get your share."

In the meantime, the word was out that Dr. Joe was balking at accepting the state's offer. This did not set well with the teachers' union who feared their future salaries would be adversely affected. Local town officials felt if he did not accept the money, huge tuition increases would be levied if a competitive salary structure was adopted. Dr. Joe would soon be subjected to local political pressures. Several town officials visited him at home and contacted his executive committee to apply pressure for participation in the enhancement act. The deadline for a decision was nearing. The teachers were disturbed and rightfully so. He called a meeting with his executive committee to discuss the situation and they told him they would support his decision whatever he decided. He said to his committee,

"Here's what I will do. It's very simple. When the state sends me the money, only then will I distribute the money to the teachers."

Everyone was much relieved -- the teachers especially and the towns. During that school year, the allotted enhancement money arrived in the spring and was quickly disbursed to each teacher in a lump-sum bonus fashion. It was a happy day for everyone. The following year the same arrangement was in place. During that spring, bonus checks, some in excess of fifteen thousand dollars, went to the teachers.

At the end of that second year Dr. Joe retired. A new principal was in place for the third and final year of the enhancement act. However, somehow, the new man , (trying to be Mr. Nice Guy) succumbed to union pressure and included the allocated amount for that year into the salaries beginning with the first paycheck in September. The enhancement money received that spring (the third year) would then be added to the salary account, thus eliminating the bonus check system. A smart political move by the unions and not so smart move for the towns and the state. Because boards of education, everywhere, included the allocated state money into their salary schedule and began paying teachers before the money was in hand, salary schedules, statewide, were now ratcheted upward to where it would be nearly impossible to adjust them downward. It should be noted that during the three years of the enhancement act, teacher contract negotiations continued at their regular pace. Some yearly salary contracts were increasing nearly ten percent, excluding any enhancement money.

After the third year -- no more enhancement money. Boards of education now were faced with severe budgetary problems. The state surplus money was gone and the state found itself in a budgetary crisis. The new incoming governor's solution to the crisis was to levy an income tax.

The previous governor was a smart politician. He found himself with surplus monies and the opportunity to assure his party's re-election by courting the two largest unions in the state with pay raises -- the teachers' and state employees'. (A classic example of "money talks").

If boards of education had the intestinal fortitude to do what Dr. Joe did, maybe, an income tax could have been averted.

· · ·

The closing years of his tenure were marred by several tragic events. He watched his very capable assistant as she fought a long, losing battle with cancer. A very sad sight to see a once lovely, statuesque woman wither away into a shriveled old lady before her time. Too many students were mourned because they lost their lives to auto accidents. Dedicated faculty, young and old, died unexpectedly. A faculty friend who just retired but never lived long enough to collect her first retirement check. Events seemed to be sending a message to him.

He would lose a good friend in Dr. Loo, and an ardent supporter of his school. It was Dr. Loo's generosity that started a beautiful tradition of planting flowering cherry trees. Each graduating class complemented his original donation by planting two cherry trees on campus. Over the years the walkways would be lined with flowering trees and springtime would display beauty to behold. He would never forget his last walk with Dr. Loo as they admired the beauty of the flowering cherry blossoms. He commented to Dr. Joe that this would probably be the last time he would see this beautiful sight. Was this comment made to be a prophesy? It was. Before the next flowering season, Dr. Joe was one of the honored few who was chosen by Dr. Loo's spouse to shovel dirt onto his coffin, a Hebrew ceremonial tradition, as it lay at the bottom of its resting place.

The eerie sound of shovelfuls of dirt hitting the vault, in which lies a friend, was never to be forgotten.

The unexpected death of a student always cast a pall over school life on campus and visibly affected those personally acquainted. A serial killer in the area took the life of a senior girl and shocked everyone on campus and surrounding communities. She was to be his last victim. He was caught and charged with her murder along with several others not only in this state but in a neighboring state as well.

This horrifying event seemed to be the last straw. It was time to get away.

Dr. Joe had given his executive board ample notice of his intentions to retire in the past but they were never taken seriously. They wanted him to stay, at least until age sixty-five, and thought they could convince him. It meant postponing retirement an additional six years. In Dr. Joe's mind, thirty-five years in this business was enough and he was riding at the top of the wave of his popularity. He decided he would announce formally his retirement at the annual meeting of the corporation.   The announcement came as a surprise to the corporators and the trustees as well. It was front page news. Within forty-eight hours of the breaking news, the student body presented him with a petition listing over four hundred student signatures requesting that he stay on as their school's leader.   It was noted that these more than four hundred signatures represented all classes with the exception of the graduating senior class; this class, by design, was purposely excluded. To gather so many signatures in so short a time was a testimonial to Dr. Joe's popularity among his students.

He was surprised and deeply touched by this reaction -- never dreaming the students thought that much of him. A greater honor they could not have bestowed upon him.

Maybe, he should rethink his decision to retire at his time?

• • •

Soon, a national search for his successor would begin. He would be asked by several board members to stay on and continue to serve the school as a trustee. This he would not do. He didn't want to be put in a position where he could be looked upon as a big brother watching over the new person. This decision was one he would live to regret.

His replacement lasted only a stormy four years and changed forever the tenor of the school. Dr. Joe had been the eighth headmaster to serve the academy in its one-hundred-thirty-two year history (1856 - 1988).

VII

From 1988 to 2002

~ *THE RETIREMENT YEARS* ~

Early in his retirement years, as luck would have it, Dr. Joe managed to survive a near lost at sea experience when sailing a friend's newly purchased yacht from Florida to Connecticut. He and three other friends sailed the twin diesel engine vessel northward in eight days consuming nearly six hundred gallons of fuel daily. They sailed from sun up to sun down, docking at nightfall. Twice during this memorable trip, Dr. Joe may have used up two of his nine lives. The first was when they were sailing the intercostal waters on the Alligator-Pungo River. He decided to climb up on the ship's uppermost deck, which happened to be slightly higher than the roof of the bridge, to take video pictures of alligators in the river. As he stood looking into the murky waters below, a barge coming toward them forced them starboard resulting in the ship running aground on a sand bar. The unexpected abrupt stop caused Dr. Joe to fall. Miraculously, he fell backward and landed in a life raft that was strapped to the roof deck. The first reaction from his friends on the bridge was to call up to him,

"Joe, are you OK ?"

"Yeah, I'm OK. But, I think I stained my underwear."
Everyone laughed. He was joking of course.

Had he fallen into the murky river he could have easily become alligator meat; thus, putting an early end to his retirement. The next morning, rising before the others, he purposely stained his undershorts with brown shoe polish and hung them on the forward masthead. Once underway, the breeze caused them to flap in the wind, calling the attention of everyone on the bridge and generating a good laugh.

There would be no laughs on the next near disaster. Sailing in the open waters of the Atlantic, off the coast of New Jersey, the seas were smooth and the ship was steering on automatic pilot. This ship's automatic pilot allows steering only of three to five degrees to either side. Everyone was on the bridge. One of the more experienced friends noticed that the waters ahead had a sinister look and decided to turn off the automatic pilot and take manual control. No sooner had he assumed manual control than, a thirty to forty foot swell came from behind, picked up the stern of the ship as if it were a cork, and plunged it downward into a long trough. Luckily the person at the wheel knew how to ride the downward side of the giant wave and saved the boat from a broaching disaster (if the bow had gone under, the ship would have toppled and gone right to the bottom). For two hours they battled heavy seas damaging many items and furniture aboard. The near broaching happened so quickly, they had no time to batten down. To make matters more frightening, everyone caught on the bridge at the time, had no access to life jackets because they were stored on the lower deck. *Anyhow, they most likely would have been rendered useless in a broaching accident.*

The harrowing experience was temporarily forgotten as they sailed into New York Harbor and The Statute of Liberty came into view. Dr. Joe was at the wheel and he was able to see what his parent's eyes saw when they came to America. Dr. Joe's eyes welled with tears as he reflected on how they must have felt seeing this magnificent and lovely lady for the first time. He felt it too.

They were looking again, only this time, through his eyes.

• • •

The retirement years became filled with many varied activities. His interest in education would take him to other levels. He accepted a full time position as the director of graduate studies at a university branch campus with the academic rank of assistant professor. Concurrently, he became a university lecturer and an advisor for a doctoral program in educational leadership at another university. He continues to this day as a university supervisor for student teachers and teacher interns. He served as chairman of the board of directors and trustees for the local hospital and served on its board the allowed maximum fifteen years; and now continues to serve as chairman of the hospital building and equipment committee. His most recent appointment was to the board of directors of a regional hospice organization. He has ventured into several more areas. All have their extraordinary stories to tell. The retirement years would bring him a second Italian Man of The Year award in the year 2000. (His oldest grandson, Christopher, surprised him by coming all the way from

Florida to be with his "Gregor" at the awards banquet. What a joy that was for him to have Chris there with the rest of the family.) Later that year, the academy corporators, his Alma Mater, would surprise him by naming a building in his honor. The dedication ceremony left such an impression on his ten-year old grandson that shortly after he told his mother he wanted to change his name to be the same as Dr. Joe, and to include the Ph.D. after his name. His lovely granddaughter, Cailynn, was equally impressed and proud. After all, her "Gregor's" school was soon to be her school.

~ A HOLE-IN-ONE -- NOT ONE but TWO ~

Retirement did allow some time for golf. It was on a vacation trip to Florida that Gregor would bring home a trophy. Gregor's golf game had progressed, *or maybe the word should be depressed*, to a point where he resorted to playing with only two clubs -- a 2-iron and a putter. Using two clubs didn't seem to have any adverse effect on his game. One day he was able to better his son-in-law by six strokes in a eighteen hole match. The son-in-law was so embarrassed that day, to be beaten by an old man with two rusty clubs, that he never invited him to play again. For Christmas that year he gave Gregor a custom made, shiny 2-iron. A month later, for his birthday, he presented him with a specialty club that was designed to serve as seventeen clubs in one. With a twist of a coin, the head of this club could be positioned to the same angle of any regular golf club.

It was this club that would accompany Gregor to Florida. There, a friend of a friend invited him to a game of golf. When Gregor arrived, at the rather exclusive golf course, his new friend told him it was doubtful he would be allowed to play the course without a golf bag full of clubs. The problem was easily solved. His friend had an extra golf bag and clubs in his car trunk. Gregor's one club now had some companions. Twosomes, on this particular day, were not allowed to play unless they were paired into making a foursome, so, a teamup with a couple from Canada was arranged. This was going to be a day long remembered. The course was crowded. When Gregor approached the first tee with his strange looking club he could hear the mumbling of golfers who were standing-by, watching and awaiting their turn. The first hole was a par-three hole. They were probably thinking, "What's this guy doing driving this hole with an iron?" Gregor got off a decent drive; however, he scored an eight on this hole. On this day, he would experience everything a golfer could possible do on a golf course. A nice long drive would embed itself in the top of a palm tree; one of his shots landed in a neighboring swimming pool; a ball was lost in a snake infested area; he was in and out of sand traps; the ball would be hit onto the wrong fairway .... If it could happen, it did. On the thirteenth hole golfers were nearby teeing off, back to back, in three different directions. On this 165 yard hole, Gregor drove the ball high and straight for the green. Someone commented,

"Look at that, it's headed right for the pin."
The golfers on the neighboring tees turned to look just as the ball hit the green, bounced twice, and gently took a long roll into the cup. A hole-in-one. Everyone cheered. Congratulations, handshakes, and even some kisses from lady golfers he never met before were showered upon him. Apparently, Gregor didn't show much excitement. He was thinking about what was in store for him when he arrived at the clubhouse. He had only ten dollars in his pocket and no credit cards. His wife was out shopping miles away. How was he

going to foot the bill for all the drinks he was expected to buy? They arrived at the clubhouse at five minutes to six. The bar and the restaurant were closing at six o'clock that day for the beginning of a renovation project. Gregor was saved by Lady Luck. The next morning an engraved trophy for his hole-in-one would be ready for him to pick up.

On the way back to the car, his friend asked how he could be so calm about his hole-in-one. Gregor smiled and said,

"Oh, that's my second one. No big deal."

"Second one? I 've played all my life and always hoped for one and you got two?"

"Yeah. I really got my first one when I was about twelve years old."

That did it. Now his friend was really amazed. Gregor proceeded to tell him of that experience.

One day he was caddying with another caddy for two good golfers. It was hot and the golf bags were heavy leather bags with a full set of clubs. There were no such things as golf carts -- motorized or hand pulled carts in those days. A golfer carried his own bag or engaged the services of a young caddy. They approached a short and steep uphill green where the caddy would give his golfer a 9-iron, then scramble to the top of the hill and position himself at the back of the green to watch for any ball that might roll into a heavily wooded area. From the golfer's view he could only see the top of the pin (flag) from the tee. The other caddy's golfer shot first. The ball rolled past the pin to the far edge of the green and into the rough. The caddy, standing nearby, kicked the ball back onto the green toward the pin.

"What did ya do that for?"

"Ah, let's speed up the game."

The other golfer shoots almost the identical shot. The ball rolls to the edge of the green and Joey, with the side of his foot, kicks the ball toward the pin about twenty feet away. Guess what? Yup, it went into the cup. Both caddys stood there looking at each other. *Truly an indecisive moment.* Then, Joey headed for the cup to retrieve the ball. By this time the golfers are part way up the hill and in view of the green. It's too late to take the ball out of the cup without being seen. The golfers arrive on the green and seeing only one ball one of them says,

"Where's my ball?"
Joey sheepishly points to the cup and said, "It's in there."

There was much joy. Hand shaking. Clubs thrown in the air. Joey never saw anything like this before. Until this day, he never knew the real significance of *hole-in-one.* This hole-in-one was to be his secret for many years. Especially when he learned what the "lucky" golfer had to endure back at the clubhouse. Out of fear that his friend might tell someone what happened that day Joey never returned to caddy that year. *Neither did the other caddy.* He threatened the other caddy,

"You keep your mouth shut or I'll crack your head. Remember, this was your idea."

Joey would not tell that story for many years and always wondered who might be out there and still alive to brag about "his" hole-in-one.

~ *GREGOR TURNS a BIG SEVEN-O* ~

Everyone in Dr. Joe's family calls him Gregor. He's Gregor to his grandchildren, his children and even his spouse, Dorothy, calls him Gregor. That name has also appealed to many family friends. Sometimes when the grandkids address him as Greg for short, it becomes somewhat disconcerting because Dr. Joe gets the feeling that others who are not in the know may think the kids are being disrespectful by calling him by an apparent first name. *He really doesn't care. He likes it.*

Gregor's seventieth birthday party was to be a special one. His children decided they would surprise him with a gift he wouldn't be able to return to the store if he didn't like it. Many times he would exchange a gift for a different color or style he wanted instead. If that were not possible he was known, sometimes, to pocket the refund and forget about replacing the gift. This time they decided to give him a trip to Italy. The money was given to a travel agent. Gregor always wanted to visit Italy, especially the village of his parents. He attempted to take his mother back for a visit several times but she was always adamant about not wanting to go. He would *not* go without her. How could he possibly explain to her sisters and relatives that he was there without her? *Old-world Italians would never understand any rationale as to why she wouldn't go and most likely would be insulted.*

By this time, Gregor's mother and all her sisters abroad had passed away. Only cousins were left living in Italy. Gregor did not want to be a part of a tour group. He was fluent enough in the Italian language to find his own way. The travel agent made all the hotel arrangements, airline tickets, and purchased rail passes. The rest would be up to Gregor and Dorothy. First stop, Milan, Italy. Here, they were met by a driver sent by one of Gregor's high school classmates, Bob, to take them to where he was staying on Lake Garda, an absolutely spectacular place located at the foot of the Alps. They were to be his guest for the visit. Bob had purchased a villa, formerly occupied by Mussolini during World War II, and was in the process of restoring it to its former beauty. It was a magnificent historic structure. *Bob promised Gregor he could sleep in il Duce's former bedroom on his next visit when the room most likely would be ready.*

Gregor and Dorothy toured Florence, Rome, Naples, Pisa, the Isle of Capri, and a town named Levanto, his surname, located on the Italian Riviera, before going on to Sicily. He wanted to know if his father's family was somehow related to the naming of the town. The first place he inquired was the local police station. They could not answer his question but recommended he go across the street to a school and ask there. No help there. The local historian was not there to help. After enjoying the town and before catching the last train out he would try one more time at a local hotel. The desk clerks in Italy are usually informed people. Again, without mentioning his own name, Gregor would ask the clerk and she responded with,

"I don't really know, but, I'm quite certain it was not named after any significant person."

How's that for an answer to deflate one's ego? It was time to catch the last train back to Florence.

• • •

During all the conversations with Italian people, Gregor had little difficulty with their language. He communicated fluently, by speaking in a Sicilian dialect. This was very apparent to Italians on the mainland. They quickly identified him as a Sicilian. When he arrived in Messina, Sicily, and spoke the dialect he was reared on, he was surprised to learn the Sicilians were quick to identify him as a Tusan; since he spoke the dialect that was common to his parent's village of Tusa, Sicily. There are more than a hundred dialects spoken in Italy!

Upon their arrival in Messina, Gregor and spouse were met by their cousins. This was their first meeting. They had never met nor spoken to each other. After introductions to many cousins they all insisted they have lunch together. Later, they were driven to the mountain village of Tusa where they were the guest of one of the families. Only one steep, winding road leads to and from this ancient village with a history dating back to the thirteenth century. Not much has changed since the last earthquake destroyed the village. The cobblestone streets are narrow, so narrow that some of the small cars need to fold in their side view mirrors in order to pass. The houses are so clustered together that windows appear only on the front walls of the houses. Most house are three or four stories in height -- the ground level floor was designed to house animals. Today, those who do not have animals, use this level as a garage, or work space, or a place to make olive oil or wine. The next levels were bedrooms and the top level serves as the kitchen and dining area. To look at the exterior of these ancient houses, one would be reminded of the worst of slum housing in our country; although in Tusa the streets were clean with no litter to be found anywhere. However, upon entering inside they are immaculately clean with a surprising abundance of highly-polished marble floors, stairs, and walls. Almost all the modern lifestyle appliances found in our country can be found there. Bathrooms rival those found in upscale housing in America.

For the seven days of their visit with Gregor's cousins, they would be wined and dined, banquet style, every night with hospitality befitting a king and queen. Dorothy, not being able to speak nor understand a word of Italian, was made to feel so very special. She would be honored with a personalized toast at every dinner, in Italian of course. She always had a cousin at her side to help her understand or explain what was going on around her. The hand gestures and the body chemistry between them was a delightful sight. They would walk the streets arm in arm, never allowing her to be alone..

This visit was an emotional experience for Gregor. Much of what he saw brought back memories of what his parents described to him with photos when he was a curious young boy. He walked the same streets, visited the simple home his mother lived in, a very small two bedroom house where six children shared one bedroom. They were so poor that on Sundays the children went to church in shifts because they needed to swap shoes. There were not enough dress shoes for each to have their own. Gregor attended services in the same church where his parents were wed. It was as if they were there with him. He experienced a very strange feeling as if nothing had changed as he was taken back in time. He felt as though his mother and father were there walking the streets with him. In the church he could envision them standing at the same altar on their wedding day. He would learn many interesting facts concerning his relatives who had passed on, and the hardships they endured to survive living off a landscape that seemingly had more rocks than soil. He learned of family feuds and the primitive forms of justice that were administered. His own grandfather's brothers were the mafiosi of the village who ruled with an iron hand. It's no wonder why so many left their native country for the promise of a better life in America. It was hard to believe that the breathtaking beauty of this land could be so harsh on its people. Only strong-willed people with strong backs could survive the challenges they faced.

Before Gregor left this beautiful island he was told by his cousins he should remove his shoes and put his bare feet in the ocean as a symbolic gesture because he, Gregor, belonged to this land; the land of his ancestors and the birthplace of his mother and father.

~ *GREGOR and the TURKEY* ~

It would be awhile before Gregor could get his mind off the emotional visit to his parents' homeland. The Thanksgiving holiday was fast approaching and his family here in America would gather for the traditional family celebration. This year, the preparation for "turkey day" would be one that would long be remembered. It seemed as though everyone at the dinner table thoroughly enjoyed the story of the events leading up to this day -- so much so, that Gregor was encouraged to write the story and share it with the local newspaper. To his surprise they published it. More surprising was reader response. The following appeared in print:

The holiday season is upon us and I hope my wife doesn't decide to have another turkey on the table. We're still "enjoying" the leftovers from Thanksgiving. The freezer is full of turkey soup, turkey stuffing, turkey this, and turkey that. I shouldn't be complaining for having so much when I know there are others out there who are not fortunate enough to enjoy the bountiful pleasures available to so many Americans.

I think Emeril LaGasse is partly to blame for my plight. You say you don't know Emeril? Well, he's the wacky chef on TV who can capture the attention of non-cooks like me with his flashy antics in front of a stove. I even give up watching John Wayne movies to see him perform. That should tell you how powerful his charismatic image is portrayed on the tube. He convinced my wife she should try some of his techniques of food preparation. So, for Thanksgiving this year we had to have a fresh turkey. Yes, a fresh turkey from the farm -- not a frozen one. She placed her order well in advance of the holiday and on "D-day" she sent me off umpteen miles to the turkey farm to wrestle a twenty-two pound bird and bring it home. With a few grunts and groans I got it into the sink where my wife gave it a sponge bath. You'd think she was washing a baby the way she held him (maybe it was a her, I couldn't tell), gently rubbing her wet hands over its entire body. My job at this point was to get onto Emeril's web site and download the detailed instructions for our next adventure -- the prep job -- soaking the bird overnight in a brine solution and other goodie cooking hints for preparing a delicious turkey dinner.

We have some big pans but none big enough to completely immerse the entire 22 pound bird in the brine solution. Emeril's instructions noted that if the pan was not big enough to immerse the bird completely in the brine we could put the bird in a plastic garbage bag, fill it with the brine solution, seal it, then put it in the pan. (Clever idea Emeril). Did you ever try to pick up a 22 pound turkey in a bag filled with better than two gallons of brine setting in a roasting pan? Definitely not an easy task for an old guy like me. Schwartzenager I'm not and I'm not sure I can spell his name, but between the two of us we managed to lift this contraption and carefully ease our way over to our spare refrigerator which is in the next room. Picture this -- me, with both hands lifting some of the weight, by the neck of the bag, and my wife crouched under me carrying the rest of the weight supported in the pan doing the side step -- a hernia prevention maneuver without music. We must of look like The Three Stooges minus one.

We made it over to the refrigerator only to find the bottom shelf is made of glass. Stop everything. That's not strong enough to carry this load. So I leave my wife holding the bag while I run down to my shop to cut a piece of plywood to reinforce the glass shelf. Now we can ease the turkey into its overnight resting place -- right ... Wrong. When I let go of the neck of the bag it just spreads itself out over the edge of the pan like a massive hunk of Jell-O, making it impossible to close the door without chancing bursting the bag. "Emeril I love you." (that's not what I really said). "Dot, hand me some of those twelve-packs of soda and we can prop this thing up in the corner." Now the door won't close. A little re-arranging ought to do it. The door now closes, but ... slowly it opens as if the turkey inside is trying to get out. No, it's the twelve-pack in front trying to get away from the bird. (Something I wish I could do about now). I can fix that. A couple of gallons of wine propped against the door should hold it shut. That does it -- I'm ready for bed.

Now with another set of holidays coming, forget that delicious turkey and let's plan on a nice roast beef dinner. Please ... no more turkey.

~ THE 50TH CELEBRATION ~

At a family gathering, several weeks before Gregor's and Dorothy's 50th wedding anniversary, their children happened to comment on the approaching milestone in their parents' life. Before the discussion could get started, Gregor said to his children,

"Look, I don't want any big parties on our 50th. We don't want you spend a lot of money on us. I'd be very happy if we all went out to a quiet dinner at a nice restaurant with just the family."

"OK Dad, we hear ya," one of his daughters replied. Dorothy then commented on their 25th celebration long past. Their kids really extended themselves for that surprise celebration and, in her mind, that was enough for her. That ended the conversation on that topic and nothing more was ever mentioned until a few days before the golden anniversary date. Two days before the anniversary date was Gregor's birthday and the children were gathered at a party for him when reference was made to the coming anniversary on Saturday, Gregor asked,

"Where are we going to dinner Saturday night?"
A long pause -- it was like no one heard the question and finally one of the daughters answered,

"Jeannette will be here tomorrow and we'll decide then."
Jeannette and her husband arrived early on Saturday morning from their home in Pennsylvania. Usually they traveled with their pet dog. This time, however, they left the animal at home with a friend. Gregor was relieved to see that. He

wasn't looking forward to this huge animal, a Rhodesian Ridgeback, in the house with his two smallest grandchildren, one of whom was very much afraid to have any dog come anywhere near her. Gregor could never understand why anyone would want such a big dog. *Why not a small horse instead?*

At the dinner table that night Gregor asked Jeannette where they planned to have the anniversary dinner. Jeannette, without hesitation answered,

" The Lighthouse Inn, Dad."

"Great, I like that. It's a classy place and the food is good there." No more was said.

Saturday evening everyone was getting dressed to go out and Gregor wanted to wear casuals. Dorothy thought that was not appropriate dress for the Lighthouse Inn and insisted he wear a suit and tie. So be it. He didn't like the idea, but he wasn't about to argue. The marriage lasted this long and he wasn't about to shorten its longevity now. He just mumbled his usual grumble. Before he could dress the phone rang; it was his cousin Sarino calling from Australia to wish them a happy anniversary. Within a few minutes after the long distance conversation ended there was a knock at the door. Dorothy answered and was surprised to find a pretty girl at the door who announced she was the limo driver sent to take them to dinner. Joe had been told the rest of the family would meet them at the restaurant. After all, the family count would require several cars for the trek.

As Gregor and Dorothy approached the long white limousine, with its doors open awaiting their entry, the first thing that caught their eyes was a pair of good looking legs wearing silk stockings and fashionable shoes. At this time of day, the tinted glass windows and the evening darkness made it impossible to see through inside. A few steps closer and they saw their young grandson, Cody, dressed in his best, neatly-groomed and wearing a big smile. He sat facing the beautiful young lady who at this point was quickly recognized as his sister, Cailynn. Dressed in a long black dress, she could have passed as a model. They came with the limo driver to escort their grandparents to the restaurant. *What a nice touch. A better choice could never be found to equal these two. That's a grandfather talking.*

Gregor and Dorothy, along with daughter, Jeannette, and Steve, her husband, entered and were seated. Before the limo started, Cody presented champagne glasses to everyone and removed a bottle of champagne from its wall rack. He was about to uncork the bottle when the limo driver asked him to wait until she was able to drive the limo onto level ground and then she would help him. Up the driveway and onto the level street she came to a stop. She convinced Cody it would be better to uncork the bottle outside and keep everyone from a possible soaking in champagne. He was somewhat disappointed when the driver asked if she could be the one to pop the cork outside the car. A smart move on her part, most likely avoiding showering the occupants and their finery. The girls appreciated that.

Besides, it would be such a waste of good champagne.

Cody carefully poured the champagne into the outstretched glasses, (Coca-Cola for him and his sister). With glasses in hand the limousine went on its way. Gregor would soon

273

wonder why the limo driver was not taking, what he thought was, the best route to the Lighthouse Inn. As they passed the academy, the driver suddenly turned onto the campus and headed toward the Museum Building. As the limo made the turn, Gregor exclaimed!

"What the hell we go'in in here for?"
The driver in a calm voice said,

"I need to stop to see Ron for a minute."
Ron happens to be the owner of the limousine service and he and Joe are good friends. The limo stopped at the museum entrance and the driver went inside. Gregor noted the many cars parked on campus and thought nothing of it. It was Saturday night and he thought, most likely, there was a basketball game in progress. The driver returned and opened the door on Gregor's side and said to him,

"Ron wants to know if you can come inside and talk for a minute."

While the driver was inside Gregor recognized several car license plates parked nearby and began suspecting something was wrong with this picture.

"Ron wants me inside? Oh sure he does. I think we've been had. "

By this time, everyone had gotten out of the limo. They all entered the foyer of the building. All is quiet as they climb the long stairway to the Museum Cast Gallery. Many coats are seen hanging on racks just outside two massive wooden doors leading into the gallery. Cody leads the way and attempts to turn the knobs on the big doors and is unable to because of a broken finger he suffered in a previous night's basketball game. Gregor takes a deep breath and helps with turning the door knobs.

They are greeted by a sea of faces all applauding their entrance. They stand motionless looking about the gallery as the applause and camera flashes seem to be never ending. They look to their left and there, displayed on Dorothy's old dress form, spotlighted from above, is her wedding gown that she made and wore fifty years ago. It was made from World War II parachute satin her uncle had given her. Gregor's eyes begin to fill with tears and he tries hard to hold back his emotions that start to overtake him. He turns to look at his wife. She appears to be in a state of shock and choked with tears. He stares at the form with the tiny waistline that once was. A few feet from the gown, a young lady fills the air with music from her beautiful harp.

A more beautiful setting would be difficult to imagine. Placed among the plaster casts, replicating many world famous sculptures, are beautifully decorated dining tables. The museum is known to have the largest collection of plaster casts in the USA. A collection of famous Greek and Roman statues ranging from Winged Victory to Michelangelo's Pieta. On each table is a centerpiece -- a large clear glass vase adorned with white gladiolus and with live goldfish swimming among their stems; the white gladiolus reminiscent of the wedding flowers of fifty years ago.

Gregor and Dorothy stood motionless and speechless with eyes welling with happy tears. Many memories must have flashed through their minds. It was such an elegant affair and they were so taken by it that neither of them would be able to eat any of the delicious food served that evening.

Young Joe, their son, standing on the balcony next to Michelangelo's Pieta, gave an eloquent toast quoting and relating ten special commandments written and presented by the priest who performed at his own wedding. It was a very emotional moment for everyone and especially for the honored guests.

• • •

This was the perfect celebration. A memory etched forever in the minds of Gregor and Dorothy who were so thankful for their children and many friends who came to share this special evening with them. Gregor was especially grateful to his Alma Mater for honoring them by allowing the Museum to cater this affair, a first in its long history. The elegance of the surrounding architecture added a touch of class fit for royalty. It was awesome.

Gregor's only wish would have been for both their parents to be with them to see this wonderful celebration. It was a party they wished would never end ... the end did come at two in the morning.

Deep down in their hearts, they knew it would never end.

~ *EPILOGUE* ~

Life's journey has been interesting and fulfilling, especially for one who started school not knowing the English language, a kid born to hard-working, uneducated parents who struggled through life to provide, unselfishly, the bare essentials for their family. Growing up in a home with no family car, no telephone, no books, not even a dictionary, nor magazines, no one to help with homework, no newspaper, and no TV, only a radio with the local six o'clock news for contact with the outside world. A home where Mama made the bed sheets from flour sacks that were bleached out and sewed together. Homemade bread was toasted atop a hot coal stove. Hard, stale bread was passed under the water faucet and coated with a spoonful of sugar -- a special treat.

It was unheard of, for children of immigrant families, to receive a monetary allowance for assigned chores. Gregor was not the only one who grew up in such conditions. Children of many immigrant families, Italian, Greek, and Polish alike, experienced similar upbringing.

Most family homes had two parents, a father who was a strict disciplinarian and wage earner, and a mother who maintained the home and was *always* available for her children. They never spared the rod to spoil a child. The word *no* meant *no* and seldom would it be repeated or need an explanation. It was tough love and although today's generation would find this kind of upbringing unacceptable; however, it was rich with love. There was no greater pride for immigrant parents than to see their children grow to become respectable and successful people in their community.

The lessons learned from caring and loving parents carried Gregor throughout his life. Was he ever a rebellious youngster? Sometimes. Was he ever a bad boy? Sometimes -- but always respecting and honoring his mother and father. As he looks back on his life he has a lot to be thankful for. He did not walk this far alone. The road of life was not always straight and narrow. There were many side streets where one could have gotten lost. There were many temptations along the way that could have resulted in an entirely different life. Caring people most likely had the greatest impact on his life. There always seemed to be someone there at critical times who cared enough and took an interest in him. They kept him from venturing too far down the side streets. Dorothy, his spouse of more than fifty years has been his guardian angel, his best friend, and a mother to their four wonderful children. Together, they molded a family of respectable, successful, and caring individuals.

Gregor will tell you he is one lucky guy who has experienced a good life. A good life to him he defines as one filled with many good memories and good memories that far outweigh the bad ones. Serving as an educator for nearly fifty years has been a most rewarding experience that no amount of money could duplicate. There is no other profession in which one individual can have such a profound effect in the development of young minds. Now, with the aging process well underway, to be remembered as a good teacher or a good coach by former students takes on a new meaning. To hear someone say, "I remember you, aren't you ... " or, " Do you remember when we played ... " or, "I always remembered what you said to me in class one day when I ... " It's impossible for Dr. Joe to remember what was said so many years ago. To reminisce and listen to what was remembered invigorates his soul. There is no greater reward than to be held in high esteem and fondly remembered -- and to be alive to enjoy it.

Gregor's grandchildren motivated him to put into writing some of his life's experiences. It has been a joy and a blessing to watch them grow. Christopher, about to finish high school, is a handsome and multi-talented youngster aspiring to be a writer. *Hope he's not too critical of this book when he reads it.* Cailynn, a very pretty high school freshman who always professes her love for her Gregor, can unarm anyone with her kindness and beauty and still is able to display a formidable and competitive spirit in athletic competition. Cody, a fifth-grader and a wannabee future New York Yankee or a candidate for the NBA, whose keen wit and humor captures the attention of old and young alike; is a proven and popular leader in school who has Gregor as his greatest fan. *No ... I think it's his mother.*

Last, but not least, the two youngest grandchildren, Sierra and Mia, who, too young at this writing to read and know what this is all about, hopefully, in later years will learn a few things about their Gregor and develop an appreciation of their heritage.

There is an apparent message that comes from Gregor's life story: Able to come so far in life, when in the beginning all the cards seemed to be stacked against him, may be attributed to a don't give up attitude and determination, a little bit of luck, and a strong belief in oneself. Never, never, sell yourself short or, for that matter, anyone else. That kid you thought was stupid or a troublemaker could grow up to be your Mayor or Governor, or even your President ... *Or maybe your boss or next door neighbor.*

• • •

Opportunities are here to be found and everyone has a chance. You can be what you want to be -- *only in America.*